THE LIBERTY TREE

THE LIBERTY TREE

DRUNK TO SOBER
via Love, Death, Disintegration & Freedom

SUZANNE HARRINGTON

Atlantic Books
London

Published in Great Britain in 2013 by Atlantic Books,
an imprint of Atlantic Books Ltd.

Extract from 'Vers de Société', *The Complete Poems* by Philip Larkin, reprinted
by permission of Faber and Faber Ltd.
Extract from *The Beach* by Alex Garland, reprinted by permission of Andrew
Nurnberg Associates.
Extract from *Trainspotting* by Irvine Welsh, published by Secker & Warburg,
reprinted by permission of The Random House Group Limited.

10 9 8 7 6 5 4 3 2 1

A CIP catalogue record for this book is available from the British Library.

Trade paperback ISBN: 9780857899415
E-book ISBN: 9780857899422

Printed in Italy by 🦅 Grafica Veneta SpA

Atlantic Books
An Imprint of Atlantic Books Ltd
Ormond House
26–27 Boswell Street
London
WC1N 3JZ

www.atlantic-books.co.uk

For Leo, for all that he gave.

'You see that stunted, parched and sorry tree? From each branch liberty hangs. Your neck, your throat, your heart are all so many ways of escape from slavery...'
    SENECA

CONTENTS

PART TWO

7 September 2006

It's one of those early summer mornings when the sun and the moon are in the sky together, the moon's fullness fading to a thin silver sliver as the strong light rises. The sea is flat and calm and glittering. Everything is fresh. Along the seafront, the white houses stand grandly like wedding cakes, blinding white in the sunlight. The empty beach stretches west, deserted except for the solitary dots of dog walkers, their faraway dogs leaping into the rush and suck of the tide, chasing tiny sticks. A lone truck collects rubbish from the beachfront bins.

From the top of the hill you can see the pier jutting into the glitter, its fairground hovering on tiny black metal matchsticks over the water. The helter skelter, the ghost train, and the roller-coaster are all still and silent in the distance, the lights and music off, the wooden boardwalk empty. Everything is pale blue, gold and silver. The whole morning is illuminated with fresh, clean light. Its newness dazzles.

A mile or so east of the pier, the town ends where the soft hills roll down to the sea. You can see miles of coast from up here, the town laid out below like an architect's model, spreading west and blurring into the next town. Up here, there is nothing except wind and air and huge sky. A few trees hunch like old women caught in a gale, their leaves and branches angled permanently inland by the sea winds. The grass is short and soft, and bright with wild flowers.

There is a dip in the hills where some trees have grown straight and tall, protected by the side of the hill; it is a place to hunch down and smoke a cigarette away from the wind. There are a few old cider bottles amongst the brambles, their labels faded, and a blackened patch on the ground where fires have been lit. A plastic crisp wrapper flaps in the tangle of thorns.

And hanging from a tree in this sheltered dip, up here on the windswept hill, is a body. It swings very gently in the breeze, feet not far from the ground, a blue nylon rope cutting into the neck. The head is at an unnatural angle, the tongue bulging and blue. The face is bluish too, blue like Lord Shiva. A small rucksack has been kicked away, and a mobile phone lies switched off, face down in the earth. The body has been hanging here for a while now, since the moon was at its highest and brightest last night. It is already stiff.

Nobody has found it yet. No dog has come bounding through the dip, in a frenzy of sniffing and barking. No rider has cantered up the hill and wheeled their horse around after seeing the sway of its silhouette. No lone morning runner has glanced this way and seen its terrible stillness. Not yet. It's still too early. In another few hours, police will be knocking on a door, watching impassively as faces collapse. But for now, the body is just hanging there, stiff and silent and alone in the soft bright morning.

Part One

'You can only write what you know, even if you don't know that you know it.'

William Burroughs

SEVEN YEARS, TWO MONTHS, SEVENTEEN DAYS

Since your father liberated himself on that sorry tree branch, he has faded away. There is a photograph of him in each of your bedrooms – in a Stetson and red and black fringed cowboy shirt at Gay Pride, and in a swirly psychedelic shirt, necklace and Lennon glasses walking behind two women dressed as Blue Meanies at the Children's Parade, at the start of the Brighton Festival. He looks great in those photos – bright and alive. He was always good at dressing up. In that respect he was a bit of a show-off, a bit fabulous, which I always found attractive. He wasn't the kind of man who would slob out in knobbly grey tracksuit bottoms and a baggy top. Not until nearer the end, but that's still some way off.

There's another photo of him in a tight sparkly silver t-shirt and a horned devil's hat handmade from red cotton, pushing one of you through the mud another year at Pride, with Petula Clark singing in the background and me posing next to him, fat from pregnancy in a bright blue African muumuu, clutching a parasol. There's a jacket of his in your wardrobe – outrageous pink plush, a girl's jacket that he used to wear clubbing with his big chunky boots and black snakeskin jeans. He was a bit of a disco king, your dad. He loved it.

But we don't really talk about him so much anymore, do we?

It's hard to know just how gaping the dad-sized hole in your lives is. It's hard to know how it will all turn out.

Yesterday you were complaining, high on pick'n'mix, after some garish 3D Disney film at the cinema, how predictable the story always is – a princess, a hero on a horse, a quest, a castle, a happy ever after. Why can't it be more realistic? you said. Why can't they die in the end? Or at least one of them? Because, I said, people think that kids can't handle stuff like that. And the two of you scoffed and said rubbish, of course they can. You're right, of course. It's the adults who can't.

Anyway. You've dealt with a dead dad, but you still don't know the full story. Neither do I, other than how and when he died. I still don't really know why, but I knew him a bit longer than you – although not that much longer. You were five and three when he died, but I only knew him for seven years, two months and seventeen days. Even if I had known him longer, I doubt I would ever have really known him, because he was like a magic mirror: he reflected back to you only what you wanted to see.

He was the kind of man who would have brought a suitcase on a camping trip. He knew how to eat lobster, but not how to pitch a tent. He had been on lots of holidays, but never travelled. He could link up a network of computers, but had not the faintest idea how to ride a bike or drive a car. He could cook, but only with a cookery book, and only certain dishes – so he could make a splendid lemon drizzle cake, but could never just throw a meal together. If fenugreek was a listed ingredient and he didn't have any, the curry remained unmade. He was not big on improvisation or thinking on his feet. He was a whizz with wires, but had no idea how to do anything with wood. He had great skin, and fabulous teeth.

So although I don't know his story, this is the story of me and him, and our seven years. You may not like it much, because it will tell you things you may not want to know, and neither he nor I may come across terribly well, although how you read it is really none of my business. But better honesty than a pretty story. It would be lovely to write you a heart-stirring tale of heroes and bravery, of selflessness and compassion, but instead you'll be reading the story of a suicide written by a drunk. Only you can make your own happy ending.

Just remember – this is a story that is filtered through me. His version would have been different, but he's not here, so this is the only version you're going to get. It is my truth, which is not necessarily *the* truth. But is there ever any such thing as *the* truth? I doubt it.

1 LONDON

We met at a party in New North Road in Islington in June 1998. Not the kind of party you're thinking of – there wasn't any food, and nobody brought a present. It was a big house that seemed like a squat even though it wasn't – big dark rooms empty of furniture and full of people and noise. Staircases crowded, strobe lights in the basement, bodies everywhere. It was all very minimal and functional, the music semi industrial. The doof-doof-doof of techno. Gabber drilling in the basement – that mutant strain of dance music that made your ears bleed, undanceable at 160 bpm, like a kanga hammer inside your head. I was never a handbag house kind of girl – I liked my music fast and hard – but gabber was ridiculous. Your dad loved it.

That night was my first night out in the city for ages. In any city. For three months I had been moving between remote beaches around South East Asia, where the drugs were few and mellow (apart from at the end, on Koh Phangan where we had acid and tooth-splintering Thai speed pills at a full moon party on the beach at Haad Rin), and so I believed myself to be shiny and clean of brain and body after my three months away from London parties. I wasn't at all – my brain chemistry was extremely precarious, like a dodgy lab experiment just waiting to blow, although I didn't know that at the time. I had no idea that years of cumulative hedonism was doing my head in. How could I have? Besides, I was feeling really good. This meant good on the surface, because the surface was tanned and backpacker-slim and bleached on top. The night I met your dad, I was a blonde, with an orange bindi on my forehead, wearing an orange furry bikini top with a zip down the front, and orange Thai fisherman's trousers that made peeing complicated. I looked like a traffic cone with a tan. In a good way, of course.

I suppose I might have been on the pull. It wasn't conscious. Nothing ever was with me. It happened when I was lying on a giant floor cushion, being softly swallowed and devoured by my first pill in months. It dissolved me into benign mush and I was breathing in and out, in and out, eyes half closed, lost in the huge pleasure of it. It's not called ecstasy for nothing. I was inside a huge, beautiful softness.

Someone was saying 'This is Leo,' and I was smiling at him and he had the most beautiful eyes, dark brown melty sparkly, dark brown skin, jet black hair, perfect features. Small faced. He was hunching down and chatting easily and naturally and I was chatting back even as my veins expanded and my blood turned to air. His pupils were big, but mine were bigger.

And then he said, 'I wish my surname was Nine, because then I would be Leo Nine. You know. Like feline,' and even in my marshmallow bliss, I knew that this was a terrible line. But he said it straight faced. Was he being ironic, or were his drugs stronger than mine? He didn't seem particularly out of it, but then in a houseful of a hundred people off their heads, it was all relative. We kept talking. I remember feeling surprised and flattered by the fact that he stayed talking to me for ages, rather than extricating himself as soon as was proper. Back then I was all big ego and small self esteem: there must have been something wrong with this good looking, charming bloke to be scrunched down chatting, rather than looking over his shoulder at the fitter, cooler party girls.

When the blood returned to my legs and we eventually stood up, I saw immediately what was wrong with him. He was short. Very short. Even in those New Rock boots that were briefly fashionable in the nineties, and which added a few inches to his height, he was still eye level with me. And I am not tall. Damn, I remember thinking. Why couldn't he have been a foot taller? But we kept talking. Later, there was a floaty kiss in an empty room, the walls juddering from the sound system, the ecstasy rushing though our veins and our brains. He moved in a few weeks later.

Why did we do that? Was it love at first sight? You are our children. I want to tell you that it was, so I will. Yes, it was love at first sight – if love means two unformed people collapsing towards each other in the hope that each will catch the other and prop them up. If love at first sight is a mistaken belief that each will rescue the other. Then yes, it was love at first sight.

'I love you,' he would say, as we lay around staring at each other.

'I love you too,' I would say back, crumbling hash into a king-size Rizla.

'You're perfect,' he'd say.

'No, you are,' I'd reply.

Because in those first few weeks and months, he was. And I was, and we were.

So what was it that attracted me to your dad, apart from his looks? He was posh, for a start. You have to remember that I was living in East London and had been for quite some time, much longer than I had ever planned. Not the cool arty bits around Whitechapel and Shoreditch and Brick Lane, or the groovy ethnic bit around Green Street, but the grim nowhere bits that are never mentioned anywhere except in government statistics on poverty: Forest Gate, Plaistow, East Ham, Manor Park. This was a long time before the Olympics and giant shopping centres and posh super-markets. My East London was rows of grimy terraced brick, plastic-fronted curry houses, chewing gummed bus stops, steamy greasy caffs, crowded pound shops and shabby charity shops, Kwiksaves and kebab shops, cavernous pubs called the Prince This and the Queen That that smelled of ashtrays and Harpic, warehouses, tower blocks, DSS hostels, squats, broken windows, boarded up doors; dirty streets that formed a great grey sprawl stretching from the Bow flyover along the Romford Road to the nothing-ness of Ilford. You got around on the 86 and the 25, or in cheap minicabs, swerving between the white van psychos and the care-free drivers from Karachi and Dhaka and Delhi and Accra and Lagos, for whom the Highway Code was as foreign as jellied eels. I've never taken you there because it's not worth the journey. There's nothing to see.

Your dad, on the other hand, was living in Little Venice in West London. While I was a twenty minute trudge east of East Ham tube station, he was overlooking Regent's Canal and seconds from Warwick Road Station in dapper, accessible Zone 2. The first time I went to his flat, which he shared with a bunch of people in their early twenties, even though he was already in his mid-thirties, it struck me that he was not like the men I knew out east. There was moisturizer in his bedroom, and his clothes were on hangers. There were proper pots and pans in the kitchen, and even though there was almost no furniture in the flat – the twenty something flatmates were suits by day, stoners by night, and seemed never to have lived away from home before – it felt studenty, rather than just poor, a world away from the cracked plates and damp walls I was used to.

'I love you,' he said, that first time I visited his place.

'I love you too,' I said, staring at his hair product and hand cream.

Leo was posh in that minor public schoolboy kind of way, which appealed to my unconscious desire to escape East London, my stint there as accidental tourist having gone on far too long. I was thirty, and I needed to get out, needed to stop living like an extra from some druggy version of *EastEnders*; but when I first met your dad, I had no idea that I even wanted to escape, until I made the decision a bit later and scarpered within a fortnight. I was not big on conscious thought back then. I knew I didn't I want to hook up with some middle class white boy, though; the idea of having a boyfriend called Tom or Giles or Freddy filled me with horror. Not that Tom or Giles or Freddy would have been beating a path to my grotty East Ham door. Not unless they had become extremely disoriented from too much acid.

What I liked about your dad was his otherness – he was black Asian, with the very dark skin of Sri Lanka, Kerala and Tamil Nadu, and he had English cut glass vowels. Being common or garden white Irish, I was determined to outswim my gene pool; the further the better. What's more, he had a job, a proper one that paid a salary rather than cash in hand. Something in an office to do with computers. This meant that he could pay for his own pints, were he the kind of man who drank pints, which of course he wasn't.

He knew what to do with a fish fork, though. He could read a wine list, and work a room. Although I had been reared with such skills, they had been largely eroded after years of feral living. The first time he took me to his flat, we stopped for sushi somewhere near the Westway, somewhere which was nothing fancier than a Yo Sushi, but back then, after all those kebab shops and chip shops, it felt like an afternoon in Nobu. 'Wow,' I said, wondering what I had done to deserve this. 'Thank you.'

'It's my great pleasure,' he said, and he was beaming.

I did wonder if he was gay, such was his dedication to grooming and fashion. I looked like a storm-tossed haystack in comparison. I remember asking him, as we snuggled up to each other, 'Are you *sure* you're not gay?' and he laughed and said I had spent so long in East London that I was mistaking civilized for queer. Maybe he was just ahead of his time. On his second visit to my place, he brought me a V05 Hot Oil treatment for my hair. He said he had noticed that it was 'a bit dry' after my travels – he was being polite, as always; my grooming regime, other than soap and water, was non-existent, as was my hair care – and so he thought my hair might 'need some help'. There he was, this short muscular guy in a tight t-shirt, advising me on hair product. My only references were gay friends in Barcelona: muscular guys in tight t-shirts with shiny hair; the East End blokes all wore baggy t-shirts – emblazoned either with Om or Motorhead, depending where their heads were at, and wouldn't have known hair product if they were drowning in a vat of it. I remember wrapping a towel around my hot oiled head, and wondering about this new boyfriend who had suddenly appeared out of nowhere and moved into my life overnight. Who was he?

He told everyone I was the woman of his dreams. Everything

about me: my accent, my orange furry top with the zip, my fondness for Earl Grey tea, my appetite for chemicals, my face, my
love of animals, my vegetarianism, my devil-may-care attitude –
he loved it all. I didn't really have a devil-may-care attitude, I was
just less uptight than him, less English. Less polite. More fuck-it,
more impulsive. Less considered or considerate. When your auntie
River met him later that summer, she said he was the politest
man she had ever met. And with that level of politeness comes
inscrutability.

So there he was. Small, polite, trendy, middle class. A 'pocket
sized Adonis,' one of his friends called him. Meterosexual to a
fault. A Leo, the same as me, but a few years older – he was born
in 1963, I was born in 1967. Much later, in Brighton, I interviewed
a psychic for work (I was a journalist by then – well, kind of), and
she told me lots of things about myself that went beyond guess-
work. The only thing she seemed to get wrong was about my
'other half', as she called him. 'He's quite a bit younger than you,
isn't he?' she said. When I shook my head, she looked puzzled.
'Yes, he is much,' she insisted. 'Much younger.'

Looking back on it, she was right. Just not in calendar years.

The things that I liked about him were as superficial as the
things he liked about me: his face, his eyes, his clothes, his accent,
his love of animals, particularly cats, his kindness, his middle
class social skills, the fact that he was not on the dole. Like a high
quality hair product, he was soft and gentle and smelled lovely;
he worshipped me unreservedly, while telling me how selective
he was when choosing women. After the teenage-style warfare of
my last relationship, he was a dream. He would make me cards
by cutting out pictures of fifties pin-ups and sticking them on
coloured paper, then write me lovely messages in his distinctive

all-capitals writing; he always signed himself 'Luv Me.' He was extremely dyslexic – later, when we become more domestic, he would leave me notes. My favourite ever was 'I will make you super.'

Having established for now that he wasn't gay, I decided very quickly that your dad should come and live with me in my rented terraced house in Manor Park. He had never been to Manor Park before, or anywhere further east than Hackney. I mean, why would you?

The house was undistinguished, small and basic, but with a lovely garden. The garden was the best bit. It was long and narrow and had a cherry tree that dripped cherries in summer, and a Dingly Dell of overhanging lilac and buddleia that you could hide inside, lying on rugs – a secret camp behind the hanging green. I was living there by myself for the first time in ages, and needed someone to share the rent. Leo was tired of living with stoner twenty-somethings, and we believed that we were hopelessly in love. So he moved from the relative civilization of West London to the barren wastelands of almost-Essex. And then realized his mistake. 'This place is dead,' he complained. 'You can't get a cappuccino anywhere. Or the *Guardian*.' No, I agreed, you can't – but you could get a mug of PG Tips and the *Sun*, and the local offie did an extensive range of £2.99 Bulgarian red. I was used to it – having to get a tube to the nearest book shop, and always being told by the Sikh brothers who ran the corner shop that they could order me the *Guardian* if I was prepared to pay up front (I never was, because I was always broke). But Leo found it hard to adjust to the sheer nothingness outside the four walls of our love nest, once he'd settled into his new room. We had a bedroom each, because it was a two bedroomed house and it seemed sensible and luxurious and modern to have a room each, where we could have our own stuff and our own space. But this only works if you are regularly dragging each other into one another's rooms, pouncing on each other like tigers, and savaging each other. That was another thing. From the very start, we never quite ignited in the bedroom. It's just that for a long time we pretended not to notice. We looked the other way.

'I love you,' he'd say, and we would hug.

'I love you too,' I'd answer, and wonder why we weren't – you know – hammering each other off the walls.

Now I know the last thing you want to hear about is anything to do with your parents and sex. You may want to skip this bit. But the lack of sexual energy between me and your dad meant that it's actually a bit of a miracle that you two exist at all. It also said a lot about us individually: for both of us, our desire to be rescued manifested itself in sexual passivity; we both wanted the other to be in charge, to take control, to sort everything out – in and out of the bedroom. We just didn't realize it at the time. I had always been with beefy blokes whose sexuality was never too finely tuned – traditionalists all, apart from one unhinged trans vestite, though that's another story that perhaps you might not want to hear – but Leo was different.

He'd been to fetish clubs with his female friends, and gay clubs with his male friends, and unlike my previous boyfriends – for whom sex was something that only happened under the duvet after a few cans of Red Stripe and a spliff – he was very open to sexual otherness. He would talk easily about the friend who was a domme, and another who enjoyed tying up and deliciously torturing men at fetish clubs. One of his male friends liked to put on make-up, wig and cocktail dress once he had come home after a hard day's work. Leo himself had been a podium dancer at some club – he was a fabulous dancer, the muscles of his chest pulsing to the music. And he'd been to boarding school, birthplace of British pervery. His female friends were all extremely dominant; his male friends had a tendency to dress up as women.

All of this attracted me hugely. At last, I thought, someone whose sexuality extends outside the box. I was thrilled to be with someone who promised to take me to interesting clubs. I was so repressed in those days, so uncomfortable in my own skin and ill at ease with my own sexuality, so fearful of being ridiculed. I was embarassed to even think beyond vanilla. But ordinary sex, nice as it was, left me wanting; I longed for something more, something deeper, something that would connect me to my innermost secret self. But I was locked up tight, desperate to release myself but too ashamed to even know where to start. I was an Irish Catholic after all. Sexual shame was in our DNA. I thought Leo might be able to unlock me. He probably thought the same about me.

I remember a specific moment in Brighton, when I had an early moment of clarity about the true nature of our relationship. It was in that little one bedroom basement on Abbey Road by the hospital, with the gloomy patio out back that I whitewashed and strung with fairylights and decorated with a mosaic flower I made out of broken blue ceramics. It was our first proper shared home, and we loved playing house together. We would sit out on our subterranean terrace all evening, me drinking wine, him drinking tea, until the old queen upstairs, the one with the puffy face and plummy voice who had religious mania and a drink problem, would shriek down to us in a despairing contralto: 'In the name of Christ don't you people *ever* stop talking?'

This was our honeymoon home in our honeymoon period, straight after my escape from East London. It struck me suddenly one day, one warm afternoon not long after we had moved south, that something was not quite right. There he was, coming down the mossy basement steps, putting his key in the lock, and there I was, his new wife, home in the afternoon, and there was nobody else around. You two didn't exist back then. We hadn't even got Carmen the crazy Labrador yet. There were no distractions, no responsibilities, nothing and no-one except us. And your dad put down his newspaper amid all the bright Hindu clutter on the sideboard, and came over to me, smiling his beautiful smile, and pecked me on the cheek. 'Tea?' he said, tootling off to the kitchen.

No. I did not want tea. I wanted ripped shirts and hiked skirts and hot breath all over my face and animal grunting and the discomfort of wall or furniture digging into my back and the side of my face and carpet burn on my knees and elbows and sweat and gasping and dishevelment and joy. Instead I got a lovely cup of Earl Grey and a biscuit.

But I'm getting ahead of myself. I had to go mad before we moved to Brighton. Let me tell you, by the time I got out of East London, I was not a good ad for drugs. I was barking. I was beyond barking. I was fucking Upminster. That's a District Line joke that you won't get, because I had the good sense to make sure you were born at least three counties away from it. Obviously, at the time, I didn't realize I was going mad. That's what happens when you take more drugs than your brain can handle – you start to short-circuit, but you don't realize you're losing the plot until it is already lost. You think, given that they have always been such an immense source of fun, excitement and pleasure, that they are the only things keeping you sane, while in fact the total opposite is true. But you never think you're taking too many, because you're surrounded by people who take far more, far more often. And because I never went near heroin or crack, I always thought I was safe, because I was only ever sorted for Es and whizz... and pot and acid, and vats of cheap booze. After all, what harm could nice non-addictive recreational drugs do?

I know this is meant to be about your dad, but I need to tell you a bit about my life before him, so that you have some backstory around my plot loss: where I was coming from, and why I was increasingly not of sound mind; the people I hung out with, and the inescapable aimlessness of my life; why I leapt on your dad as though he were a lifebelt, to stop myself from sinking. And about Harry, the boyfriend before him. You know, the one who thought that if you cut an avocado in half, the centre would be full of prawns. I'd not had a boyfriend since Harry. It had not ended well, and while we were together, we had not always been the poster couple for true romance. He was a big burly beer drinker from south of South London with a soppy heart and about the same level of emotional maturity as me. Although he did have considerably more emotional intelligence: he would say things like, 'It's not where you are, it's where you're at.' And once he said that although I was cleverer than him, he was wiser than me. That, children, would not have been hard. Wisdom was not something I possessed. Not even a tiny bit.

Harry wasn't really an East End geezer, but he had lived there so long that it was hard to tell the difference. He had done a lot of travelling, and had this magical ability to find his home no matter where he was on the planet, but his tastes remained simple. Beer, mostly, and prawns. Curry and cigarettes. Base speed. Me. And he was quite old-fashioned about certain things, like the word 'cunt' – he couldn't bring himself to utter it, even though he effed and blinded the same as everyone else. Once I made him come with me to a Chapman brothers exhibition at the ICA, and after one glance around the fake garden of hanging plastic foliage filled with shop dummy children with penises and vaginas moulded onto their faces, he legged it. I found him outside, smoking a roll-up, more outraged than the *Daily Mail*. Another time, at the Malda cinema in Barcelona, he spent most of an early Todd Haynes film about Jean Genet leaning out the window of the cinema toilets, smoking a hash pipe; the film was too gay for him. Too arty. Too pretentious.

Harry and I should never have got together. It began in Barcelona, after I had been dumped, at twenty-three, by someone to whom I had foolishly and disproportionally given my heart. Harry was the ex's friend. He came out to see us, except we had broken up and the ex had taken up with another (she had the same name as me, but she didn't drink nearly as much as me, and was said to have been stable and mature and nice). Boo hoo, I wept, drinking even more and smoking myself senseless with grass cultivated on my roof terrace. Boo hoo. My life is over. And Harry had put his arm around me and said, don't be daft, no it's not. I'd clung to him like a drunken barnacle. 'But she's just sad and lonely,' the ex said to Harry in disgust, when he heard that we had hooked up. Harry, apparently, had shrugged, and said, with considerable self-deprecation, 'So am I.'

That's the abridged version. The longer version is tortuous, and does not reflect well on how to handle a break-up from someone desperate to get away from you, or how to treat the instant follow-on man whose gruff reluctance masked a shyness and fear of getting hurt himself. And I hurt Harry all right – hurt people always hurt people – but I didn't hurt him right at the start. At the start, I was the only one hurting, and he was like a big soft blanket who wrapped me up in his daft jokes and unthreatening jollity and kindness. And he was brilliant at drinking.

After a million platonic bottles of Estrella during the first half of that stifling Barcelona summer, Harry and I got together romantically after being stuck on a bus together for three days. EasyJet had not yet been invented, so we were escaping the '92 Olympics on an overnight coach to London, where I planned to sign on and sofa-surf until the TEFL schools reopened again back in Barcelona, and the Olympic hoopla had ended.

We had not factored French lorry drivers into our journey. From Perpignon to Calais, every major road – and quite a few minor ones – was blockaded by militant truckers. By day three, we were franc-less, fractious, and stinking like the runny cheese and over-ripe peaches being fed to us by the lorry drivers. They were distributing their perishable cargo free to everyone they were effectively holding prisoner on the hard shoulder, amongst the hot bright fields of beige cows and giant sunflowers. I still can't drive past a field of sunflowers without having trucker flashbacks.

But during those three days, while I gnashed my teeth and stamped my feet and wailed and moaned and thundered, Harry stayed calm and solid and even tempered. Some nice ladies who must have lived through the Blitz bought us bread and cheese in a hypermarche, and we got to Calais just as they were closing the port. We were the last to get onto the ferry, joyously clutching pints of gassy English lager as we sailed towards the white cliffs. When we finally got back, filthy and wrecked, to the shabby house in Forest Gate where Harry had a room, he let me use the bath first. It was this great kindness that made me advance on him later than morning, damp and scrubbed clean of coach fumes and sweat, and in a moment spin our sensible, uncomplicated friendship into a slow-motion car wreck of a relationship that would take years and years to grind to a bitter halt. (We are friends today, Harry and I – and for that I am grateful, because he was a good man and I treated him badly. But not as badly as I treated myself.)

And when I was with him during those few years after that bus journey through France – it was very on/off, with lots of bust-ups and dramas and door slamming and break-ups and make-ups – it meant I was part of the crowd. His crowd. I was desperate to be part of that crowd, because that was where the drugs and music and sense of belonging were. His crowd, it has to be said, was about as far removed from the people I had grown up with as you could imagine. I could never visualize any of them having ever been children – it seemed as though they had emerged fully grown down the pub, pint in one hand, pool cue in the other, snorting drugs off the cistern in the bogs. And that was just the girls.

Everyone was linked by the parties. You were as likely to see the same faces in the Bamboo Jungle in Anjuna, smeared in fluorescent paint and flying high on liquid acid, as you were at that old factory in Tyssen Street in Dalston, dancing to the same trance and techno, except with a roof over their heads instead of the Indian full moon. Harry used to constantly take the piss out of the middle class end of the psychedelic spectrum: 'Oh hallo darling, mwah mwah,' he'd say in a terrible plummy voice, rolling his eyes back in his head to simulate being out of it. 'Sweetie! Haven't see you since Vagator! How are your chakras?'

Harry's crowd was not like this. There were one or two middle class casualties who had got shipwrecked in Stratford or Forest Gate or East Ham and never found their way back to North or

West London, and a few who had blown in from further away – France, Spain, Greece – but they all had one thing in common: they were blokes whose primary purpose was getting wasted. Lists are always handy, so here's one that might show you where they were at:

INTO	NOT INTO
Organizing parties	Restaurants (except curry houses)
Going to parties	Sport
Music	Dinner parties
Drugs	Theatre/Cinema
Booze	Healthy living
Pubs	Nine to five
Caffs	Education
Festivals	Family life
Signing on	Marriage
Shared housing	Children
Goa	Pension plans

The thing was, I was shifting slowly from the first list towards the second, except I didn't know it at the time. I didn't realize that you could cherry-pick bits of both and create your own kind of life; I thought that in order to avoid going straight – that is, mortgages and sensible shoes – you had to give up everything on the first list. Remember, I was not coming from a place of logic; I was always chasing something. Happiness was always around the next corner, and I was in relentless pursuit, like a blind monkey in a maze. A bee in a jam jar.

One of the best things about Harry was that he was protective, so I always felt safe and comfortable with him. Bored maybe, and frustrated at our lack of common ground beyond booze and powder and pills, but the upside was that he looked after me. If I was off my head, he knew where I'd dropped my jacket; if I was wobbling down the road the morning after on a pair of break-neck platforms, he would provide a steadying arm. One of his favourite phrases was, 'Consider it done.' He was good like that. He was kind and funny and generous, the kind of bloke who would make a fantastic uncle but an unreliable dad. He'd have left the baby down the pub, or in the back of a cab. Not that anyone was thinking about babies back then – at least not consciously anyway. No, not consciously.

So what's this got to do with your dad? Well, he and Harry were polar opposites: big/small, black/white, posh/not posh, you name it, they were the opposite of each other. Your dad was one of those party-heads who liked getting wasted too, but not like the others; he would still go to work on Monday mornings. He was a week-ender. He would swallow pills and trips, but he never seemed to be out of it. I couldn't figure it out. He'd do a microdot, the kind of acid that could make an elephant hallucinate, and he'd seem perfectly fine, apart from being wide awake forever. Sometimes I wonder if he didn't just pretend to take drugs, like those mental patients who pretend to swallow their medication but secretly spit it out. He hardly drank at all – he liked a gin and tonic (and I mean *a* gin and tonic, a single, moderate, civilized G&T) – and he smoked like a teenage girl: shallow inhalation, instant exha-lation, ostentatious hand waving. He didn't really do spliff. He couldn't skin up, which seemed bizarrely unmanly. Yet his taste in music was more extreme than any of the trance crowd; he used to say, in his smooth public school voice, 'I like my music *hard*.'

Leo was not, however, one of the Bald Men of Techno, who differed from the psychedelic trance crowd in that they all had shaved heads, flight jackets, and a devotion to blistering noise; for a start, he was too well turned out. He would turn up at filthy squat parties full of people off their heads on ketamine as 10k rigs battered their senses with that awful gabber, and he would be immaculate in his snakeskin jeans and skintight black nylon t-shirt with an orange rectangle on the front. His hair was shiny, his nails were clean, his teeth were white and intact. He was never ragged or unkempt, even if he had been up for days. Eager to assign him a pigeon hole within the culture, I found I couldn't. I remember asking someone about him just after we'd met – because we really were complete strangers to each other – and they said, 'He's all right, Leo. He's sound.' And that was enough for me. The idea of actually getting to know him never crossed my mind.

There was just one snag, which didn't become obvious until he had already moved in. Although your dad knew how to debone Dover sole, dress for dinner and dance using mostly his pectoral muscles, he was not protective. He was too small. I don't mean physically (although that didn't help), but emotionally – he didn't have that big masculine presence that I didn't even realize I craved. He was suave and charming and lovely, but he didn't look after me as much as look up to me, and I didn't want to be the leader – I was still emotionally about twelve years old myself. I should have listened to those alarm bells that began ringing slowly yet distinctly when he moved in and placed a framed photo of dozens of teddy bears next to his bed, and an old toy stuffed sheep on his pillow. At the time, after the emotional bluntness of Harry, I thought Leo's teddy thing was merely quirky and ironic; I didn't interpret it as what it really was: the manifestation of a lost boy inside a thirty-something body. 'This is Daffyd,' he said, unpacking the tatty, old toy sheep from a box of his stuff.

'Uh, hello,' I said, staring not at the sheep but at Leo. But his face was impassive. Smooth and perfect.

Anyway, I was far too self-involved to really register too many of Leo's psychological potholes, so long as he was being nice to me. And he was always nice to me. He was the nicest, kindest person ever. Despite this niceness, however, I was just about to go completely around the bend.

2 HALLOWEEN

Christ who does she think she is... look at all that
fucking food, like Abigail's *fucking* Party... *all that*
pretentious shit she has hanging on her walls... she
looks like something from a horror film when she's
out of it... keep it away from me, I don't want to have
to talk to it... shit party anyway... how did Harry put
up with her for so long... shhhh, she's looking over, she
can hear you...

It happened at Halloween. I know it's hard to imagine going mad
at Halloween, seeing as it's the best night of the year. Our favourite
night, the one we look forward to for months. It's pumpkin lanterns
and dressing up as dead aristocrats or zombies or whatever, and
feasting on chocolate eyeballs and doing that blindfold game
where we stick our tongues into plates of awful combinations
like cat food and harissa – it's the night when everyone comes
down from London and we spend hours making ourselves undead
in front of the mirror, and we film ourselves and march through
the darkened streets, a screeching troop of highly animated multi-
generational horrors, exuberant in our panstick and our death-
liness.

The Halloween I went mad, it was from a different kind of horror. It was four months after I met your dad, and I thought I would never, ever come back from it.

I decided to have a party. I made pumpkin pie and lots of other orange food and put it on a table in the front room, because I wanted the kind of party where people would eat food, and have conversations, as well as getting off their heads and dancing until lunchtime next day. This was perhaps a bit naïve of me – maybe if I'd been living in Notting Hill (or Little Venice), such parties would be possible, but not out this way. People didn't do food. They did ketamine. Still, the house looked suitably ghoulish, decorated with swathes of fake cobwebs and hideous giant spiders that I had bought a few weeks earlier in New York.

Now, being on the dole in East London does not usually stretch to weekends away in New York – back then you got around forty-four pounds a week to live on – but your dad had stepped in and played Fairy Godmother. He bought me a plane ticket. River and Joe had won a prize for some music quiz to go to the MTV awards at Madison Square Gardens, and as I lolled about moaning about how jealous I was, Leo suddenly said, 'Wouldn't it be nice if you could be there the same time as your brother and sister?' and paid for a seat on Virgin Atlantic. Just like that.

I was amazed. I had never been to New York before, and could not believe that this man, who lived in my house but whom I hardly knew, would do such a thing – especially when he couldn't come himself because of work commitments. (The concept of 'work commitments' amongst everyone else I knew, especially myself, remained just that – a concept. A very abstract concept. Leo was the only person I knew who had an job. I hadn't had a proper job since my mid-twenties, because I had made backpacking and parties my full-time pursuit, and because I hated working for other people, to the extent that I chose poverty as the lesser of two evils, topped up with the odd day's cash in hand here and there. But nothing too strenuous. Instead I lived on rice and lentils.) 'Are you really paying for me to go to New York?' I asked him, half disbelievingly. He nodded. 'I love you,' I said. I couldn't believe anyone could be so kind.

'I love you too,' he said.

So. Off I went to New York, and spent three days walking around on my own craning my neck at giant buildings and three nights getting progressively more trashed with my siblings, culminating at Sound Factory on the last night, where we danced until the morning to Junior Vasquez, the three of us off our nuts on $25 pills called Versaces. That won't mean much to you, but Junior Vasquez was a house god, and even though River and I weren't into house – too many vocals and plinky plonky piano samples, not enough doof-doof-doof – the Versaces meant we didn't care. We were still flying high as we crossed the Atlantic later that day.

Back in Manor Park from Manhattan, laden with Halloween tat from those cheap stores by Union Square that sold everything from teeth whitening kits to vibrators, I announced I was having a party. Leo's input was background and minimal. I can't even remember if he invited anyone, but he must have done because I vaguely remember being introduced to people the next morning after my mind had already left the building, and being unable to do anything other than grind my jaw in their general direction and avoid all eye contact.

I thought it would be fun. Certainly lots of people came. None of my intimates were there, though, apart from Syd, but that night I was too fried to connect even with her. River had gone straight from New York to Australia or Ireland or somewhere, Saskia had just had a baby. Harry was in California visiting someone, and anyway he may not have been too keen on me since I had replaced him with someone half his size and twice as educated, even though there had been a respectable gap since our break-up, and, given that our paths overlapped a lot we had had to reach a kind of uneasy truce. I didn't know how he felt, but I still desperately wanted him to like me. I still needed him to like me.

It was like that Philip Larkin line:
    'The big wish
    Is to have people nice to you, which means
    Doing it back somehow.'

It was the doing it back that completely stumped me every time.

The night of the party, the house seemed to be mostly full of people I knew, rather than friends. Now this is fine, providing that the people you know are (a) nice and (b) think you're nice too. Unfortunately, this was not entirely the case, particularly as the night progressed and my grip on reality diminished. There were forces of evil operating that night, although in retrospect I think they were mostly – but not wholly – inside my head. That's the thing with paranoia – you can never truly know the difference between reality and delusion, because what seems as real as your feet may not actually be real at all. Then again it might be. You just can't tell.

I still can't, thirteen years later. Paranoia is awful. The blindingly obvious question is why on earth anyone would put themselves in that situation in the first place, but it's quite straightforward. Over a prolonged period of time, I had been losing my grip without realizing it. My inner self – the intelligent self – was rebelling against my outer, more stupid self and the pointlessness of my life as I headed towards thirty with nothing that fed my soul; the conflict, being played below the level of consciousness, was wreaking havoc in my mind. As were the drugs, although I had no idea about that either. I thought the drugs were my friends. William Burroughs once said that paranoia was when you knew a little of what was going on, and psychosis was when you found out exactly what was going on; I made the transition that night.

It was also the night when I realized how much I had relied on Harry as a safety net, a deflector shield, a bulletproof vest. And how ineffectual your dad was, and how much of an outsider.

A bloke at the party terrified me. He was off his head on ketamine, and I was off my head on E and speed, and he seemed to be telling me that he would like to stab my eyes out. Now, he may not actually have been saying this at all, but when you are off your trolley, you become super sensitive to other people's energy. You didn't have to have special powers to pick up the fact that he didn't much like me, though – he seemed sneering and snide, to the extent that someone else murmured to him to take it down a notch. He was everywhere – no matter which room I went in, there he was, glaring and mumbling and radiating hostility. At least I think he was. It certainly wasn't love and peace.

Now what would you have done? Well, you wouldn't be in that situation in the first place, because you are functional and have healthy self-esteem. You'd have asked him to leave, obviously. That would have been the sane, sensible, grown-up thing to do. That is what I would do now. But back then, I wasn't sane or sensible or grown-up. I was a mollusc whose shell had been forced open. If I had still been with Harry, I would have found him and just sat next to him, and felt safe against the creaking leather of his coat, because nobody would have been mean to me or taken the piss out of me when I was with him. But Harry was up a mountain in Santa Somewhere smoking pot with an old friend and I was in a house full of gurning strangers, stumbling from room to room, unable to find a safe place, my terror growing, my brain on fire from too much E.

And what did your dad do? He gave me more E.

'Open wide,' he said, every time we passed each other in the thumping crush, shoving another pill on my tongue, like some kind of disco priest, while our living space became a mini rave full of heaving bodies, the Technics on the kitchen table spinning out techno as people spilled out into the garden where a fire blazed in the firepit. We didn't have to worry about the neighbours – they were in the thick of it, selling pills to everyone for a tenner (that's what they cost back then – these days I believe you can get them for fifty pence, but I can't imagine they would be much cop).

Anyway. The night took on a catastrophic aspect. The scary bloke crashed into me coming down the stairs and snarled something; I was paralysed with fear, with humiliation, with terror. Everyone was laughing at me, whispering about me. The paranoia began eating me alive, feet first, so that the watching crowd could see me being devoured in front of them, raw and wild-eyed. I sat on the floor of the crowded sitting room, surrounded by people but unable to join in. Everyone was talking behind their hands about me. Bursts of laughter cracked over my head, and I heard snatches of jumbled acid banter mixed with poisoned words.

She's looking at us... no don't look up... she'll only come over, talking about herself... she never shuts up about herself... fucking hell.

I moved from room to room, my heart jumping inside my ribs as if it were going to burst, mouth bone dry, eyes giant black saucers. Someone gave me a line of speed. Another pill. Obviously I said yes to everything. I tried to tell Leo what was happening, but he didn't seem to get it. I tried to tell someone else, but it seemed as if they were just humouring me. I moved from room to room, garden to house, house to garden, but nowhere was comfortable or safe. I heard someone laugh the words 'amphetamine psychosis'. Leo looked frozen. He was locked inside his own drugs, inscrutable. Was he as terrified as me, and just pretending everything was all right? He was on lockdown. Fuck. Harry would have known what to do. 'I want to go home,' I whispered to him, digging my nails into his arm, jerking my head at the roomful of people.

'You are home,' he said, looking at me as though I were insane.

'I want them to go home,' my voice a shaky whisper.

'You can't just throw people out,' he said, jaw tight, eyes wide. He was right. How could you ask a whole house full of people on drugs to disperse, to take themselves out into the dark empty street where there was no music, no firepit, no sofas? That would have broken the first rule of parties: don't change your mind halfway through. Unthinkable.

It went on forever, that fucking Halloween party. People were still there the next day. The house was trashed, the garden full of ash and half burned bits of old wood. By now there was nobody in the whole place that I trusted, except Leo, who, although trustworthy, was useless. I was beyond speech, just wide-eyed and grinding my jaw, and desperate for everyone to fuck off, desperate for the warm sanctuary of booze. When the house was finally empty, I finally cried. I drank and drank and cried and cried. I never cried, but now I couldn't stop. That was it. Everyone hated me. It was over. It was the end.

EMERGENCY SMOOTHIE

- Place a large banana (potassium, for the existential dread) in a blender.
- Add freshly squeezed orange juice (vitamin C) and some plain yogurt (easily digestible protein).
- Squirt in some honey (energy) and spirulina (apparently it's good for you).
- Add at least 20 mg crushed valium, 1000 mg vitamin C, and a few vitamin B12s.

If this had been a film, a magic fairy godmother figure would have appeared and whizzed up one of these smoothies for me, to soothe the blazing chaos inside my head. Cool hands would have massaged my tight, hard shoulders and clenched jawbone, while telling me in a low voice that everything was fine, that none of it was real, that nothing bad had happened. Then the chemical warmth of the smoothie would have washed over every cell in my body and I would have slept.

In real life, I didn't have a fairy godmother, or any of the ingredients to make a valium smoothie. Not even a banana. In the end I just drank myself to sleep on rough, corner-shop vodka, but this just meant that the day after the day after, I had a hangover on top of the horrendous comedown.

It was one of the lowest points of my life.

Actually the Halloween party turned out not to be the end of my life, but the end of my life in East London. Although it really did feel like the end of my life at the time. Every day for three months after that fucking party, I thought about killing myself, fantasized about how I would loop the belt of my towelling dressing gown around the highest banister and let myself drop, swinging gently, my face going blue. Blue like Lord Shiva. Logistically, this would have just broken the banister – although I didn't weigh much back then, the bannisters were like matchsticks and you couldn't have hung a hamster from them. But I still thought about it every single day, as I sat at home alone in the smoke-fugged kitchen in my dressing gown, day after day, numb and lost, rolling cigarette after cigarette.

I was less popular than the clap. In retrospect this was not just paranoia at all – I would never have won Miss Congeniality because, in the words of various people who knew me over the years, 'your entire world revolves around yourself'; 'you don't connect with people'; 'you're on your own bus'; 'you only call when you want something'; and – from Harry – 'everyone hates you, even your own sister'. (I think he was a bit miffed at that particular juncture – it was a couple of years before I met your dad – because I had just run off to India with this cross-dressing, deranged guy who happened to be a mate of his. But that's another story.)

So I sat at home thinking suicidal thoughts, dreaming of nooses and overdoses, and under the cover of darkness at the weekends I carried on as usual, going out to parties because I had no idea what else to do, and convinced that if I avoided the scary people I would be fine. Which I did, but I wasn't. Because soon everyone became one of the scary people. The ones I deemed safe began freaking me out too. This only happened when I took drugs. Isn't that weird? Well, no. Not really. I just couldn't quite make the connection between drugs and terror.

How could these little round pills, my beloved friends for years and years since we'd first met in 1989, suddenly have turned on me? For so many years, they had given me the best nights of my life; filled me with empathy when I had none of my own; given me the energy to dance for ten hours straight; connected me to a fluorescent tribe where the currency was hugs, sweat and beats. Hands in the air. Shrieks of joy. Pounding hearts. A feeling of belonging.

It simply couldn't be. It was unthinkable. So it couldn't be the E turning on me, it must be the humans. And yet by Christmas that year there were no safe people left – they had all become scary. Time and time again, I would grab Leo, wild-eyed at 4 a.m., and tell him that we had to leave *right now*, because somebody was vibing me, or had said something nasty under their breath, or was speaking in that exhausting side-mouthed acid babble which you had to be hypervigilant to decode, about me, always about me, being snidey and snickering. I would absolutely insist that this had really, truly happened, because in my head, it really, truly had. Sometimes it happened when Leo was right next to me, and I would be nudging him, and hissing, 'See? See? Come on, we have to go. They hate me.'

I think because I was so convinced myself, he began to believe me. He wasn't like Harry, who would have said sharply and emphatically, 'Don't be daft, you're imagining things, lay off the pills. Shut up and have a drink.' When Leo confirmed that yes, quite a few people we knew peripherally disliked me, it just made it worse. 'But why do you care so much about what these people think of you?' he would ask, bemused. 'You don't even know them outside of the parties.'

But I did care. I couldn't bear the idea of being unpopular, yet it was beginning to dawn on me that I was in no way as popular as I would have liked. All I wanted was for people to like me, yet there was a gap in my brain where the empathy and the ability to connect were meant to be. These days – and I apologise in advance for sounding like a self-help book – I realize that the only person who should really like you is yourself, but back then I had no sense of who I was; I was just an empty wall of ego unable to imagine the feelings of others.

And then Harry was putting the boot in, slagging me off to anyone who would listen. I didn't imagine this. It was entirely real. He was bored stiff, having put up with me as a friend, girl-friend and ex-girlfriend over a period of many years. His good-will was all used up. I'd worn it out. Yet I kept hanging out with him. The paranoia got worse and worse, because it seemed that all my fears were real. Years after I read Nicholas Saunders' *E for Ecstasy* in 1993, I found an old copy of his 1997 follow-up, *Ecstasy Reconsidered*, which looks at what E can do to your brain. It seems the pills were doing nothing more than 'impairing psychic defences against anxiety-generating material in the unconscious'. In other words, I was already a basket case, and the pills just burned away my defences, exposing the raw, weak innards of my mind.

3   BRIGHTON

You're probably getting bored with this now. Don't worry, it gets better. I didn't end up killing myself, which I consider to be one of my better decisions. Instead we moved to Brighton. Your dad knew someone who lived in Kemp Town, and we went down one weekend and hung out in the gay bars on St James Street and went to Revenge and Sunday Sundae, and it was the first time I had experienced any of Brighton beyond the Pier. I loved it, mainly because it wasn't East London. And that was before you ever stepped out into the light. There was sky everywhere, and white royal icing houses along the seafront, and the endless sea. There didn't seem to be any poor people, and nothing was ugly. The air was clean and fresh. I remember walking along the beach with your dad, crunching over the stones, and it suddenly hit me, that this was the solution. 'We could live here,' I said. 'We could move here. It would be easy. We could do it.' Two weeks later, we had a flat in Kemp Town. Your father didn't know what had hit him.

Because things were frequently so distorted inside my head, you might be wondering just how your dad and I were doing. We still barely knew each other. My memories of this time are dominated by my own paranoia and self-obsession, so that your dad, who was never a forceful presence, was almost peripheral.

But it wasn't all paranoid meltdowns. For our first New Year's Eve together, before we moved to Brighton, we went to Madrid. Neither of us had been there before, even though I had spent years in Barcelona before I set off on my travels with the deranged transvestite, whom I'll tell you about another time. From the balcony of our hostel in Puerta del Sol, we watched as thousands gathered in the plaza below; we drank our cava, counting down to midnight before Feliz 99 flashed up in giant lights. I was already drunk, because I had been drinking all day, and I forgot to eat the grapes we had bought earlier: in Spain you eat a grape for every second being counted down, so you have twelve grapes crammed in your mouth in twelve seconds, with juice running down your chin. Except I didn't. We found the grapes all squashed and bruised the next day.

Leo was starting to notice my drinking. Because things had been so overshadowed by the regular paranoid meltdowns that dominated my life at the time, my boozing hardly got a look in. In Madrid, we spent the afternoon drinking rioja in a bar full of the giant mounted heads of bulls killed in the ring. The waiters were dressed as toreadors, and the more I drank, the more I felt like Ernest Hemingway, even though I was vegetarian and would have rather shot myself in the head than go to a bullfight. But I was so happy when I drank. Nothing mattered. I loved Leo, who was a rubbish drinker, when I was drinking. I loved everything when I was drinking. Most of all I loved drinking when I was drinking. 'Te quiero,' I told him fuzzily, in that bar in Madrid.

'What?' he said. 'Look, can we get the bill?'

There's a photograph of me at the station next day, waiting for a train south, looking like death warmed up.

When I remember that trip to Spain, there's a slideshow of amazing colours in my head, pierced through with an underlying, unspoken, clawing anxiety. It was nothing to do with Leo. He was so easy to be around, happy just to follow me on and off trains, in and out of doors, up and down stairs. It was probably just as well that he didn't understand anything. The racists in Spain come mainly come from the plain; like most racists, from the middle of nowhere. At some dusty nowhere station in the middle of Castilla La Mancha, waiting for another train, the old man at the station bar said to me conversationally, 'Isn't he too black to be English?' Loads of places would ignore him – I had taught him how to say 'excuse me, two beers please' – but outside of Madrid he remained el hombre invisible until I marched up to whoever wasn't seeing him and bellowed 'Hola!' Then they would turn away from mute, mono-lingual Leo, and focus instead on the unusual colour of my hair. It was pink at the time.

The Alhambra was a dream. The mountains behind it lit up at sunset, making the snow glow pink. It was freezing up there, even though we were in Andalucia. I'd forgotten about the altitude. We spent days lost inside sacred Islamic symmetry, mirrored pools and mosaic'd arches, hidden passageways and closed rose gardens where Moorish princesses had taken secret lovers and been hacked to death by jealous sultans. At night we sat on cushions in small dark Granada cafes lit by Moroccan lanterns, eating hummus, falafel and pitta. And drinking. Always drinking. 'You're always drinking,' he would say.

'And?' I would answer. '*And?*'

Anyway, when you take someone to a new country, it's your duty to introduce them to the drinks menu. It'd be rude not to. Go on, I'd say. Try this. Try that. Your dad would have a sip, then hand it back to me. He was happy enough with a glass of rioja.

And I mean a glass. 'You have to try the fino before dinner,' I'd say. 'From the barrel.'

I loved drinking from the barrel, watching the man turning the metal tap and catching the pale liquid in a long sherry glass. It made me feel like an extra from *Carmen*. Leo hated fino, and everything else from the barrel – probably because it was like paint stripper, but so moreishly cheap. You could get a glass of fino for about fifty pence. So I would drink his. 'You must try Licor 43,' I'd tell him, after we'd eaten. He hated that too. It was a sticky sweet vanilla-tasting drink popular with old ladies, that I loved over ice. So I'd drink his too. Then we'd have carajillos – espressos with cognac – and a cognac chaser. Except the cognac, which was always ropey cheap stuff like Sobrano, gave him heartburn, so I would drink his. I'd drink his wine too, once he'd had his glass or two out of the bottle.

The morning we left Granada, I was careful to cover the mattress on my side of the bed with extra blankets to hide the huge wet patch underneath. Then I instantly banished all thoughts of it from my mind, so that by the time we had walked up the narrow cobbled street to an old man's bar for coffee, Diet Coke and Neurofen (my standard breakfast – I only had Bloody Marys in an emergency, because I never drank in the morning unless I was close to death) it had never happened. What had never happened? Exactly.

If we kept on the move, everything was all right. All the best times I had with Leo during our seven years together involved movement. I didn't know how to be still. I felt like one of those sharks that die if they stop swimming. We took a bus down the mountains from the Sierra Nevada to the beach, travelling from winter to summer in an hour or two, and spent the day lying in the sun on warmish sand, reading our books and drinking cold fizzy cava out of the bottle. There was nobody there at all, apart from a few fishermen and a sad man in a beachside café with no customers.

That night we took a sleeper train back to Madrid, and went to the Prado first thing the next morning. Poor Leo. It seems to be a bit of a pattern of mine, dragging unwilling men around art galleries. A few years later, at the Pompidou, when our relationship had lost some of its deference, he simply sat down on the floor, ignoring the Warhols and Pollocks and Kandinskys and Picassos and Matisses. And when I said, 'But you'll never get a chance to see these again!' – which sounds like a premonition now, but at the time I was just trying to make him get up – he looked up wearily, and said, 'You go and memorize them all for me.'

At the Prado, all I really wanted to see was *The Garden of Earthly Delights*. He was so patient. Three times we accidentally ended up going through the wrong door out onto the street, where the queue stretched around the corner. Three times we jumped the queue and explained we had taken a wrong turn and could we please go back inside. Three times our tickets were reissued, and we walked in huge circles past Goya, Velazquez, Caravaggio. Past Dürer, van Dyck, Breugel. Warmer, warmer, through another big door. And then – fuck! – out in the street again. Until at last we found it. We stood transfixed. Actually, I think Leo was not quite as transfixed as me, but he hid it well, and he bought me a hard-back of Bosch colour plates in the gift shop, which the dog we hadn't got yet would chew up a few months later. It's still on the bookshelf somewhere, covered in bite marks. There are bits of Leo dotted around everywhere. They're just not very obvious. Well, apart from you two of course.

*

We got married. It was my idea. I'd just been prescibed anti-psychotics, which – although they remained unopened under a heap of red lipsticks in my make-up box – gives you some indication of where the doctor thought my head was at. In hindsight getting married may have been a subconscious – if somewhat drastic – diversionary tactic; I didn't so much marry your father as take him hostage. I didn't even believe in marriage, which made it seem like an act of inverted subversion: let's get married just for the hell of it, for the party. My reasoning really was that simple, with no sense of the future whatsoever, other than that he was an awfully nice man from whom I had no plans to break-up.

Also, getting married was such a lovely way of taking my mind off the fact that I was still hearing voices every time I took drugs. Which was quite a lot, still. Like a laboratory beagle that had been let out of its cage, I still followed my nose back to East London for the parties, even after we had made our escape south, barreling down the M23 in a rented van full of tatty furniture and boxes and boxes of my books.

Once we had left East London, we only went back up to the fluffy parties with the fluffy party people, mostly at the Alice In Wonderland house on Margery Park Road with the sunken garden and the wonky tree house and fluorescent mannequins in the flower beds. No more scary blokes in grimy squats. But there were still shedloads of MDMA involved. Obviously.

I remember one particular morning with the sun coming up over the garden, and everyone lounging around bug-eyed, the music less intense, Syd walking down the garden path with a tea tray of chipped mugs and a carton of soya milk. The djembe drums were coming out, people were skinning up in the early sunlight, there were flashes of colour everywhere, light catching on glitter and bindis and clothes made from recycled saris, and everyone was mellowing after a hard night's dancing. It was a safe place – no spiky geezers from down the pub, just a garden of assorted hippies – but I still managed to flip. I ended up locking myself in the upstairs bathroom, my fingers rammed in my ears to block the wafting chatter from the garden. 'We have to go, we have to get out of here,' I whispered, seizing Leo in the kitchen and dragging him away down the road to West Ham Park, where we walked in despairing circles around the rose gardens as I tried vainly to convince him that those dreadlocked crusties visiting on their bus from somewhere rural were bitching about me, that the one with the shaved head and all those piercings was sniggering at me. That my friends – the ones I trusted – really despised me, and were only pretending to like me because they were kind. I remember the bewilderment on Leo's face, as he repeated over and over than I was imagining things. And then I wondered whether he wasn't in on it too. Whether it wasn't all a giant conspiracy.

Now, as your mother, I am supposed to be giving you all kinds of useful advice, whether you want it or not. Like, always moisturize your neck, because one day it may be your face. Or never imagine you can outrun a rhino in a straight line – throw off your shirt and zigzag. And if you are going to take drugs, at least wait until you are out of your teens. I didn't start until I was in my early twenties; had I assaulted my still-forming teenage brain with chemicals, I imagine I would now be rocking backwards and forwards on a locked ward, and not sitting here writing this for you. So if you must do them, at least do them intelligently. Familiarize yourselves with concepts like rehydration and nutrition. Understand what dehydration, low blood sugar and sleep deprivation can do to your mind, before you ever start adding mind-bending substances. A banana here, a milkshake there, can make all the difference.

I would swallow pills on an empty stomach ('eating's cheating'), then dance manically all night, subsisting for twenty-four hour stretches only on water, nicotine, hash, and more pills, before bringing myself down via a vat of alcohol the morning after. It was usually around dawn that I had my worst attacks of paranoia, as exhaustion, dehydration and plummeting blood sugar combined with the high wearing off, and I would start to crash. Of course, everyone else was coming down too, some more jaggedly than others, but for some reason, it only seemed to be me who was hearing all those voices and getting those tidal waves of fear. I would be the one in the horrors, at least until I started boozing – and I didn't always have booze in the house, because I was so disorganized. As time went on, I made more and more sure to have beer in the fridge – or, as it got worse, vodka in the freezer.

Back in lovely, blue-skied Brighton after another fraught Sunday morning, I finally went to the doctor. She was a locum, all fresh from medical school and with eyes that visibly widened when I told her that I kept hearing voices talking about me and laughing at me every time I took drugs. She wrote me a prescription for more drugs – a supply of anti-psychotics – which I immediately hid, because I didn't trust official pills from giant drug companies, only the ones that came over from Holland hidden in the side panels of friends' cars. But I did stop taking E, at least for a while, to let my mind cool down again after all its boiling over. And that left a gap in my life, one that needed filling. Nature abhors a vacuum. 'Why don't we get married,' I said to your dad one day in late spring. It came out of nowhere, a random thought. 'It'd be fun.'

'Okay,' he said. I think he was quite chuffed.

What I probably meant was that the wedding would be fun. Although everyone from the Buddha to the Twelve Steps recommends living in the moment, I lurched from moment to moment so blindly that the concept of anything beyond the immediate present did not exist. I couldn't think beyond the weekend, never mind the rest of my life. But because we didn't argue, because we were having a nice life in our Kemp Town basement by the sea, and because it would be a great excuse for a party where we could all get dressed up and prance around, I decided we should get married. It wasn't volatile with your Dad, the way it had been with Harry, or insecure, the way it had been with all the other boyfriends before him. It seemed highly unlikely that he would leave me. He was always nice to me. And that was enough reason for a bloody good day out.

Your Dad didn't hesitate, which was just as well, because he didn't really have a choice. Luckily he liked a good party as much as anyone else, and to be honest I think he was quite pleased that someone actually wanted to marry him – he said it made him feel terribly grown up. And the funny thing was, I thought he *was* terribly grown up, because he had a pension plan and went for regular health checks and owned a colander and a garlic press.

He did, however, complain a lot about all the debt he was in. While my financial situation was beautifully uncomplicated – I had not a pot to piss in – he spoke endlessly of his debt. How could it be, I wondered, that a man of such means could be so perpetually impoverished? He earned twenty-four grand a year, which to me made him a veritable Croesus, and he lived rent free thanks to my ingenuity around such matters, our bills in general so tiny a churchmouse could have managed them. When pressed, he would go all mysterious and mutter about owing money to Bad People I Didn't Know. Truthfully, I never got the straight of it. I never met these Bad People I Didn't Know, or understood what he owed, or how much, or how. Maybe those Bad People I Didn't Know were called Visa or MasterCard – I never found out. All I know is that your dad never, ever had enough money. From the night I met him, when he borrowed fifty quid from me on the way home from the New North Road party, to the very end, he was always skint. Not mean, not ungenerous – quite the opposite, as you will recall, buying gifts of everything from Hot Oil hair treatment to Virgin Atlantic airline seats – but skint. Skint, skint, skint. Financially, he was a black hole through which money was sucked, never to reappear. By the end, he made me look like Bill Gates. 'How will we afford it?' he asked of the wedding.

'Don't worry,' I said cockily. 'So long as you don't want it at Westminster Abbey, we'll be fine.'

So we had a lot of fun figuring out how we would put on a wedding with almost no money whatsoever; back then, I had no income other than the dole, plus a few quid here and there occasionally teaching English as a foreign language. I was also starting to get tiny bits of my writing published, but the pay was erratic and pathetic. Luckily, I was very good at being poor. I knew how to pov-shop, and could do a lot with dried chick peas and rice. Having grown up in comfort, paradoxically, I was relaxed about having no money; I was not particularly materialistic. I assured your father that, like most things, getting married could be done on a shoestring with a bit of imagination. It wasn't as if we wanted a banquet for three hundred guests. I don't want a normal wedding, I told him. Just a party for our friends. And nothing churchy. He was in full agreement. Having been raised Catholic, he was as anti-church as I was. But, unlike me, he was very, very atheist.

So we sat on the cheap nylon carpet of our living room floor, him making lists, me making wedding invitations out of sparkly silver paper and pink fake fur, as our new puppy Carmen ('As in Carmen Miranda,' Leo always pointed out, whenever people began humming Bizet) chewed on our shoes. Carmen was our new baby, and we adored her. Half Labrador, half Boxer, she was a fat black velvety little thing with huge eyes and floppy ears, who peed everywhere.

We were happy then. Well, relatively speaking. We were living by the sea, in a neighbourhood where not only were cappuccinos and the *Guardian* freely available, but where all the shops sold expensive nonsense instead of things costing three-for-a-quid, and further down St James Street you could, if you so desired, buy poppers and leather body harnesses, then dance the night away in gay discos. It was a long, long way from the kebab shops and bus shelters of Manor Park.

Not that we really wanted to dance our nights away any more – we were too busy playing house with Carmen. She would grow into a gigantic, bouncy thing who needed miles of walking a day, and trashed the place every time we left her alone for more than half an hour, and who really needed to live in open countryside instead of a one bedroom flat; but we never thought any of that through. I just told Leo we were getting her and when he saw her, he fell in love. Had he known that he would be the one who would end up walking her every morning as I lay in bed too hungover to remember where I'd put my feet, he might have objected more. But that first summer in Brighton, nothing could go wrong.

'Do you take this man to be your lawful wedded husband?' asked the registrar at the town hall.

'I do,' I said. And so I did.

Of course the wedding was fun. Well, apart from the night before and the day after, and the bit in the registry office, which was sweaty and uncomfortable and made me want to giggle like a schoolgirl and pull faces; but the rest of the day was a hot blur of colour and laughter. We came out of the town hall in a confetti blizzard and a swarm of fairy wings – even Carmen the wiggly black puppy was wearing some, handmade by me from sparkly gauze and a coat hanger. There were about thirty of us, dressed up as if it were carnival, pouring out into the white of the square on that blazing August day, relieved to be away from the registrar in her serious suit and the unnatural formality of the seven minutes or so the legalities took. I would say 'ceremony', but it was nothing of the sort – we just wanted to get that bit over with so that we could get on with the fun stuff.

Your dad looked amazing. He wore a sharp black suit and a shirt that seemed to be made from purple tinfoil, which glittered in the sun. The same shirt he wore to his funeral. All of our friends dressed up, in red sequins and orange taffeta and pink gauze, in crumpled suits and harem trousers and funny hats and many pairs of fairy wings (they had not yet become a festival staple, or become synonymous with hen nights); outside the town hall, a mariachi band materialized as if by magic and played the jolliest music as we all trooped out. Nobody had booked them – they just turned up out of nowhere. As we made our way through the Lanes to the Pavillion, tourists stopped and filmed us, and asked us if we were a street theatre performance. Which we kind of were. We didn't look much like a wedding.

I had gone up to Green Street and bought an electric blue salwar kameez, and then spent most of the wedding budget on hair extensions because a week before the big day, in the Alice in Wonderland garden in East London after a long night of loud music and no sleep, I had drifted off while sitting upright in a chair as Saskia began giving me a pre-wedding trim. All I remember is thinking that it was taking ages, as I nodded in and out of a spaced out dream, the rising sun warming my face as she snipped and snipped. I think she must have been fairly mashed herself, because when I woke up I was knee deep in my own hair and looked like Gwendolyn from *Wallace and Gromit*. It was a horror bob, slashed to my ears, the worst haircut you have ever seen. I just remember sitting there, opening and closing my mouth like a fish lost for words. Which is why, after emergency damage limitation in some snotty overpriced salon, I turned up to my wedding with flowing blue and red pretend hair as unnatural as Leo's tinfoil shirt and no money left over for anything else.

There was a shoe shop in Brighton at the time called Buffalo, which was briefly fashionable – the Spice Girls used to wear those towering Buffalo platforms in the nineties – and your dad had bought me a pair of silver platform mules there, for sixty pounds. That seemed like an awful lot for a pair of shoes – more than a week's dole money – but he insisted. So I was actually taller than him on the day, because I was elevated on those glittery wedges, but he didn't seem to mind. He said his smallness was part of who he was. I still have those shoes. I never wear them, because they're too uncomfortable, but I will keep them forever.

The day itself was a bit like India – functioning chaos. You know how weddings are planned down to the very last meticulously anal retentive detail, with every little moment filled with colour coordinated thoughtfulness? Well, imagine the total opposite and you'll have some idea of ours. We had no photographer, no wedding album, no flowers, no best man, no bridesmaids, no speeches, no band, nothing. We barely had a venue. We just turned up, signed our names on the dotted line, then made our way over to the Pavilion where someone who knew how to use a camera snapped lots of lovely pictures.

There was a gap before dinner, which was upstairs at the Sanctuary Café – that place off Hove seafront where they had vegan cake and lesbian poetry nights, I think it's closed down now – so River scouted ahead and found a pub with a garden which would accommodate thirty or so oddly dressed people for a spontaneous round of drinks. We had planned nothing. Leo left everything to me and I left everything to chance. It was chaos theory in action. 'To the bride and groom,' someone called, as we sat at the trestle table in the courtyard of the pub. Everyone raised their glass. Leo nudged me. 'They mean us,' he said. We smiled, and I drank mine fast.

No-one seemed to mind that our wedding was a bit all over the place. Everyone seemed to be having a terribly jolly time. One guest was already tripping his face off. Another managed to hold off until we sat down to dinner before swallowing his acid. There was a lot of giggling. Upstairs at the Sanctuary, it was all wood and windows and a relaxed seaside feel. After dinner, once we had finished the cake (each table had its own homemade carrot cake, instead of wedding cake; the tradition of sending bits of wedding cake in envelopes to people we had not invited struck me as insane and unhygienic), tradition got the better of us and there were some attempts at speeches. A terrier called Padstow, now deceased, barked continuously throughout, even as my dad stood up and made an impromptu declaration in unfamiliar London slang that 'Love is the guv'nor.' Someone else read a poem. The cava flowed.

The cava had been flowing all day. Since I woke up, in fact. Leo had stayed somewhere else the night before, in keeping with tradition. I can't remember where. I can't remember much about what I was feeling other than numb; excited, yes, but also trying to drown out the clamour, the voice in my head that was screaming at me to run away, to stop, to not do this insane thing, to put the brakes on. *WHAT ARE YOU DOING?* screamed the voice inside my head. *WHY ARE YOU DOING THIS? DO YOU WANT THIS? DO YOU? DO YOU? DO YOU REALLY?*

But obviously it was far too late for those kinds of thoughts, so instead, the night before I became somebody's wife, I got drunk. I vaguely remember telling River that actually getting married was all a bit of a mistake and that really Leo and I were just a fling which had gone on too long, but by the next day I had killed those thoughts by filling my head with frocks and flowers and fairy wings, and more cava. Everyone gets nervy just before they are due to get married, I told myself. It's perfectly normal, this feeling that I am totally doing the wrong thing. And then the taxi came and took me away.

I didn't actually get married drunk. That would have just have been wrong, like smoking when you're pregnant or snogging your friend's boyfriend. No, I held off, apart from a morning glass to steady my nerves – that is, to celebrate the specialness of the day

– until after we were officially Mr and Mrs. Then I began drinking like a woman dying of thirst.

The adrenaline neutralized it for the first few hours. After dinner, once any older guests had been dispatched back to hotel rooms, we went down to the dance space in the basement of the Sanctuary, and the pills came out. The friend who had originally introduced Leo and me played a blinding set, all our old favourites, and we danced and danced until it was all over, and we were out in the street saucer-eyed and joyous. When we retired to our flat for our wedding night, there were about fifteen of us. Leo spent his first night as a married man lying squashed in a tiny corner of his own bed as various bodies sprawled around him, including the dogs Carmen and Padstow. I never went to bed at all.

Inside my head a storm was brewing.

Looking back, you don't have to be a medical genius to understand what happened. A wedding is a big event, especially if it's your own, no matter how informal or bohemian or totally disorganized. My adrenaline levels were already in overdrive when I added the vat of cava and fistful of ecstasy – the prolonged over-use of which had recently resulted in a prescription for anti-psychotics. And I'd had no sleep. I had no concept of self-care. I thought that being vegetarian and eating a lot of tofu was enough to make me bullet-proof – and for a long time, it had been. Just not anymore. The morning after the wedding, we were all still awake, tired and wired, in the mess of the flat. There were wilted flowers everywhere, and sparkly gift wrapping from opening our presents in the middle of the night (because no, we did not have a wedding list at John Lewis). There were bodies everywhere in various states of disrepair, and two bouncy dogs desperate for a walk.

I wonder what Leo was thinking, waking up to this post-wedding carnage (unlike everyone else, he had actually managed to get some sleep). I never thought to ask him, to be perfectly honest, although over that first summer in Brighton when the East End massive kept arriving en masse on our doorstep – always at my invitation – he had murmured a few times about my insatiable need to be surrounded by a crowd all the time. 'There are always so many people in here,' he would say, waving his arm around the tiny flat, and I would attack him for not liking my friends, missing the point entirely. He did like my friends, he just didn't like always having to share his bed with half a dozen of them and their dogs.

But back then I had no empathy, with him or anyone else; I thought he was being a fuddy-duddy when he objected to the eternal cry of 'all back to mine', because I was working entirely off my own agenda. One of the few times he seemed genuinely cross with me was when I made a vat of curry for everyone (I was good at feeding lots of people at very little notice, so long as they weren't expecting anything gourmet). 'For God's sake,' he hissed at me. 'You've made it too spicy – now Syd can't eat it. Not everyone has the same taste as you.' And I had looked at him, uncomprehendingly.

Anyway. The morning after our wedding, people decided that a visit to the beach was in order – it was a beautiful day outside, hot and sunny. Our London visitors wanted to make the most of the seaside. Ill prepared for either heat or hydration, I sat dumbly in the blazing sun, toxic and exhausted. The idea that maybe I should have gone to sleep somewhere peaceful and quiet never occurred to me; I might have missed out on something. Syd, Ted, River, Leo and I and a few others sat in the sun, and it blazed on our heads, and the day got hotter and hotter as the sun rose higher and higher, and there was no shade, and the stones were hot and hard, and as we sat there for hours and hours, I became convinced that Ted despised me. Like slow inward-spreading poison, the idea consumed me until I was dumb with it. As it looped around inside my brain, I became paralysed by fear and discomfort. And insanity.

Now back then, Ted was quite a lot spikier than the Ted you know today. This was before Lotus and Vishnu were born, when Ted and Syd were not the long established couple that you know and love and dress up with at Halloween and go camping with in the summer. Ted had been part of Forest Gate's acid army, a semi-feral squatter still slowly being domesticated by his relationship with Syd, and later by fatherhood and age. Back then, he was a bit scary. A bit twisty, a bit tweaky. And inscrutable – was he laughing with you? At you? At least, that was my perception of him anyway. He was not yet the Ted who liked to sit around on Sunday afternoons drinking tea and eating cake and talking about this and that. Back then, he wasn't exactly what you'd call fluffy. And I wasn't exactly what you'd call stable.

And so on that hot, demented morning on the beach, the day after I got married, sitting amongst a group of people I definitely counted as friends, people who liked me enough to come down to the seaside for my wedding, the switch inside my head had flipped again, and I began imagining that every word from Ted's mouth was a barbed jibe. Then they were all starting to do it, all using double-speak. They either hated me or felt sorry for me. Someone asked if I had read any good books lately. This meant, *'Read any good books lately, you pretentious tosser who thinks you're everyone's intellectual superior?'* I couldn't answer, I was too busy chewing the inside of my mouth, too afraid of eye contact. Whoever asked me looked away. Everyone had been up all night, everyone was frayed around the edges, but I was the only one who was collapsing inwards because there was nothing inside me to hold me up.

I was on a loop: I was irritating Ted by my very presence. Syd pitied me. Everyone who didn't loathe me thought I was pitiful.

Not to labour it, but here's what seemed real to me at the time: Ted and Syd were hand-cuffed together – someone had given Leo and me a pair of those joke sex shop hand-cuffs, and Ted and Syd had put them on, then lost the key. Such was my paranoia by late morning – or my heightened perception, as I thought it was – that when Ted said I was getting on his nerves, I actually asked him in a whisper if I really was annoying him, because I desperately wanted some reassurance that no, I wasn't, that everything was all right. I don't think he heard me in any case – my memory is hazy and distorted, and in fairness, I wasn't the only person off my tits – because he pointed to the hand-cuffs biting into his wrist, and said quietly, 'Yeah, it's starting to get on my nerves a bit now.'

Oh. The hand-cuffs. Not me.

It's really hard to describe paranoia because it's like trying to describe a dream or an acid trip – nobody but yourself is in there, so it only makes sense to you. But the mathematics of it are simple – low self-esteem plus addictive personality plus too many drugs equals meltdown.

Later that day, back in the flat, my face was all swollen from chewing the inside of my cheeks, and my skin was burnt raw and puffy from over-exposure to the sun. I had a dehydration headache, and was shivering. Then I threw up all over the floor. Sunstroke, drugstroke, madstroke. I remember River, on her way out to a post-wedding dinner with our family after no sleep herself, a dinner which I was supposed to attend, telling me quite seriously, 'Lose the drugs or lose your friends.'

The next day, all the friends who had stayed over after the wedding drove to Cornwall for the solar eclipse, leaving me behind. They told me there wasn't enough room in a half empty car. Can't say I blame them.

So it took not one, but two deeply horrid experiences – and dozens of lesser occasions of terror and teeth-grinding and hiding in locked bathrooms with my fingers rammed in my ears to block out the sound of people's voices tearing me apart – before I finally got it. The drugs no longer worked. At last, it sank in properly. Like the dancer Michael Clarke, who once said that he had been 'misled into believing that as an artist you were meant to explore different states and then report back to normal people', I too believed that it was somehow my job to explore my consciousness so that I could write it all down, while neatly avoiding normal nine-to-five living. But that only works if (a) you are Oscar Wilde or one of the Beats or Carlos Castenada, and (b) you are not too fucked up to actually write it down. And it definitely doesn't work if the drugs have turned on you, changing from fluffy puppies to rabid attack dogs.

It was time to say goodbye to a part of my life that had sustained me for a very long time.

Goodbye then, little round pills, little pink calis, doves, rhubarb-and-custards, mitsubishis, leahs (after Leah Betts), little pills that gave me empathy and let me dance away all those years. Goodbye lines of MDMA that made me feel like I was made of fluff and candyfloss and love. Goodbye, tiny bits of blotter stamped with Bart Simpson, purple hearts, Californian sunshine, cartoon elephants, Daffy Duck, the Buddha; goodbye little black microdots that turned my brain inside out – sometimes in a good way. Goodbye white lines of everything that ever kept me up all night, from rock star coke to washing powder speed. Goodbye ketamine, cooked up on a silver spoon under a silver moon in India. Goodbye creamy black charas from the mountains of Manali, goodbye cheap Moroccan hash smoked from cheap Moroccan pipes, goodbye giggly weed grown on the roof, goodbye skunk that always floored me, goodbye 2CBs and blueys, goodbye squidgy black opium so dreamily beautiful that it made throwing up a languid pleasure. And goodbye magic mushrooms, the most magical and benevolent of them all, goodbye to the chirruping mushroom fairy flitting around the room, and the beautiful geometrics and fractals in front of my eyes, the ancient and sacred portal to the divine. I realize how nuts that might sound, but still – we didn't get on our hind legs without them. Goodbye, goodbye, goodbye.

Still, at least there was always the booze.

Sorry, this is meant to be about your dad. Your dad, who loved boarding school food like mashed potato and fish finger sandwiches and custard and burnt toast, who never talked about his past, who wasn't in contact with anyone from his past, who had no family apart from an auntie, who lived miles away, and some relatives in South Africa whom he had never met.

Your dad, with his dark-chocolate skin and his hot-pink polo shirt, his short muscular body that shone in the sun, his rugby-playing thighs in yellow denim cut-offs, his big boots and cropped blue-black hair. That was what your dad looked like going to work. In London, he'd head off to East Ham tube station at 7 a.m. looking like he was going to an all-nighter at Trade. He worked at King's Cross for a charity and was on Islington Council's payroll; it was a cushy number, doing something techie and finishing early afternoon every day. 'You have such an easy job,' I said idly, barely able to remember what a job felt like.

'No I haven't,' he would reply. 'You have no idea what it's like.'

But I did, as it happened. Between the ages of seventeen to twenty-seven I had worked many full time jobs. I'd worked in a bakery decorating cakes at three in the morning; I'd worked in a comic warehouse humping dusty boxes of *X-Men* and *Spiderman*. I'd spent far too much time in offices, answering phones and typing up words so pointlessly dull my brain used to vomit, surrounded by people so alien they might as well have had green lizard heads coming out of their suits. I'd worked on market stalls in the snow, and helped homeless people get into night shelters. I'd been a youth worker, an administrator, a secretary, a salesperson, a shopworker, a TEFL teacher, a dishwasher, a personal assistant, a wardrobe assistant, a cleaner, a private language tutor, and when I couldn't bear any of it any longer, a temp. So I did have quite a good idea of what it was like to work in a job I disliked, because I disliked pretty much all of them. And so I legged it – onto the dole, so that I could be free to do what I liked doing – writing, backpacking, going to parties. Penniless, but free. (This was long before the global economic meltdown, when those kind of options still existed, when the dole was still viable.)

Anyway. Even before we ever moved south, I began to notice how much your dad moaned about his job, and the people he worked with. How enslaved he was, because of his mysterious debts to the Bad People. How hard done by he was. He seemed to worry a lot about things that didn't exist in my world: salary increases, pension plans, old age, annoying work colleagues, health, overdraft facilities, not being able to afford stuff. At the time, I was more concerned with the voices in my head, and and I couldn't countenance Leo's being anything except utterly forward-looking, strong, confident, organized and together. All the things I had not yet become, all the things he would never see me be. It took a while to realize that I was barking up the wrong man.

One summer evening in Brighton, very soon after we had moved here, we were walking along the seafront towards the Palace Pier, our new puppy waddling along joyfully on her pink puppy lead. It was almost sunset, the light was gold and the air was warm and soft. We were strolling into the sun, hand in hand, the sea sparkling. 'Wow,' I said. 'Could this get any better.'

It wasn't even a question, but a statement of fact. And without missing a beat, Leo had began to complain bitterly about having to take the train to London every day, and how awful it was, and how he hated his work, and everyone at his work, even though he couldn't really explain why. And I began to realize that behind your dad's elegance and charm and kindness, there was a way of looking at the world that was very much glass half empty.

Of course you know how rotten it is to commute to London – whenever we do the train journey, never in rush hour and only for fun things like visiting Tate Modern or the South Bank, it's long and boring and tiring. But still. Surely, I asked, the trade-off between an extra half hour on the train and coming home to the sea and fresh air and space and Regency splendor and gay bars and Waitrose balanced it out? Didn't it?

In my world, if something isn't working I tend to do one of two things: accept it or leg it. The obvious thing for your dad to do was change jobs. Get a local job. Do something new. Drop the old stuff that he had been doing for years, that he said he hated. Branch out.

And thus began a chapter of extreme tedium between us, as I appointed myself his manager, and he became the opposite of Mr Can-Do. How he struggled over the next few years with his work life, and how little sympathy I had for it all. How he laboured. Job applications that took days to complete because of his dyslexia, interviews after which he didn't get the job, scanning the appointments pages and finding nothing, signing with a dozen agencies, and all the time the same refrain: 'There are no jobs for me in Brighton.'

When he did quit his office job in London, it was still as if he had had the weight of the world upon him. And that was before we ever had any real responsibilities, apart from Carmen. By responsibilities, obviously I mean you.

I bet you want to get on to the bit when we went to India, and made one of you. That's much more interesting than job applications. So, after Leo had quit his old London job and before he shackled himself to a new one in Brighton, we went to India for our honeymoon, three months after our wedding. Back then, you could go away for up to thirteen weeks and not lose your housing benefit, so that's exactly how long we went for – thirteen weeks.

Your dad had never been away that long before purely for pleasure. Before I met him, he had been employed by some big bank or other and had worked briefly in New York and Hong Kong, and although he said he had made a fortune while doing so, he had nothing whatsoever to show for it other than a fancy silver watch. He said he had put it all up his nose. I wonder. He had also told me, very soon after we met, that he had been to Glastonbury many times, and that he had once owned a huge motorbike, but had witnessed a crash which had put him off bikes for ever.

It turned out that he had never been to a proper festival in his life. A month after we first met, I dragged him to the Big Green Gathering, which was still a fledgling eco-festival on Salisbury Plain. (Later, during the years when you two came along with me, it was a far bigger affair at Cheddar Gorge, before it went bankrupt and was closed down by sinister forces allegedly directed from Westminster. Too radical, apparently. The festival since restarted in Wales – when we went last summer, it was bliss, wasn't it? All the usual delights: Weirdigans Café, the Magic Hat Sauna, Buddhafield Café, dragon-shaped mud ovens baking spelt bread and vegan brownies, pedal powered hemp smoothies, Welsh anarchists and English hippies. All the lovely people. Loads of lovely people.)

Anyway, the summer your dad and I met, the Big Green Gathering was still pretty rough and ready – wind-powered and solar-powered, just not yet the big green activist event it would grow into; back then it was knit your own tofu, and brew your own mushroom tea. Leo hated it from the moment we bunked in under the fence rather than pay the then tiny ticket price. 'It's a bit basic, isn't it?' he said, looking around at the scruffy pop-up community doing ingenious things with solar panels and recycled chip oil. (Glamping hadn't yet been invented, but I know for sure your dad would have far preferred it.)

As a festival regular, I was mystified by his reaction. And then mortified. The morning after we – that is, I – put the tent up on that flinty windswept hillside, I was sitting in Ted's ambulance with Syd and some other women, drinking strong tea out of metal mugs and smoking roll-ups, and a woman I didn't know, a no-nonsense hippie who lived in a horse lorry with her children, looked out the window, and laughed. 'Christ,' she said. 'Aren't men so vain?' There was Leo, my new squeeze on his first group outing with us, shaving in the wing mirror of the ambulance. *Shaving.* I will never forget it. Scraping away with a razor, his neck craned so he could see what he was doing in the mirror, in a field full of eight hundred soap-dodgers, with compost loos and mud ovens and a single vegan food stall, on a hill in the middle of nowhere.

There he was, shaving, and – oh, how my face flamed – dabbing on aftershave. It was the only time in our early relationship that I actually wanted to kill him, that I felt genuine shame, that I felt he had really shown me up. And when I remonstrated with him, told him that it really was an inverse faux pas, he admitted he had never been to a festival before. 'Not like this one anyway,' he said, waving his arms at the prayer flags blowing in the hilly breeze, and the converted ambulances and ex-horse lorries and old buses, and the bell tents and teepees and bigger tents where people congregated. Later, as it got dark, he hated that it really did get dark, because there were no generators allowed on-site; it was natural light only, candles and lanterns, and someone on a bicycle hooked up to a sound system so that the music in the communal space was literally pedal powered – and as the stationary cyclist got tired, so too did the music slow down. Leo was appalled. 'This is so – so *primitive*,' he exclaimed. 'There's nothing to *do here* at night.'

As if it were a holiday resort, instead of a bunch of well-meaning hippies trying to change the world via permaculture and urns of chai on a remote Wiltshire hillside, the Ministry of Defence doing loud, low flyovers just to remind us who was really in charge. I remember patiently explaining to Leo that this was not a rock concert or a techno-festival, that you made your own entertainment, that you made your own music, and hung out and had a laugh and built a fire and cooked over it, and no, there were no flashing lights or 10k rigs or techno DJs. I wondered what the fuck he had been expecting. He left a day early, because he had to catch a train from Warminster back to London for work, and I exhaled. He had been an urban disco fish in a distinctly alien pond.

In India, another small but significant untruth was exposed.

I wouldn't call them lies, because that makes it sound like it was something devious or dishonest, whereas really I think it was just your dad trying to sound more impressive than he thought he was. One paranoid morning-after, soon after Leo and I had met, there had been a group of us around at Harry's, after a trance party with some Japanese DJ, and Leo had talked about he used to ride a big bike, and how he had witnessed a terrible bike crash, after which he never rode again. I thought no more of it.

A year and a half later in Hampi, on our south-Indian honeymoon odyssey, the only way to see the ancient Vijayanagar ruins scattered around the wide dusty radius in the blistering sun was by motorbike. It became immediately clear that Leo had no idea how to ride one. How odd, I thought. Hadn't he had a ginormous bike before he had met me?

I'd learned to ride a bike the hard way on my first extended trip to India, by getting on and falling off, getting on and falling

off, getting on and driving into a ditch, getting on and driving
into an Indian field worker on a bicycle, both of us sprawled in
the dust, with cut shins and expressions of great surprise, until
I got the knack of it and ended up with a Suzuki 200 cc for the
rest of the season. By the time I left five months later, I was driving
in a similar manner to all the other Western trance-heads – bare-
foot and tripping. The only harm that ever befell me was three
broken toes on my left foot, and exhaust burns on my inside leg
– a small price to pay for the no-helmet, no-papers, no-driving
test, no-insurance, no-rules freedom that used to be motorbike
riding in Goa. You just got on, and took off. I used to feel as if I
were flying, the wind blowing in my face on those red dirt roads
where brightly painted statues of Ganesh jumped out from the
deep green of the jungle. I had always liked bikes, but I fell in love
with them that first time in India.

But Leo, despite his biker talk, had obviously never been on a
bike before. In Hampi, he rode pillion with me, on a zippy little
scooter thing, and disliked the sensation so much – or perhaps
he just didn't like my driving – that he got off and walked the
last few miles back to the huts by the river where we were staying.
I don't know why, but we never talked about it. But it did make
me wonder about other things he had said – had he really earned
a fortune with Bank of Satan? And if so, then had he really had
done as much cocaine as he said he had? Because if he had,
wouldn't it have left more of an imprint on his personality?

Cocaine is such a me-me-me drug; it turns even the nicest people
into babbling wankers. Leo just didn't fit the coke profile. (I never
got into it either; like any drug, if it was put in front of me I would
do it all night – but given a choice, I preferred more mind-altering

stuff, rather than just stuff that made you talk shit louder and faster. I can honestly say that the only drug I have never been remotely interested in trying is crack cocaine. Coke itself seems so horribly unrelaxing. Heroin, on the other hand, sounds so heavenly divine that my often faulty sense of self-preservation always made me avoid it like the plague. One snort and I would have been done for. I would have been jabbing needles into my eyeball within a week.)

And as for your dad, I can't imagine him ever really doing vast amounts of any drug – he liked his pills and his acid, but could he really have been a coke monster? Or could he have been telling porkies not to be cool, but to gain approval? I wish I had been a bit more attuned to the warning signs earlier. He didn't need to gain approval. I liked him as he was.

4 INDIA

GRAND HONEYMOON ITINERARY

November 1999 – March 2000

(unplanned)

Maharashtra	Bombay – Matheran – Bombay
Goa	Anjuna
Karnataka	Gokarna – Om Beach – Half Moon Beach – Mysore – Bangalore
Tamil Nadu	Kodaikanal
Kerala	Calicut
Karnataka	Om Beach – secret Rainbow Tribe beach – Om Beach – Hampi
Maharashtra	Matheran – Bombay

Although he was racially south Indian, the nearest Leo had ever been to south India was Vijay's Chawalla on Green Street for a masala dosa and a bowl of bhel puri. So when we landed in Mumbai – although in my head, it will always be Bombay – and the heat hit us in the face and wrapped itself around us like a wet bin liner, and the smell of shit wafted from the slums around the airport, for the first time your dad was surrounded by throngs of people who, to some degree, looked like him. 'Wow,' I said, as we battled our way through the mayhem. 'Do you feel at home?'

He reminded me that his ancestors had left a different part of the subcontinent hundreds years ago, and that some of them came from Persia and Mauritius, but I didn't care. It was the first time I had ever been with him in a crowd where he looked like everyone else, and on some level that must have been exciting for him. Well, it was exciting for me. Especially as I had thought we would not get there at all – at Gatwick, about to board a Yemini Airlines* flight via Cairo and Sana'a, Leo announced that he didn't have his tickets. He had his passport, yes, but not his plane tickets. 'I thought you had them,' he said, his eyes widening as I jumped up and down hissing and spitting at his assumption. It turns out I had, but only because the issuer had stapled them to the back of mine; he had never thought to ask, and I had never thought to look. One of Leo's favourite expressions was, 'In the land of the blind, the one-eyed man is king.'

I was that one-eyed man.

If you drew a scribbly line up and down and around south–west India, you'd have a picture of our meanderings. Hubli, the place

---

* By the way kids, when it comes to your turn to travel, if there is any oil left, my advice is to spend that extra few quid and avoid the very cheapest airlines; you will pay in other ways, believe me. You will never want to spend hours of your life stuck in Sana'a airport's departure lounge, with its bare concrete floor and thin melting cups of instant coffee. You won't want to be frogmarched off into a cubicle and roughly frisked by a stern woman in a niqab. And you certainly won't want to change planes, so that bits of the ancient one assigned for the last leg of the journey literally drop on your head during take-off. Trust me. It's not worth the money.

where one of you was made, is not listed because we stayed there just one night on our way to somewhere more interesting, but that's all it took. It was February 5, in case you want to know. Except you probably don't. In fact, the very idea might be making your toes curl, because it involves the two words you should never read in the same sentence – parents and sex – but bear with me. It's part of the story. Pretend you're reading about someone else and you might be able to stomach it better.

As honeymoons go, ours was untraditional in that River, Syd and Gimli were there too, as well as all the people we met along the way and travelled with. I had done India alone before, months of being thrown in at the deep end, of full-throttle madness, all the way from Anjuna to Kathmandu and back again. By the end of it, I had gone feral from nearly half a year of sleeping on cowdung floors and eating with my hands and traveling on the tops of buses alongside the rice sacks and caged chicken, clinging on for dear life rather than being smothered to death inside.

I had arrived with a fiver and the promise of a job and a roof over my head; when those promises almost instantly fell through, I improvised with a few hundred pounds from a credit card and did massage at Anjuna Flea Market every week, living on a couple of quid a day. You don't need much money in tropical paradise – just the beach, the sea and a good supply of books. I even learned how to live without plumbing, but I won't go into that, or you really will throw up.

This time, it was nice to have company and a tiny bit more cash in my pocket. I wasn't sure how your dad, Mr Urban Fastidious, would adapt to India, but he took to it like an Englishman to curry. By the time we got to Om Beach – once my favourite place in the world – he had almost gone native, swapping his shorts for a lungi, and shaving only every few days, often at the barbers in Gokarna, where you could get hot towels and head massage and a deadly looking cut-throat razor shave for a few rupees. From his head to his guts, Leo was loosening up. 'I love you,' he said, as we sat on the beach eating freshly cut pineapple that dripped juice, from the pineapple lady with the deadly machete and the heavy fruit basket on her head.

'I love you too,' I said. 'Want to share a mango?'

Travelling with your dad gave me a totally new experience of India. It gave me access to conversations without any subtext or agenda. A white woman travelling alone can get pestered – not hassled, or threatened, but pestered. (The earliest Hindi I learned apart from 'How much?' was 'Chalo Pakistan', which is quite rude 'piss off to Pakistan' but occasionally necessary when your head wobble – which means 'yes please' and 'no thank you', and 'later maybe', and 'I acknowledge what you're saying but please go away' – is ignored. Still, it was safer than most places in the world; safer yet quite insane and unpredictable, which is why I love it.)

Now I was treated with great courtesy because I was with an Indian-looking gentleman. And *he* was source of great curiosity because he was with two white ladies, scruffy and dusty though River and I invariably were. On trains and buses, men would speak to him in Konkani or Kannada or Tamil or Hindi, and when he looked blank, they would try English, because as a rule Indians are fantastic at languages while we are utterly hopeless. 'What is your country? What is your job? How much do you earn? Is this your wife?' they would sing, in their beautifully accented Victorian English, with their immaculately pressed trousers and oiled hair and perfect moustaches. It seems to be the law to have a moustache in India, and high-waisted trousers and crisp shirts, if you are a non-field worker. Leo would tell them that he worked with computers, and the men would beam and say that they did too, and they would talk for ages about techie stuff and I would sigh dreamily and read my book because if he had not been the object of their fascination, it would have been me, and I had answered all the questions many, many times already. Food would be brought out, offered and shared; Parle-G biscuits and samosas and sweet chai bought from the young boys who went up and down the carriages calling 'Chai chai chai chai' in urgent singsong voices.

For Leo, as a commuter, the experience of people chatting charmingly to each other on trains was something extraordinary – and especially their chatting to tourists, to whom so many rural Indians showed a particular courtesy, unlike in London, where tourists were generally perceived as irritants clogging up the transport network with their bags and maps and cluelessness. Only once did we end up on an actual commuter train during morning rush hour into Bombay; thousands and millions of slim brown perfectly groomed men squeezed and squished their way onto the slow, mile-long, lumbering brown train with the metal bars over the windows instead of glass; it was like shoving toothpaste back into the tube. We were sitting at the back, as the carriage became so full that it was just one seething heartbeat, the men closer together than atoms. At each suburban station into Victoria Terminus, more and more got on. At no point was there any sign of discomfort, ill-temper, or a fight for space. Everyone wriggled and squeezed to accommodate everyone else. Briefcases were passed over heads, and tiffin boxes. It was the most insane overcrowding I had ever seen, potentially panic-inducing, yet co-operative and dignified as you could never imagine on rush hour tube, or First Capital Connect.

Obviously, despite such dignity and deference, this was my idea of hell. My favourite places in India are rural backwaters where there is no hint of modern life. I've heard that in the past ten years Om Beach has changed and modernised (just as Goa is now all jet skis and package tourists), but back then it was heaven on earth, provided you weren't bothered about things like electricity or plumbing. A long, hard, hot walk over the baking headland from Gokarna (these days there is a road), you'd be on the point of death with a 30 kg pack on your back in 100 degree heat, the sweat running off you in shiny rivers, and suddenly there it would appear, lying below you like a vision of paradise, with nothing down there apart from a few sunbathing cows and three or four palm leaf chai shops – huts with woven palm leaf walls on three sides, a beaten earth floor, and cow sheds out the back where you could sling your hammock on the cobwebbed beams for around fifty pence a night.

MENU

Banana lassi

Banana pancake

Banana craps

Fruit craps

Browny

Special browny

Backed micoroni with spinesh

Mixican tootills

Creambod eggs

All you did all day was lie in a hammock reading, lie in the sand, reading and writing, lie on your back in the sea, thinking, or lie in the chai shop, eating. That was it. The evening's entertainment was uncomplicated – watching the sunset, playing backgammon, or, if you weren't too stoned, maybe even chess, and every now and then venturing to another of the handful of chai shops for the same menu with different spelling mistakes. You might walk over the headland to Gokarna every few days for a coconut ice cream, or some bindis, or to visit the post office where there were often no stamps (this is the country, remember, where it is not unknown for restaurants to close for lunch). Back on the beach, days passed in a golden haze of sun, heat, salt and charas. My drug ban didn't extend to charas – I just didn't smoke it in chillums. Well, not too often anyway.

We read a lot. River brought great bricks of books with her; I remember trying to read *Dr Zhivago* when she had finished it, and wanting to throw it into the sea with frustration, because even though both my life and my brain had slowed down sufficiently to digest such a thing, I still couldn't stand the bloody misery and long-windedness of it. Instead I read *Crime and Punishment* for light relief. Everything is relative, especially when your supply chain – that is, access to a Waterstones – has been cut off. Your dad, with his terrible dyslexia, was the world's slowest reader. He would lie in his purple hammock, in the hot shade of the chai shop, spending hours on each page, taking it all in, slowly, slowly, even when it was something as slim and simple as a Graham Greene. He had faintly scientific taste in books, like those by Stephen Jay Gould and James Lovelock, but lugging a back- pack full of books around was never a problem for Leo; despite his ability to read science – something entirely beyond me – his dyslexia meant he did it very slowly, so that one book would last him for months. Picking hungrily through the rubbish left behind by other backpackers – the John Grishams, the Tom Clancys, the endless dogeared copies of that fucking *Celestine Prophecy* – I used to almost envy him. But even now, with the Kindle, I still lug books around. There are never many clothes in my luggage – they take up too much room.

Around New Year, the beach got busy. Goa used to go party crazy at New Year, the beaches filling up with whiskey-drinking men from Bombay – which meant that Om Beach was suddenly flooded with people escaping. As the 'Goa heads' began descending with their noise and their party drugs, we left our huts with the smooth shiny cowshit floors, untying our hammocks from the cobwebby beams, and trudged over the next headland to Half Moon Beach. This was even more remote and inaccessible than Om, and hardly anyone went there. There was just one small chai shop on Half Moon, owned by a local Brahmin called Raj and his beautiful young wife Rani; there was nowhere to sleep, no huts, no showers, nothing, so we strung our hammocks under the trees next to the beach, and lived like shipwrecked pirates for weeks on end.

Our needs were completely pared down. Rani made us food; Raj smoked with us and played chess and backgammon and talked philosophy, mostly with the menfolk, and at night we had candles in glass jars and each other. The sea was often phosphorescent, so we would swim at midnight in the warm water, and come out like human fairylights, covered in millions of green twinkling sparkles, which died to darkness in seconds. We spent Millenium Eve on Half Moon Beach, and the only way we knew that the Millenium Bug had not caused the faraway outside world to end was that a lone plane, a dot miles up, flew over in the middle of the night. At dawn, monkeys would come to our jungle clearing and steal our stubby sweet bananas, hung from branches on string to keep the ants off; we would hear them chirruping in our sleep, and wake to banana skins everywhere and no bananas. Life was blissful.

Your dad, though, he was a bit funny about it all. As in funny peculiar. For a start, although he wore a lungi all the time, he would not take off his t-shirt. He had this idea that he was no longer as svelte as he had once been. He wouldn't swim either, no matter how hot it got. 'Black people don't swim,' he'd say, from his hammock in the shade. Except they did – Indian men swam all the time in their horrible baggy brown Y-fronts, and Indian women waded into the sea in their saris, the material spreading out around them in colourful wet circles so that they looked like tropical water lilies.

But weirdest of all, every evening half an hour before sunset Leo would roll up his hammock and head off, up and over the rocks back to our hut on Om Beach. He refused completely to sleep outside. 'I like to have a door between me and the world when I'm asleep,' he would say, trotting off on his own as the rest of us gathered on the sand to watch sunset (like telly, only better).

That I know the exact time and date of your conception is no accident. We spent huge chunks of our prolonged honeymoon sleeping with a few miles of beach and headland lying between us. Him in the cowshed on Om Beach, me in my hammock on Half Moon. Unentangled, unentwined.

Intermission

The Rainbow Gathering

'...this amazing beach hidden somewhere, but no one knows where it is.'

Alex Garland, THE BEACH

'There is a Rainbow Gathering happening at a secret beach near here,' said the German hippy with the pink dreadlocks and pixie tattoo, one morning as we sat around having chapatti, chai and chillum for breakfast. Again. Sometimes you just longed for a bowl of muesli. The German wrapped a safi – those damp dirty strips of cloth used for cleaning chillums – around his big toe, and began running the hollow clay pipe up and down, scraping it out, before repacking it with more tobacco and charas. 'I know the name of the beach,' he said mysteriously. 'You can get there by boat only.' Then he sucked on the chillum and shouted 'Bom Shiva!' to the ceiling, before passing it on and coughing out smoke until his blue eyes watered.

The Israeli took a break from playing his huge drum. 'I have been to many Rainbow Gatherings all over the world,' he said, rewrapping the safi around the mouth of the chillum before he sucked on it. 'It is a very *shanti* vibe. You bring food and everyone eats together. Everything is shared. It is beautiful, man.' Then he gasped and coughed, and his eyes glazed a bit.

So we made an escape plan. We walked over the blazing headland to Gokarna and bought sacks of rice, dhal and unidentifiable vegetables. Leo and the German found a fisherman who knew where the beach was, and fixed a price with him. We told nobody what we were doing – we didn't want those awful noisy Goa kids turning up a day later. At dawn the next morning, Leo, River and I, the Germans, a few Dutch and Japanese and the Israeli with the drum waded out and climbed into the wooden boat, carrying the sacks of food carefully on our heads. We saw the Indians do it every day, but it was much harder than it looked and we nearly snapped our necks trying to keep upright. The boat was a wooden dug-out with nothing to shade you from the white glare of the sun. A primitive engine spluttered out dirty clouds.

The fisherman, silent in his tattered vest and lungi, didn't quite know what to make of us. His face was thin and serious and almost black from the sun, and his teeth were red and black from chewing paan. He spat the red juice over the side of the low-slung boat all the way, as the Israeli sang happily and played his drum, and the Japanese boys – who spoke nothing except Japanese – shared around small, fat sweet bananas. A few miles from Om Beach, a pod of dolphins leapt out of the water, doing backflips and showing off in the blaze of the day. We grinned. The vibe was indeed most *shanti*.

The boat chugged along parallel to miles of empty bleached out tropical coastline, then turned around a sudden headland. On the other side of the headland, dark rocks stuck out of the water like huge black teeth, hiding the land behind them. The fisherman manoeuvred the boat slowly and with great care through the rocks, eyes narrowed, a beedi clamped between his lips. And there it was. There was the beach, an empty stretch of perfect white sand hidden behind the wall of rocks. He'd found it. We'd found it. It was beautiful. 'Beach,' he said. It was the first word he had spoken all morning.

The ten of us climbed out of the boat into a few feet of pure clear water, our sacks of food once again balanced on our heads. The fisherman stared open-mouthed as a naked Western couple came racing along the sand. 'Welcome home!' they shouted in English, before skipping off down the beach like an hallucination. The boat sputtered off, the fisherman paid a few rupees more than we had agreed, for so skillfully negotiating the rocks and not drowning us all. He had smiled and wobbled his head, and then he was gone, twisting his way back out to sea in his stone-age boat. We looked at each other a bit blankly. We had no idea what to do now. 'Come on!' said the Israeli, hoisting his drum on his shoulder and taking charge. 'We go and say namaste to everyone.'

We followed him up the deserted beach, miles of empty whiteness with nothing but palm trees in the distance. Then we found them. Behind another row of rocks was the Rainbow Gathering, completely hidden from view. You couldn't see it from the sea, or from lower down the beach. There were at least a hundred people, all Westerners, some with clothes, some without, scattered around the rocks. Everyone was thin, tanned and dreadlocked. There were an awful lot of beards. Everyone looked very, very *shanti*, to the point of inertia. Nobody seemed that surprised to see us, or particularly interested.

The Israeli disappeared, shouting greetings in Hebrew at someone; we stood about sheepishly, wondering what to do with our food. A young, earnest-looking man with an especially straggly beard bounded over. 'Welcome home,' he said. He had an Australian accent. 'I'm Zib. Is this your first Rainbow? Do you want to know anything?'

'Yes please,' we said, awkward as children arriving at a party.

'Okay,' he said. 'You brought food. Good. Put it there. The shit-pit is back off the beach. You'll see it – there's a yellow flag tied to a bush. Don't shit anywhere else. There's spring water half way up that hill over there. There are no drugs or alcohol. Respect that, yeah? Everything is communal. There are talking circles and drumming circles and if any of you want to do a workshop on anything, feel free. We are a very organic community here. Peace to you all.' He said it like a command. He was quite bossy for a hippie. 'Um, thanks,' we said. And then he bounded off again.

We set up camp under the only palm tree lower down the beach, and wondered why nobody else had thought of using its shade. I had a sudden, desperate desire for an ice cold Diet Coke. I drank some warmish water instead. We lay back and decided it was all very utopian.

That night it was full moon. After dark, a girl in a loincloth ran around the beach from group to group, shouting, 'Food food food!' and pointing at a flat area of scrubland beside the beach. We dutifully followed her, carrying our metal plates and spoons, and joined a huge circle of people sitting cross-legged in the bright moonlight. It was a strange sight, this great assembly of strangers sitting in a big circle on an unlit beach in the ass-end of nowhere. Everyone else seemed to think it was normal, so it must have been. In India, your idea of normal shifts from day to day, hour to hour. Normal can be anything. There is no normal.

'Now we say Om!' yelled the girl, when there seemed to be hundreds of people in the circle. Everyone stood up, joined hands and raised them over our heads, and went 'Ommmmmmmmm!' very loudly for ages. Then we sat down again, and a spindly mad-eyed elder hippie ran around the circle with a few younger assistants carrying huge pots of food. They slapped rice, dhal, vegetables and chapattis on our plates. We were starving by now. The food was basic, but good. The context – a huge circle of strangers eating together on a beautiful deserted beach – was fantastically idyllic, in theory anyway. Nobody talked much. You couldn't quite make out people's faces in the moonlight, and there were a dozen different non-Indian languages going on, although like everywhere else, English was communal. After everyone had eaten – there were no seconds – somebody near the cooking pots stood up and shouted in broken English, 'Tonight we feed one hundred seventy-two people!'

Everyone cheered. 'So now you give to the magic hat!' Three hippies danced around the food circle singing a song about the magic hat, and everyone threw some rupees into a knackered straw hat. Then people started drumming and chanting, and we watched, too repressed to join in.

Apart from the full-moon high tide flooding our camp that night – which is why nobody else had camped under the palm tree so low down the beach – and the sun rising early and frying us alive, we slept quite well on the sand. When we woke up, we were hungry. Really hungry. Rumbling belly hungry. The communal breakfast was too hideous to contemplate – awful, grey, watery porridge, and something that was being called 'halva', but which absolutely wasn't. We searched the bottom of our bag for any remaining bananas and peanut butter, and ate them off stale bread.

By the middle of the next day it was becoming clear that despite the we're-one-big-family ethos of the gathering, there were hierarchies within the group to rival the caste system. We felt our daytripping, blow-in status keenly from the indifference of the hardcore in charge of the cooking. Our offers of help with the food tasks were coolly rebuffed. One of our party, a gregarious young Dutch woman, went to the Talking Circle in the afternoon, and came back an hour later, fuming. 'These people are not humorous!' she said. 'I ask a simple question and I get from everyone that I am authoritarian! What do they mean!' We started explaining 'authoritarian' but she interrupted, exasperated. 'No, no, I know what "authoritarian" means, it is the mentality I don't understand. I finally get the Talking Stick—'

'The what?' We were giggling helplessly by now.

'The Talking Stick!' she thundered. 'You cannot talk unless it is passed to you, but the same handful of men keep holding it and not letting others talk! And so I finally get it and I ask them, very nicely, why is it that they say no drugs and everyone is smoking chillums all the time. And so they are too stoned to collect water from the spring, but they are talking about this being a community where everyone helps each other and there are no drugs'. She paused for breath, flinging her dreads over her shoulders. 'I am not anti-smoking! I am fucking Dutch, I smoke all the time! I only ask a simple question and then they all start saying I am authoritarian and need to open my heart more! It is – what do English people say – bollocks!'

'Yah,' said the German with the pixie tattoos. 'I collect water five times today and the spring is way over there, because the water-collecting guys are too stoned to do it. I don't care about that, but they don't even say thanks or nothing. Not,' he added gruffly, 'that I want thanks, but these guys are so unfriendly. It is stupid!'

'Maybe by drugs they mean acid,' someone ventured. We shrugged. Personally I felt that a crate of cold Kingfisher would make everyone interact better, but then I turned out to be an alcoholic, so what did I know.

It was developing into Us and Them, becoming perhaps ever so slightly Lord of the Flies, except everyone was too stoned to do much. We couldn't take it seriously anymore. I remembered what River always said about civilization only ever being three meals from anarchy.

The nearest village was five miles away, but only if you knew the way ('Turn left at the big tree an hour from here over that hill,' someone said vaguely). We sat staring out to sea, and when we saw a tiny fishing boat, we waved frantically at it. It came in, full of fish. The boat man agreed to come back once he had delivered his catch.

When we reached Om Beach, we all but kissed the sand. Food and shelter and running water. We were sunburned and dehydrated and very, very hungry. The stoned guys at the Manakarna chai shop made us rice and dhal and chappattis, and we drank bottle after bottle of lemon soda, and lay in our hammocks, exhausted and happy, like the Famous Five after some big adventure.

The next day the Israeli with the drum came back. 'Guys,' he said, flopping down on the sand where we were lying, surrounded by fresh fruit and more lemon sodas. 'I am home. Those people, they couldn't laugh. And everybody needs to laugh. Otherwise it is not funny.'

'When a call is triped it may result in meter reading one way speach getting wrong number in such cases calls are chargeable'

Sign in phone booth,
near Gokarna bus station, Karnataka

Leo and I did occasionally get time alone together on our honeymoon. In Hubli, for instance. On 5 February. There's nothing to tell you about Hubli – it's just a town where you have to change trains in order to eventually reach Hampi – apart from that when we left there, one of you was inside me, a little zygote dividing and multiplying every twelve hours. It's just as well you didn't know me then, or you might have wished you were wriggling up someone else's fallopian tube, someone who had been regularly taking folic acid instead of the other kind.

This is a diary entry from a few days before we left for Hampi, the journey on which you were made. I wrote this after sitting on the rocky headland with the solitary palm tree that juts out between Om and Half Moon beaches; in retrospect, it seems almost psychic, but then again the background gnaw of baby hunger had been quietly upon me for a while now. Not in my rational mind – I don't know if I possessed one, nor did I have any idea about the reality of babies, or whether I was even particularly keen on them, having always preferred puppies – but under its surface, there was an unnamed throb, a soft insistent drumbeat, a tug.

'I saw the outline of the land behind me like a reclining man
(with an erection around about Kudle Beach) and the rocks
below looked like a woman's legs opening to let in the salty
surge of the filling-up sea. I am lately so focusing on repro-
duction... This morning I had the most beautiful, natural,
credible dream of Leo and I on a train to Pushkar, with our
newborn with us, lying on the train seat opposite, dark
skinned and black haired and velvety like a baby animal, tiny
miracle fingers clasped together, and when I woke up, the
dream haunted me all day. Well, not exactly haunted – but I
feel a lot of love today... I have also drunk a lot of fenny
today.'

(Fenny, by the way, is a local liquor, made from fermented cashews or coconuts; it tastes like liquid fire, gets you roaring drunk, and leaves you for dead in the morning. Stick with lemon sodas is my advice.)

We were in Hubli to get to Hospet, which is even less interesting than Hubli, except it's how you get to Hampi. Try saying that fast after five fingers of fenny. Hampi is an astonishing place, which is why people suffer the journey to get there. Leo and I left the others on Om Beach and set off inland to do 160 km of bus-train-bus; this might not sound like much, but on Indian public transport it's like 160 million km, especially as I was recovering from a bout of exploding guts and forced at regular intervals to choke down bitter mouthfuls of evil black ayurvedic stuff from the doctor in Gokarna, who had shoved a stethescope into my spasming abdomen and told me to avoid papaya.

I hadn't eaten in days, because you cannot feed whatever monster lurks within, so I was in deeply spaced out fasting mode before we even clambered onto that hot crazy bus in Gokarna with the blaring Hindi pop music, driven by a man so frighteningly eager to break his cycle of samsara that it would have made even the most robust guts turn to liquid. Syd had given me something homeopathic, which tasted lovely but I'm not sure I believe in homeopathy any more than I believe in fairies – so I swallowed my emergency Immodium as well, and hoped it would hold me together until we got to Hubli. Leo and I took turns being squashed against the hard side panel of the bus by a fat woman in a purple sari.

When we stopped, late in the evening, filthy and exhausted from heat and noise and dust and 'hello coconut, hello samosa', and 'chai! chai! chai!', I was nearly dead. We decided to take a room in an actual hotel – The Kailash Hotel, Lamington Road, Hubli, which cost about a tenner, and which is where you were sparked into being. The room was unimaginable bliss. After living under a tree on a beach, we had the luxury of an actual bed, bedbug-free, a teeny en suite with a shower that trickled tepid water, and an air cooler (like air conditioning, but warmer). There was even a television.

Downstairs there was a restaurant called the HavMor, which was brightly strip-lit and overseen by a fat jolly fellow who joyfully explained the name, once he had gone through the formalities of establishing where we were from, where we had come from, and where we were going: 'It is called the HavMor because our food is so delicious that you will want to have more,' he beamed. 'Have more. You see?'

We saw. And actually, he was right. We each had a thali, served by a serious boy in flip flops trying to do silver service in the formica surroundings, and not quite pulling it off. We didn't care. Apart from a packet of Parle-Gs and a few thousand lung-busting

Gold Flake, I had been nil by mouth for days. So boiled rice and curd and a teaspoon of dhal and subji tasted like heaven. I didn't dare HavMor.

Leo had runny pink ice cream and an extra naan after his 'executive' thali, and we retired upstairs, fed and showered and desperate to recline on a bed whose mattress was not thin and hard and prickly and stuffed with tough, spiky coconut matting. There was even a pillow each. I rolled a spliff with the Gold Flake and my chunk of charas, and we got stoned and watched *Ghostbusters I* and *II* on the telly, and we made the older of you.

You were a tenacious little beast from the very start. In Hampi, when you were a cluster of cells attached to my uterine wall, and about the size of a bean, I got sick again. We all did. We had met up with the others by then – everyone had left the beach to regroup inland in Hampi, joining Leo and me the day after we arrived – and we all took turns to be violently ill. It got to the point where we were taking bets on which one of us would be struck down that day – suddenly, someone would go pale, then green, then bolt, clutching their face and their guts, to the hideous concrete latrines behind the buffalo shed, and we became so blasé about all the puking and shitting and groaning and whimpering that it became normal. We even laughed about it, as we shared Valium and Immodium and chewed on ginger like pregnant ladies. Little did I know.

One morning when it was still dark, we all walked along the black country road through the obelisks to the bottom of a steep hill. (There are obelisks everywhere in Hampi, huge natural rock formations dotted around like giant alien eggs amongst the paddy fields and banana trees and coconut palms as though Dali had been involved in the design.) At the top of a thousand stone steps was a temple, a simple whitewashed temple perched alone on top of the world, overlooking a vivid patchwork of green glittering paddies, huge smooth rocks, and the sacred ruins of the ancient kingdom of Vijayanagar. The temple baba was expecting us – someone had told him there would be Westerners coming at dawn to watch sunrise. We had brought breakfast with us – chapattis, peanut butter and boiled eggs, like a tie-dyed Famous Five. For once, none of us was sick that morning.

It was called the Monkey Temple, in honour of Hanuman the monkey god. There were hundreds of real monkeys everywhere. But before you go all misty-eyed and David Attenborough, and start envisaging those cute little creatures in nature programmes, imagine instead a marauding gang of yellow-fanged hooligans who leapt and hissed and spat and screeched, and from whom you did not want to get a bite, because they probably all had rabies or the flesh eating Ebola virus. There was nothing at all cute about these monkeys. They were a bunch of vicious miniature bandits.

We kept well out of their way, sitting on the bleached stone ground, and positioning ourselves to face the slowly streaking sky and watch the sun come up. We were exhausted from the climb, silenced by the sheer scale and beauty of being up so high. And then a monkey ran up behind us and stole Syd's bag, with all her homeopathic remedies inside it, and her purse. We jumped up, but the horrid little goblin hissed and spat and bared its awful fangs, and bounded away, all leaping legs and tail, screeching in glee. 'Oi, you little fucker, get back here now!' we shouted, shaking our fists as impotently as Homer Simpson.

The white magnolia tree behind us began to shake. We spun around. It was the baba, somehow balancing cross-legged high up in its branches, his morning meditation interrupted by his own helpless laughter. 'Goodbye bag,' he said, his eyes watering. 'Goodbye, goodbye.' He climbed down from the tree and invited us indoors, where there were no monkeys, just his surly house-keeper who made us chai. We were half way through our break-fast with him when River suddenly had to leap up and leave abruptly, rushing past us out onto the country road and away from the group. Today was her day to be sick. 'Bring it all up for Hanuman,' we called encouragingly.

Later, it was my turn. Back at the African-shaped huts where we were staying on a farm full of buffalo (the baby buffalo, with their buck teeth, were goofy and adorable) and cows and oxen and dogs and chickens, I suddenly felt overwhelmingly vile, worse than I had done since I had arrived in India two months earlier. I puked and puked and puked, and my guts turned inside out. It was like an earthquake going off inside me, an ectoplasmic explo-sion, but you were strong and determined, like you always are, and clung on inside the chundering mothership. And all the time, as I raced to the concrete latrine or lay weakly in my hammock, I had no idea you were in there. 'This place is going to kill us,' your dad said. 'One by one.'

We left the buffalo farm sooner than we would have liked because we got worn out from playing gastric Russian roulette. It turned out the women were washing our food plates in filthy water, and we were slowly being poisoned. The women weren't doing it on purpose – they washed their own plates in the same water – but our Western guts couldn't cope. But don't let that put you off Hampi – just don't share your water supply with a herd of buffalo.

By now, your dad was making friends with the locals. He got invited for chai to the family home – that is, the family palm leaf hut in the jungle – of one of the young guys who worked in the chai shop on Om Beach. Just him. No wife – I was too white, and too female. He set off into the jungle in his lungi and his Cramps t-shirt, and came back hours later grinning, having met dozens of male relatives and answered dozens of questions. He looked pleased and bemused. He led such a white English life back home.

But it was in Kodaikanal down in Tamil Nadu that River and I actually lost him in the crowd. The three of us had gone south on an adventure, to check out a proper hill station. River used to tell everyone we met along the way, 'They're on their honeymoon and they brought me with them', and people would laugh, and look a bit confused, but as a trio it worked. I needed someone else to talk to apart from Leo, because even though we were exceedingly fond of each other, we ran out of things to say quite easily. And the more we got to know each other, the less we had to talk about. With River and me, as you are aware, this has never happened. I can't imagine it ever would. Blah blah blah, we go. Blah blah endless blah. Your dad, both as a male and an only child, could never understand it. 'What on *earth* could you possibly have left to say to each other?' he would ask, noticing we were still sitting in the same place, still deep in conversation. 'What?' we would reply, barely pausing for breath. 'Blah blah blah.'

Anyway, after a tortuous bus-train-bus-train-bus-train odyssey via Mysore (where I had become so dehydrated that I had to spend two days in a hostal room, sucking down Dioralyte and industrial headache pills and gallons of Bisleri) and Bangalore (like Zurich compared with the cows-and-temples villages on the coast) we finally arrived at Kodaikanal. It was high in the mountains, cool and wet and scented with pine, and the air felt European until you opened your eyes. Then it was nothing at all like Europe. Everything was a bit damp and shabby and ramshackle, and people were dressed differently from the heat of the coast – there were lots of woolly hats and shawls and you could even see your breath in the early morning, and the leaves dripped.

And everybody was the same colour as Leo. River and I stuck out like two pale sheep in a dark field. Everywhere we looked, there was a version of Leo. Small, dark sinewy men in lungis, wool blankets thrown over their shoulders to keep off the mist – he simply disappeared. 'Leo, Leo, you're surrounded by yourself!' we would shriek, as we lost him again in the market, and he would shrug, and men would speak to him in Tamil and he wouldn't have a clue what they were saying, and everyone would look blank and then laugh. We rented a grey stone Victorian cottage with a formal garden – it was lush and ornate, and you could imagine Alice and the White Rabbit disappearing in the morning mist – and for all this magical beauty, it cost just a few rupees a night. It was the kind of garden that should have had pale English fairies at the bottom, amid the stone statues of regal Hindu goddesses, and it felt strange, like travelling back in time, under the dripping green trees.

It rained. Apart from monsoon, I had never before been rained on in India. It was bizarre. We got wet. There was a fireplace in the cottage, and blankets, and a telly, and so we cocooned, smoking spliff and eating chocolate and I always had a small bottle of Old Monk rum on the go (or Old Drunk, made from that most volatile of substances – IMFL, or Indian Manufactured Foreign Liquor. It was foreign all right, about as rum-like as whatever you'd pour into a lawnmower, but it kept me warm at night in front of the weak smoky fire).

Up here, there were places where you could have extraordinarily foreign delicacies like real non-Nescafe coffee and proper cake, and we even found an eccentric café down a muddy track in the middle of nowhere that did apple crumble and custard; it felt strange and wonderful after the hot dry spice of the India thousands of feet below to eat something so warm and comforting and familiar. Apple crumble and custard, up a damp mountain where everyone's skin was the colour of glistening dark chocolate. Even the cows were different up here, bigger and fatter, and the market stalls sold avocados and eucalyptus oil and everything smelt different – wet and fresh and thick with mountain pine. Real pine, not Toilet Duck pine. It was bliss to inhale.

But it rained. It rained and rained, so we left.

Our time was running out. Leo and I left the others back on Om Beach, to finish our trip in the same place where we had started: a small hill station near Bombay called Matheran. There, three months earlier, after escaping the noise and heat and chaos of the city, we had retreated to a calm, spartan hotel set deep in woodland, where the only sounds were birds and monkeys and the soft thud of horses' hooves on earth pathways, and you could sit for hours on the verandah and read and drink lemon soda. (My lemon soda was generally 50% Romanov – or Ruffenuff, as I privately called this alarming non-Russian vodka; it tasted like surgical spirit, even worse even than Old Drunk. But I drank it anyway.)

That first trip to the quietness of Matheran had felt like a real honeymoon. We were together, alone and in silence, after the polluted craze of Bombay. We had played backgammon, and walked for hours in sunlit woods, and lay on clean worn sheets under a mosquito net and read our books companionably, like an ancient couple who had been together decades.

There were no cars or bicycles allowed in Matheran, and no roads – just pathways of soft clean earth under canopies of trees, high up in the mountains. The only way to get around was on horseback, or on foot. It was so enchanting, and so utterly *other* from the stoned sun-bleached beaches, that we decided to go back there before our final journey from Bombay to the grey cold winter in England.

Matheran was just 100 km from Bombay. To get to there, you take a suburban train from the organized anarchy of Victoria Terminus to a train junction at a suburb called Neral. From there you take a mini train, like something from Toytown, that groans and puffs vertically up the side of a mountain through One Kiss Tunnel (you are in its darkness long enough for just a single kiss) until you reach the tranquil woodland of Matheran. From the toy train station, a horse will take you through the woodland paths to your lodgings. No cars or motor vehicles are allowed.

This sounds easy, doesn't it? Except this time it wasn't. I was in a major grump from endless days of bus-train-bus-train-bus-train from the southern beaches, my as yet unrealized pregnancy playing havoc with my hormones, and as you know, your dad suffered from top of the range dyslexia. In these circumstances, the difference between an 'a' and a 'u', proved crucial.

Cross-eyed with confusion from trying to negotiate the Bombay suburban train network that serves seven million citizens a day, we had accidentally got off somewhere ridiculous about ten miles from Neral. Gauging my rising agitation, your dad wisely suggested a rickshaw to take us the last ten miles. (They're those tinny mechanised cockroach-shaped vehicles painted black and yellow, which make a noise like a lawnmower crossed with a hairdryer.) 'Yes, yes,' the rickshaw driver said, zipping in and out between the giant honking trucks and Ambassador cars on the highway, turning around to us as he drove and grinning expansively like a Bollywood star in his aviator shades, oiled hair and huge moustache. 'Not long only.'

Something was wrong. We were speeding up a multi-lane highway away from the distant mountains. It seemed as if we were going back the way we had come. 'Neral, Neral,' I kept shouting over the insane racket of the highway, as the autorickshaw zigged and zagged amongst the speeding traffic and hot dirty air whipped our faces. 'Yes, yes!' shouted the driver over his shoulder. 'Soon coming!' We drove on and on. You could see the mountains receding, the urban landscape bearing down on us. Finally, he pulled off the highway and into an ugly industrialised place. 'Nerul, Nerul,' he beamed. And then it dawned on me. Two places, one vowel and many miles apart.

I was in a very bad mood indeed by the time we reached Matheran. Had there been a kiss in One Kiss Tunnel, it would have been the Glaswegian kind. Yet even with my traditional lack of self-awareness, it did strike me as odd that I was in such a ferociously bad mood. After all, it's genuinely hard to be bad-tempered in a place like Matheran, because there is nothing there that is irritating. It is a place designed to be utterly unannoying. High up in the mountains, the air is beautifully soft, clean and cool. Because there are no vehicles there is no noise, traffic or pollution.

Only horses – and I *love* horses. There are no Westerners, just Indian families and newlyweds. It is surrounded by forest, and jaw-dropping views of valleys. You can ride horses at dawn through silent woodlands to the tops of huge hills to see the sun coming up over what looks like the whole of Maharastra. It's not the kind of place you could reasonably be in a bad mood. But then there is nothing reasonable about pregnancy, especially when you don't yet realize you are.

We stayed in the same quiet woodland hotel, with the monkeys on the roof and the Bihari cook who made us a delicious thali every day for lunch. Further along the silent leafy earth road was the Last Resting Home For Parsis, a kind of remote mountaintop Eastbourne for the small religious community connected with Zoroastrianism. When a Parsi died, their body was placed on a slab of rock high up in the air for the vultures to pick clean; it was the ultimate in recycling, and when the vulture population of Maharastra went into mysterious decline a few years ago, the Parsis were horrified because without the birds, the ancient death ritual was thrown into disarray.

Matheran's main drag was a series of little cafes and shops selling honey, sticky peanut brittle called chikki, and leather sandals, which we speculated were made from recycled horses. There was even the occasional 'cocktail terrace' to accommodate racier customers from Bombay – and me. It was nice to sit in a wicker chair and sip what the menu ambitiously called a 'gin fizz', people watching, and feeling fleetingly serene as the cocktails took the edge off my restlessness and irritability. The only passing traffic came from angular Indian horses ridden mostly by Bombay tourists whose legs stuck straight out at right angles, and half of whom rode in saris. It was a peaceful place.

It's the little things you remember; how the ears of Indian horses turn in and touch each other, unlike those of European horses, which point straight ahead; how Indian cats have smaller heads than European cats; and how Indian rats have lovely big round ears like Mickey Mouse, and very sweet faces. (I met my first Indian rat just a few hours after arriving in India for the very first time a few years earlier; it had fallen out of the palm leaf roof, utterly dead, onto my shoulder as I stood naked in the primitive shower of a beach shack in Goa. The dead rat was enormous, lying on my foot in the warm trickle of water, and I don't remember having any kind of Disney moment as I shrieked my head off.)

Anyway, Matheran was a gloriously kitsch, peaceful, harmless place, full of non-marauding monkeys, gentle horses, beautiful birds and mellow Indians, including the one I had married, although he was in fact from Hammersmith. But I was out of sorts. Nothing seemed right. Everything was annoying me. The place, the people, our hotel, the food, your dad, my books, even the horses with their funny ears. Surges of anger kept breaking over me. 'What's the matter?' your dad would venture, and when I would just scowl, he'd look confused, which irritated me even more.

I tried to remember my last trip to India, when I had spent five months living semi-feral and without the relative comfort of this trip – had this kind of irritability descended on me at the end? Had I experienced India fatigue before? I didn't think so. I would have stayed even longer last time, had I not run so completely out of money. What was it then? Was I already sick of being married to your dad, after just seven months of marriage and three months of honeymoon?

Surely not. Surely it would last longer than this. After all, we were properly, formally, officially married. There was no going back. So why was I feeling so cranky, so ill at ease? My automatic instinct was to self-medicate rather than sit stewing in it, so I bought a litre of Ruffenuff and knocked it back with cold fizzy tonic and sharp fresh lemon carried to the verandah by the smiling Bihari on a battered tin tray, in an attempt to take the edge off myself. But for once, the drink didn't work. It made me drunk and angry, instead of just angry.

5 BRIGHTON

We huddled with our backpacks in the vicious cold of the train platform at Gatwick that day in March, tanned and thin from all the puking and shitting, your dad so dark he was shiny black like Kali. We were desperate to get home. The wind was cutting us in half, the air stinging our skin through our pathetic cotton hippie gear, making me shiver so hard I felt nauseous.

It was beautiful finally to unlock the front door after months away. The basement flat in Kemp Town, with its knackered draylon sofa, shabby formica kitchen and damp patches on the bedroom walls was a palace of opulent riches compared with the bed-bugged lodgings of economy India. Everything seemed soft and velvety and deeply warm and comfortable and luxurious. Cushions and armchairs and bathtubs, oh my. Carpets and fridges. Extraordinary riches. Bliss.

There was half a bottle of tequila in the empty fridge, cheap stuff from Spain, I don't remember who put it there, but there it was, waiting for me that morning we got back, an unexpected welcome home present. I poured myself a glass and drank it straight. It tasted really bad. I remember choking and gasping, 'Ai, gasolina!' before hurling another glassful down my throat to get warmed up and chilled out. Leo had a cup of tea. When I had finished the bottle, I went to bed, snuggled under the lovely soft warm duvet, and slept and slept, my jetlag submerged in the alcohol.

Next morning, standing outside the Pound Shop on North Street, I thought I might die. Not from the cold, although it was icy. Not from a hangover, although the tequila had been like drinking brake fluid. Not from the journey, even though I was totally wiped out. But I knew what cold weather and hangovers and jetlag felt like – I spent much of my life suffering at least one of the three, usually the middle one. No, this was different. I felt sick and nauseous and dizzy and vile. There was definitely something not quite right. I had been looking forward to that initial amble around the chilly Brighton streets after the heat and dust of India, savouring that reverse culture shock, marvelling at how coolly ordered everything was before it all began to stifle and depress me again. But I was feeling too rough to take it all in. My plan to spend an hour mooching contentedly in Waterstones, reading the backs of dozens of books – like window shopping, except indoors, and quieter – suddenly seemed impossible, like climbing a mountain in high heels. I wanted to throw up, lie down, possibly die.

Instead I walked up the hill to Boots by the Clock Tower, trying not to vomit into the nearest litter bin, and bought a kit. I took the bus home, locked myself in the bathroom, and peed on it. And there you were. A little blue line. 'Leo!' I screamed. 'LEO! LEO!'

He came running. I was leaning against the bathroom wall, ashen, holding the small white plastic stick, grinning like a loon, shocked, thrilled, incredulous, open-mouthed. 'I'm up the duff,' I said, waving the magic wand. 'Look. Look! I'm *pregnant*!' His mouth hung open too. He gasped. Had he been able to go white, he would have. I thought he would faint.

'Wow,' he said at last. 'Wow.'

We just stood there for ever, grinning at each other.

'I didn't think I had it in me,' he said at last. He actually said those words, as though he had never considered that his sperm might be normal. Potent, creative, life giving. He looked like he might explode with pride. One hysterically over-excited phone call later, and Bertha came dashing around, clutching a giant bunch of flowers and a bottle of Mumm champagne. For the first time in my adult life, I genuinely couldn't stomach more than a tiny mouthful. I felt too sick.

I should tell you about Bertha. Or at least, about how we met, because the likelihood of our becoming friends was, like Bertha herself, extremely slim. It was a miracle really, given how it all started.

Once upon another lifetime, I worked somewhere horrible. Of all the horrible jobs I have ever had, this job was perhaps the worst. I had come back to grimy old East London with Harry after a few years of caning it in Barcelona – I'd begun to suspect that if I didn't leave Barcelona, I would end up mad or liver damaged, not realizing that madness and liver damage can happen anywhere, as long as your brain and your liver are nearby. Back in Blighty without really knowing what I was doing, I got a job in a book warehouse in Bow. Amongst its toxic dust and ugliness I had plenty of time to regret my decision to leave behind the bars, clubs and beaches of Barcelona, the architecture, the culture, the climate. Although I had been trying to save myself from death by hedonism – Barcelona is another story, which I will tell you another time – it would be fair to say I hadn't entirely thought things through in my haste to leave my destructive self behind, and restart again somewhere more grounded. I just bolted. To Bow. Of all places.

I don't know what I was thinking. Harry and I were on our last legs – again – and I couldn't readjust to a regular job after years of working five to nine teaching English to rich Catalans, instead of nine to five in a dystopian East End warehouse. It seemed like a giant step backwards, even though I had originally thought that I was moving forwards. I was bored, furious, obnoxious, resentful, and as usual, ripe for adventure.

A bloke at work – one of the upstairs blokes, rather than the downstairs drones – began paying me quite a lot of attention. He paid all the women quite a lot of attention, but I was bored and fed-up and didn't care. We got it on. He could have been anyone, I just wanted distraction from the blind alley into which I had reversed my life. He told me that he had four kids, which seemed as bizarre as saying he had four giant squid, because nobody else in my world had kids or knew kids or anything resembling kids – not even nieces or nephews. Kids didn't exist in our world. Kids were weird little aliens whose existence meant your life was over. And mine was still only starting.

Anyway, this bloke at work didn't appear too impeded by the fact that he had four kids. He seemed to be free to do whatever he liked, most of the time. It wasn't as if we were in love or anything – we were just two bored, self-involved people distracting ourselves on each other, drinking down the pub after work, and getting it on whenever we could.

He had a flat somewhere bleak on the North Circular where he propped up his monthly salary with a secret dope farm, growing giant skunk plants under hydroponic lights, back when skunk was still a bit of a novelty rather than the mind-bending norm into which it has since morphed. It was all very professional. Nobody lived there, but it was set up to look as if it was an ordinary anonymous London flat, which it was, from the outside; lights were programmed to switch on and off at appropriate times, and curtains were rigged to auto open and close.

But when you opened the door into the flat, the smell of high quality skunk hit you in the face, despite the packages of industrial anti-odour stuff everywhere, and the two bedrooms being tightly sealed. The plants were grown in those two rooms. It's not often that you find plants physically intimidating – maybe in dense jungle, or if you're Snow White in the forest at night – but these plants had presence. They were seven feet tall and vibrating in the hot wet hydroponic air, sealed off from the outside world, giant matriarchs sticky with bud. It was like the Day of the Triffids in there. It was also high maintenance – he called it 'gardening' – and highly lucrative.

That the bloke took me there at all showed just how stupid he was. I could have been anyone. I could have been Julie working for the Drug Squad. But he was not thinking with his head. It transpired he never did. So he took me to his flat that was really a dope farm, because it was the only place we could be alone together; he risked it with me, some unknown girl from work, because like me he was in pursuit only of pleasure without ever considering consequence.

I moved out of Harry's. I really hurt him, trampling on his feelings, but I was so caught up in myself that I hardly noticed. As far as I was concerned, my leaving was justified – the relationship was dead, I was feeling trapped and suffocated, and the bloke at work looked like an escape hatch. This was something of a pattern for me, seeing men as a way out. I left in the back of a minicab, going to stay in someone's squat on Murder Mile, until I found a place of my own in a shared house with some hippie blokes in Leyton who made hippie jewellery and, like everyone else I knew, smoked a lot of dope. Life was once again urban, hectic, excessive, and, as always, hand to mouth. I had no idea what I was doing, so I just kept hurtling along, doing it.

The bloke had told me he had an ex-wife who was neurotic and controlling and insane and made his life hell and wouldn't let him see his kids regularly, but in truth none of his story registered enough for me to care – I just heard the word 'ex' before the word 'wife' and that was good enough. I did have some vague sense of ethics in that I would not have become involved with someone still married, especially as there were so many unmarried – and therefore uncomplicated – blokes out there, but someone whose wife was 'ex' was fair game. That they were linked by children was academic, because I had no experience of such situations. None of us was married, or had been married, or had families, or been separated from our families; I had no concept of what it was like to have an ex-spouse or kids, and wasn't particularly interested. I was only interested in now, and fun, and me. Nothing else.

Anyway, how was I ever supposed to have any empathy with a woman who had four kids? I knew nothing of mothers, other than that they surrendered their identities the second they got knocked up; they stopped being women and started being packed-lunch-making machines, their lives made up of laundry and the school run and kill-me-now conversations about breastfeeding and food allergies. They all looked the same, with their mumsy clothes and harassed faces. (This was the early nineties – the appalling concept of the Yummy Mummy had not yet been invented.) I had no idea what a mummy was, other than fucked.

So my view of motherhood was narrow and dismissive, and my personal experience of responsibility had only ever involved cats. Four cats in total, three of whom I had abandoned in London when I moved to Barcelona, and one of whom I had abandoned in Barcelona, when I moved back to London. Well, not quite abandoned – I left them with very reluctant friends, who were none too pleased when I scarpered, leaving a pile of cash on the table to buy cat food for the rest of the cats' lives. Cats live a long time. I have no idea what happened to any of them. They could have ended up in a vivisection laboratory for all I knew – and I was a *passionate* vegetarian at the time, a real bunny militant, a supporter of Animal Aid and the British Union for the Abolition of Vivisection and hunt sabotage, an animal rights marcher, a flag waver, a naive admirer of the Animal Liberation Front; I just had no concept of taking personal responsibility for anything, from my cats to my lungs to my liver to the wife and four young children of a serial adulterer.

And then one day it was all over between me and the bloke. He came to work and told me he had to curtail our dalliance because one of his kids was very ill and he was needed back home. He was going back to his wife. I didn't really care. We both shrugged amicably. And that was that.

Except it wasn't. A few weeks later, he arrived at work carrying a book, which he handed to me. 'This is from, um, my wife,' he said, looking a bit embarrassed. He was no longer referring to her as his ex-wife. As I sat gawping at it, he said he had told her about me, and that I was a reader. *He had told her about me?* I put the book gingerly on my desk and stared at it for a long time, in case it was a bomb, but it wasn't. It was *Eva Luna* by Isabel Allende. So I took it home and read it, and liked it. When I sent it back, I sent one of my books too. I wish I could remember which one.

A week or so later, the bloke at work once more came sheepishly to my desk, returning my book and bringing another from his wife. This time it was Mario Vargas Llosa's *In Praise of the Stepmother*. I read it, and loved it. I sent it back, with another of mine. Then came Laura Esquivel's *Like Water for Chocolate*. She liked her magic realism, this wife. Then a Clare Boylan novel. Then a Wendy Perriam. A Zoe Fairbairns. A Fay Weldon. Each one I devoured – I have always had very mannish taste in books, my favourite writers the great misogynists like Hemingway and Bukowski, or smartarses like Brett Easton Ellis and Jay McInerney, and so I welcomed the women, these females on the page who wrote about things of which I knew bugger all. Like motherhood, and relationships and feelings. I read them all, sucked them all in, as she read mine. She must have liked what I was sending back, because the books flowed back and forth all summer. The bloke at work became just a carrier, a conduit. A mobile lending library.

Eventually I put a note in one of the books: a biro drawing of a cocktail – a Martini glass with a stripy straw – with a question mark next to it. Although we had been silently communicating via words for months, I was too scared to write a single word directly to her. I had, after all, been improper with her husband, who was no longer presenting as an ex-anything. In places where crimes of passion were acknowledged, she would have been legally entitled to kill me. But instead of a death threat, a note came back in the affirmative. We were to meet up. In the flesh.

Standing outside the Whitechapel Gallery that day and searching the face of every woman as she approached was actually quite scary.

'Don't worry about what I look like,' she had said on the phone, perhaps more menacingly than she had meant to sound. 'I'll know who you are.'

And so I stood there, face scanning and chain smoking, my curiosity – the stuff that killed the cat – the only thing keeping me nailed to the spot. Is that her? Is that her? Is that her?

In the end she blindsided me. Marched at me from the right as I stared straight ahead. Took me completely by surprise. Knocked me out. Not literally, although she said later that her friends had urged her to bring a baseball bat. No, what I mean is, *she* was a knockout. Tall, skinny, willowy, ethereally beautiful, dressed all in black, with clouds of pale hair and huge eyes. Jesus Christ, I remember thinking, *this* is the mad wife in the attic of that unremarkable bloke at work? This beautiful woman? I had to stop myself staring. This is a *mother*?

We skirted around each other inside the gallery, saying very little, as if on a particularly awkward first date, just grateful for the art (don't ask me what exhibition it was, it could have been dancing elephants for all I remember); when at last she suggested the pub, I almost collapsed with gratitude.

Once inside the Blind Beggar, she took a bottle of Pepto-Bismol from her bag, had a big, pink glug of it, and ordered a large brandy. She had an ulcer, she explained, lighting the first of a million Marlboro Reds. She had an ulcer from being married to a man who told other women that he was separated from his wife and four children, when in fact he was nothing of the sort. 'Did he call me his ex-wife?' she asked. I nodded dumbly, waiting for the Pepto-Bismol bottle to crack over my head. It never did. The bloke at work had done this many times before, she said. I was the first one that she had actually bothered to come and meet, because I was the first one who appeared to have some kind of a brain. Generally, she said, he went for morons. Thickos. Divvies. She wanted to meet me, she said, purely out of curiosity.

'Oh,' I said. For once, I was at a total loss for words.

The obvious thing to do was drink a lot as quickly as possible, so we did. We told each other truthfully what had happened, which – unsurprisingly – turned out to be quite different from the stuff the bloke at work had been telling each of us. By about the fifth or sixth drink we were laughing quite hard. Then we went for dinner together, and she paid for it with his credit card.

And that was how I met your godmother Bertha.

So there we were, years later, Leo and Bertha sipping Mumm in the basement flat in Abbey Road, as I sat on the wonky draylon sofa feeling like I was going to die, from excitement and nausea and exhaustion. The plastic stick with the blue line was on the table next to me, already a precious family heirloom. It's still in a box somewhere, the blue line long faded. 'I didn't think I had it in me,' he repeated to Bertha. Just as I looked like I might die, he looked like he might burst. Bertha beamed at him.

Your dad and Bertha had always got along, always approved of each other from the moment they met. They were cut from the same English-boarding-school cloth, a place of matrons and stewed prunes and emotional deprivation. They understood each other. With my very different background, I might as well have been from Mars. But the dynamic between the three of us worked, so much so that the previous summer, when Bertha had come to visit us in Brighton, she and I had made a secret pact as we walked along the seafront. 'I'll have a baby,' I'd said, somewhat recklessly, 'if you move to Brighton.' By then I was beginning to be consumed with that biological imperative which transformed my complete disinterest in mothers into an overwhelming desire to be one.

I knew nothing about actual babies, however, other than how to manufacture one; there was no way I could have had one without Bertha around. Bertha had been a midwife, and knew all about babies and births. At this stage, Leo had not been consulted, or informed of our plans. He had always said that it was not the right time to have a baby, because we had no money, and nowhere to live, but I had long since realized that there is no such time as the right time and the only right time to do it is right now.

So your cellular three month existence was presented to him as a fait accompli, and he was so amazed and delighted that he forgot about the state of our bank balance and instead strutted around the flat, chest inflated, a slightly dazed look on his face.

I had no idea pregnancy was so astonishingly all-encompassing. I thought it was just about growing a bump out front – I didn't realize I would be able to smell a smoker ten seats away on a bus, or sniff out what people were having for dinner three floors up, or that my hair would thicken, my nipples darken, my eyes go scratchy so I couldn't wear contact lenses, and that I would alternate between savage rage and blissful well-being. I didn't realize that I would need to pee every ten minutes, that my lungs would be squashed up under my armpits so that I could hardly breathe, and that I would develop the appetite of a wolf, if wolves ate mostly cheesecake and ice cream and other easily digestible combinations of sugar and fat. Your dad made risotto almost every night, because it was creamy and carby and you didn't need to chew it.

Pregnancy even stopped me being a vegetarian, something I had been since my late teens. One day, opening a can of tuna for the cat – not our cat, just a cat that had adopted us and spent most of his life purring on our sofa, and who liked us because we bought him tinned fish – I inhaled the dense ocean smell and devoured it, straight from the can, with my fingers.

'You can eat what you like when you're pregnant,' Bertha said. So I did. She was my pregnancy guru. I had no idea that I would develop a sensitivity to how fabrics felt, that seams rubbing against my skin would drive me crazy, that I would only be able to wear the same few garments that didn't irritate, that I would need giant knickers of the nightmare inducing kind. And I ate. I nurtured my inner wolf, and I ate. And ate. Not junk – apart from the cheese-cake and ice-cream – but spinach and skim milk. You are made of spinach and skim milk, which I would eat from the bag and drink from the carton. I had never drunk milk, and now I was downing litres of it a day. I was becoming enormous, like a hot air balloon billowing upward from fat swollen feet.

'You're building a skeleton,' Bertha said. It felt very safe being pregnant with her around. She knew everything there was to know. She was Mother Superior, and I was a novice. She had changed my perceptions of motherhood. Before we both moved to Brighton within a year of each other, I would go around her house in North London for dinner and be repeatedly amazed that this was a place where four young children lived. There would be evidence of them of course – toys in toy boxes, kid art on the kitchen walls, rubber ducks in the bathroom – but they were always tucked up in bed when I got there. It was Adult Time. The only experience I had of other people's children was time spent with a handful of hippie kids in East London unacquainted with the concept of bedtime, who would still be pinging off the walls at midnight, driving everyone insane.

My definition of 'mother' was infuriatingly narrow. Bertha used to say impatiently, 'I'm a lot more than just a parent, you know.' I think I had said to her that I had expected her to be an old hag with saggy tits and no teeth, and her children to be snot-nosed monsters. And yet as well as everything else, she was the loveliest mother you could imagine; you could see it reflected in her kids, who made me realize that children could actually be beautiful little beings to be around. In theory, anyway.

Of course there was always a lingering dynamic between Bertha and me: that I had done her wrong, but unintentionally, because I was emotionally retarded, and that we had overcome it. We loved to tell people how we had met. Their eyes would widen. We even made money out of it. We had each written our separate accounts of the story of how we met, and sold them to trashy women's magazines for £500 a pop, which was a lot when you were skint in the nineties. She had long since split with the bloke, who had disappeared entirely, abandoning their four children, and moving to a town where nobody knew him and beginning the whole process again with another unsuspecting woman. I was ashamed I had ever even glanced at him, but his purpose had clearly been to lead to me to Bertha and one of the greatest friendships of my life. So he wasn't a total waste of space.

Leo and I, on the other hand, ended up in relationship counselling when I was pregnant. Once the initial euphoria wore off, I realized I felt furious with him quite a lot of the time. Obviously, this is a pregnancy thing, but on some deeper primal level, I was also unable to articulate the feeling that I needed more from him. I'm not sure what – just more. I was by now exhausted from running the show – and the curtains hadn't even gone up, the stage lights were still dimmed. I would rant and rave, and he would sit there, passively, staring at me as though I were some madwoman in the street. One of those nutters who shouts at cars and pigeons.

'I am not being *heard*,' I used to shout, so that people several streets away could hear me perfectly. I remember the relationship counsellor asking what I wanted from a relationship, and me replying theatrically, 'I want it to be *perfect*.' And the counsellor had looked a bit hopeless, as she shook her head sadly. As we walked down London Road afterwards – well, I waddled, like a woman with a space hopper stuffed up her jumper – Leo stopped at a stall and bought something small, which he handed to me. It was a bar of clear soap, with the word 'Love' inside it in red letters. I still have it. The look on his face – loving, trusting, willing – when he gave it to me is embedded in my heart like a sharp sliver of glass.

6 BIRTH

You were born by elective caesarean because I knew that you would be the camel and I would be the needle's eye, and that after twenty hours of terror at not being able to control the situation – never mind the pain – I would still only be half a centimeter dilated, and that I would inevitably be rushed for an emergency c-section because you were turning blue, and your heart was on the blink. I was very determined not to let this happen. I knew quite well I was not a disciple of Sheila Kitzinger's birth-as-orgasm, despite poring over the books, and listening to Bertha's natural birth stories, and seeing photos of bloodied heads coming out of giant vaginas that frankly gave me nightmares, like watching snakes devouring cows but in reverse and with extra gore. I was not connected enough to myself to have the mental strength to squat in the dark in a room at home, or even in a birthing pool with half a dozen doulas on hand (not that you got doulas on the dole), so I thought the best option was the one where I removed myself from the process entirely, and let the men with scalpels do the work. I was too terrified of anything else.

It took seven minutes. They drugged me up – it was gorgeous, a warm flooding deadness – and sliced me open, then dragged you out. 'It will feel like someone is doing the washing up in your abdominal cavity,' said the man in the green scrubs whose breath smelt of instant coffee. And it did. The sound of you being lifted out of me was the sound of a metal spoon being pulled from densely set jelly – a deep, wet, sucking sound – and, Jesus Christ, there you were, and someone was saying you were a girl (I had forgotten the whole idea of 'boy' and 'girl'), and your hand was covering your face like a tiny starfish, and we stared at each other, your head all raw red and waxy white, the deep black glimmer of your eye. Your skin, which I had expected to be anything from dark chocolate to pale cream, was actually the colour of mushroom soup. You were hairy like a baby monkey, and your skin felt softer than a wet petal. You took my breath away. Leo and Bertha were by my head behind green masks and it was all too surreal. As Bertha held you in her capable, professional arms – for she had done this before, many, many times – Leo looked as if he might dissolve with disbelief at what had happened. It was like a magic trick, the appearance of this baby from behind a screen. Later in the recovery suite, hooked up to tubes, and catheted, and off my nut on the morphine, I gulped my champagne and stared at you from deep inside myself, from deep inside the hospital drugs. *What the fuck.*

Sorry, that sounds terrible. Now that we know each other, now that you know how much I love you, and that you are and always will be the two people in my life I love the most no matter what, after all that we have lived through, I have to tell you that actually, I was not an automatic mummy. Not even semi-automatic. 'I don't know what to do,' I would say, over and over. Because I didn't. I hadn't a fucking clue. Or maybe I never did say that out loud. Maybe I just thought it, while pretending to know.

It actually took quite a while for my bond with you both to develop, which – and I cannot emphasize this enough – was nothing to do with either of you, because you were tiny children, immense in your perfection, your purity. But there was a thick glass wall between me and the rest of the world that not even you could penetrate, in your early babyhood, your beautiful newness. I was shutdown. It took some time to discover just how shutdown I was, and to dismantle myself brick by thick glass brick.

So in those early days when I was still reeling from it all, Leo was the mummy, and I was the sort of mummy, and Bertha provided the Mother Superior support and advice hotline, and between us we muddled along. If it had not been for Leo and Bertha – well, I don't know. Leo adored you. He was so proud. He would march around with you in that navy Baby Björn, and you would fall asleep together, you face down on his broad chest muscles, now retired from dancing and making an excellent shelf for a baby-sized head. There are millions of photos of you two together: you in that caramel-coloured bunny suit, with the floppy ears, lying on Leo next to Carmen the dog, who was the size of the Sphinx in comparison (Carmen took to you, once the initial shock had worn off; Leo bribed her with roast chicken from Asda.); you and Leo asleep next to each other on the bed; Leo, looking like a new parent zombie with black bags under his brown eyes, beaming wearily as he holds you; Leo and you in the bath, your honey skin against his dark brown.

We seemed a sweet little trio. We were both entranced by you – we would lie there watching you for hours, the way other people watch the telly. 'Imagine,' we would say to each other, 'We made her.' And we would gaze at you, a bit stupefied. We used to tell people that we were in love with our baby. It was more than ordinary love – we were *in love* with you.

But in me, there was something not quite right. I was good enough at caring for you: the dressing, the bathing, the feeding (though not breastfeeding – I couldn't do it, even though I had never expected to feed you any other way), but I was not quite present. We might have been in love with our baby (and we were, don't ever be in any doubt about that), but I was still reeling. Not just from the usual stuff – the sleep deprivation, the fact that I could no longer consider my time my own, the terror of dropping you and you breaking into a thousand pieces – but the loss of myself. Who was this enormous woman dressed in flapping shapelessness, pushing a buggy along the seafront? I didn't know her, and I didn't belong to myself anymore. I remember bumping into a bloke from the London parties, who was down in Brighton for the day, and feeling so castrated, so finished, so ashamed. Not of you, obviously. Of myself. Of being just another faceless fat lass pushing a pram. I had desperately wanted you, but when you arrived, I had this chest-crushing realization that unlike all the jobs, all the boyfriends, all the addresses, all the situations I had ever crashed in on and run out of, this was not something I could change my mind about. There was no turning back. So when I looked at you, although it was with amazement and adoration, it was also with a suffocating feeling of oh-fuck-what-have-I-done. There was a terrible disconnect.

And then there was a final eviction notice, and the bailiffs came.

The little basement flat on Abbey Road was being sold. Our home, with the fairy lights and the elderly, drunk, God-bothering queen upstairs, and the anonymous, tuna-loving cat who lived on our sofa, was being sold along with the rest of the building. Becoming a parent and becoming homeless at more or less the same time is not good for your sense of security or stability; I nearly had a heart attack. Up the road, Bertha and her children were being made homeless too – their rented place was also being sold. 'We should get a house together,' Bertha said, as we sat smoking.

When it came to smoking, Bertha and I were like Patti and Selma from *The Simpsons*. I smoked Marlboro Lights, she smoked Superkings. Sometimes when I was especially broke I smoked Mayfair, or roll-ups. I hadn't smoked at all when I was pregnant, apart from those first few weeks in India when I couldn't differentiate between food poisoning and sperm poisoning. You were lucky – they made me feel too sick, as did alcohol, otherwise you might have been born with foetal alcohol syndrome and a smoker's cough. On the operating table moments after your emergence, and as they were neatly sewing me back together, I remember croaking, 'For Christ's sake can someone give me a cigarette...' Nobody did though. Back home with you, I started smoking again straight away, without ever pausing for thought. Although I did smoke out on the terrace, and not in the house, out of respect for your brand new lungs.

Your dad was working at the hospital where you were born, and earned so little that he could not come to our financial rescue, but at least he was there, and not spending all his time, cash and energy on a commuter train to King's Cross. But really, he could do nothing except leave everything to Bertha and me. We were the sorter-outers. He was the agreer. Whatever we sorted out, he agreed with it. Which is why, in the six or seven months before your first birthday, you lived in a hostel for homeless people. This is not really an experience I would recommend. Try to avoid it if you can, unless you're desperate.

Obviously, we didn't end up in a homeless hostel by accident.

We kept telling ourselves it was all part of our grand plan, our long term strategy, that actually we were there by choice. At the time it felt like choice, but really our choices were either (a) find another rented place to live, this time with a dog and a baby and no deposit or (b) get the council to house us. The other option – a mortgage – was not an option at all, because we had no money.

Looking back, this was such an insecure period of our lives that it seems like someone else's story, peopled by strangers who were actually us. Changes were happening so quickly that it felt like my life was telescoping in on itself; from deranged paranoiac twitching at the edge of East London parties to married dog owner in Brighton to sunkissed beach bum in south India to fifteen stone new mummy in a homeless hostel – all in the space of two years or so. It was too much. Too much change, too much responsibility. Too much, too much.

But still. We got there in the end.

HOW TO GET HOUSED: A CUT OUT AND KEEP GUIDE

- First, make sure you have either children or a disability or both. Being 'vulnerable' also helps. That can cover a multitude of states, conditions, predicaments, preferably combined. Be creative.
- Let the housing department know well in advance that you are being made homeless through no fault of your own. If you have dependents, the council has an obligation to house you. Pets don't count as dependents. Only small humans.
- Never leave the place you are being evicted from until the bailiffs come, no matter how many threatening letters are

sent, no matter how nerve wracking it gets. It's like playing chicken, but stay put.

- When you are finally given an eviction date, which can take months, even if the landlord takes you to court – which he will, so that he can get you the hell out of his place – go straight to the homeless department of the housing office.

- Be prepared: this is a terrible place full of extremely stressed people carrying babies and suitcases, and waving bits of paper. Do not leave until you are seen. This can take hours. Do not be fobbed off.

- Make sure everything is recorded, dated and filed in front of you. Get copies of everything, with 'date received' stamped on them. Assume everything will be lost, deleted or mislaid.

- Remember that staff might come and go as your mission progresses, and that you will have to retell your story over and over and over again to overworked, emotionally hardened housing officers who have seen it all before, heard it all before, and for whom your tragic tale of being made homeless is about as heart wrenching as an episode of *The Simpsons*. Your story is nothing compared with the stories of those suffering domestic abuse, fleeing war zones etc. But you still need somewhere to live.

- You will not be housed together as friends. No matter how much sense it makes logistically, financially and socially, for both the housees and the housers, this will not happen.

- Couples, however, are housed together. Same-sex couples, one of whom has a disability, with many children between them, have a more legitimate claim to a council property than, say, two able-bodied heterosexuals with just one child. You can see what I'm getting at here.

- If you are offered a property somewhere horrible, the threat of homophobic bullying by the local peasantry can be used to your advantage.
- If you continue to be offered hideous properties miles from anywhere, get outside help. Disability rights advocates, housing lawyers, family doctors, gay rights advocates – access them all. Get letters written on your behalf. Build up a portfolio of reasons why you need a proper house located somewhere reasonable. Hurl these letters at the people saying no. The suggestion of court action is also useful.
- Persist. Harangue. Turn up in person until they are sick of the sight of you, and house you properly just to make you go away.

This is not a manifesto for lying your way into a house to which you are not entitled. Bertha really was, amongst many other things, a disabled lesbian. That bloke, the one she had been married to, had been the only man in her life. All the others were women. In Brighton, she had finally found her true home. And over the years, she had developed a neurological illness – not of the degenerative variety, but the kind that comes and goes; it affected her mobility and her ability to do stuff like drive or work, and, when it was especially bad, even to get out of bed. That first winter down here, she couldn't even get up her own stairs and had to sleep in the sitting room. She never gave up, though. She never gave in to it.

No, it was me who told the lies in order to get us housed together instead of in two separate flats. It was me who pretended to be her wife, when I was really just her friend. And it was me who pretended that I did not have a husband, when actually he was there all the time, just not officially. During this period, which ate up our lives for what seemed like forever, your dad did not formally exist. He faded into the background. He had no official purpose.

Anyway, I bet you want to know what it was like living in a homeless hostel. As a lifestyle choice – even if you can magical-think it into some kind of Orwellian class tourism experiment, a kind of *Down and Out in Brighton and Hove* – I still wouldn't recommend it. It's grim. If they weren't grim, they wouldn't be homeless hostels, filled with desperate people who had lost their way. Naturally, we didn't include ourselves in that category – we were awfully nice, middle class people with no money, who were on a mission to get housed. So we sucked it up – the sticky, grimy ugliness, the feelings of loss of control, of being pulled into a vortex of depersonalisation. We were now government home-lessness statistics.

Initially, the housing people sent us to a hostel on the seafront, right across the road from the beach, which would have been fabulous had it not been for the fact that we were given the key to a small bare room with iron beds and stained mattresses in a piss-stinking basement peopled by individuals so spectacularly fucked up and dodgy that the caretaker, himself a wizened old creature with frightening teeth, sidled up to us and, out of the corner of his mouth, hissed, 'Don't leave your children out of your sight. Keep them with you at all times.'

We blew a collective gasket, and marched back to the housing office. I remember really shouting that day, shouting my head off at blank-faced people behind desks. *What the fuck* were they thinking, sending a disabled woman and a bunch of young kids and a baby down those steep stone steps to a reeking nether-world inhabited by people so damaged that you could not leave your small children to find the disgusting communal loo by them-selves, for fear of their safety? *How dare they* treat disabled people like this, and endanger our children? *How the fuck* were we supposed to live like this for months and months, while we waited to be housed? I roared and I yelled about legal action, about going to the media, all sorts of dire threats howled from the bottom of our well of powerlessness. We got moved that night.

We spent most of 2001 in a big old house near Preston Park that the council used for homeless families. If you drive past it now, it's all boarded up, with metal sheets nailed across the beautiful old Victorian windows, and a huge concrete slab blocking the once-elegant driveway with the huge trees. Long ago, there would have been carriages and vintage cars on the gravel drive outside the grand front door; when we got there, the only cars parked outside looked stolen.

It was, we were assured by the housing people, the top end of emergency accommodation, the Ritz of homeless units. Bertha and her children were given a shed-like prefab in the garden which was too small for two adults and a brace of kids, so you and I (and Leo, unofficially) were assigned a room in the basement of the main house – always bloody basements. Except in this case, it meant Leo and I had our own front door, and shared a bathroom and loo with just one other flat across the hall, rather than being part of the hellish free-for-all going on in the main house above.

The other flat in the basement housed a succession of the walking wounded: first a single parent fleeing domestic violence with her sexually abused daughter, both of whom who were insanely needy and always hassling us for cigarettes or sweets; then, when they had been moved on, a Middle Eastern family arrived, escaping persecution from somewhere life-threateningly repressive. I liked them instantly because they were quiet and educated and left their shoes outside in the hall, and cooked food that smelled of spice and warmth, but the mother and father avoided all contact with me the way I had avoided contact with their predecessor. As far as they were concerned, I was just another fucked up loony in a madhouse. 'No, look, I'm the same as you, I've been to university, I read the *Guardian*,' I wanted to tell them, as they passed with silent politeness in the hallway, watching me struggling with your buggy and the clinking bottles of wine in my plastic carrier bag. But they always kept a wary distance.

Still, we were lucky. Upstairs in the main house, it was like a psychiatric ward from which the beefy Grace Pools and Nurse Ratcheds had all fled. You would hear screaming and crashing and shouting and punching day and night, as nutters came and nutters went, as drug addicts attacked each other and alcoholics fell over. One inmate who briefly had the room directly above ours used to play a single soft rock ballad over and over and over again at a million decibels – that I can't remember which song it was just shows how effectively I filleted it from my memory. Much later, reading about the aural torture used by the Americans at Guantanamo Bay, I had flashbacks of that crashing guitar riff over and over all night at top volume. But this was still a few months before 9/11 had even happened.

When 9/11 really did happen, you and I saw it together. It was a month before your first birthday, and a month before we would get out of that place. I remember watching the plane flying into the Twin Towers on our tiny portable telly, that sunny day in September. You sat on the hard, grubby, nylon-carpeted floor, silently looking at me with your huge dark eyes as I watched the plume of smoke billow into the hard, blue Manhattan sky. I remember your serenity, as you sat on the floor playing with your wooden blocks, while the outside world reeled in shock from the flattening of the Towers.

I remember looking at you, and even as my heart melted at how beautiful you were, I had the awful feeling that being stuck at home with a baby was the most boring place on earth. No wonder men didn't do it. I remember feeling so trapped, and berating myself for feeling like that, and wishing I could be someone else, somewhere else, and feeling frustrated that I couldn't just enjoy being a mummy, even though it seemed that in order to be a proper mummy, you had to have had a lobotomy first. Yet all the other mummies I knew seemed happy enough and as far as I knew were non-lobotomised – so what was the matter with me?

Being in that dank basement room didn't help. Everything was unpleasant to touch. Nothing smelled good. It was all ugly, ugly, ugly. I used to count the seconds until wine o'clock, which was getting earlier and earlier. Wine was my closest ally, the softener of edges, the evening gift to unwrap, the warmth to sink into, the blurring respite.

One night, it was so noisy in the main house upstairs I thought I would go mad. It sounded as if there was a wrecking ball up there, a demolition party in progress. I remember stuffing wet cotton wool into my ears and chugging cheap wine to try and make it all less infuriating, less unsavoury, less intrusive. Next day, River rang to find out if I had received the case of delicious wine club wine that she'd had delivered for my birthday (people always gave me booze as presents back then, because they knew they couldn't go wrong). The delivery man had left the packaged case at the front door, as instructed. And then it all made sense – the extra noise, the extra falling-around-drunkenness, and the no-show of the wine. The ancient alcoholic couple who had recently been moved into one of the rooms in the main house, the toothless old woman who sometimes appeared at my door wanting money or cigarettes, the smelly old man with the wild hair: they'd had it. I told River that I would ask them to send her a thank you note. She smiled grimly. I don't think she thought it was funny.

Bertha and the children were in their shoddy prefab shed the authorities referred to as a 'bungalow' further up the garden; it was almost pleasant, if you could tune out the chaos nearer the house: the endless comings and goings, the desperate and the dispossessed, the screechy children and the harassed, hopeless parents whose lives were already mapped out for them, the young girl selling the *Big Issue* who was already smoking heroin, the other young girl covered in the livid stripes of self-harm, the dodgy geezers, the thin, fucked-looking people.

Leo would leave silently for work every morning, almost sneaking out the door in his smart shirt and trousers. How the mighty had fallen. Instead of going off to his London job in a pair of cut off shorts and a skin tight t-shirt, before returning to his bachelor pad in Little Venice to get ready to party the weekend away, there he was, trotting off to a pittance-paying job that almost – but not quite – required him to wear a tie. Poor Leo. It seemed his life had gone a bit pear-shaped since he had met me, yet he had put up no resistance whatsoever. Had I suggested we take a collective leap off the cliff, I wonder if he would have agreed. He never showed the slightest sign of tiring of this endless game of Follow my Leader, even though I was becoming increasingly fed up with my role as leader. And he continued to say, 'In the land of the blind, the one-eyed man is king.'

'Never mind,' I would tell him whenever he wondered how much longer we would be stuck in this place, but really I was trying to tell myself. 'It'll be worth it in the end.'

It was.

We moved into our housing association house on your first birthday. It was had just been built, had a teeny garden, and was in the middle of town, two minutes from North Laine. Best of all were its newness, its blankness, its white walls. No build-up of dirt, no ingrained dramas, no history of misery were held in its corners. No, it was as fresh and clean as a fall of snow. We were hideously overcrowded, of course, with children coming out of the woodwork and no room to swing a hamster, but the relief that our homelessness was finally over was incredible. Our mission, conducted through gritted teeth and held breath, had been accomplished.

Your dad and I had the main bedroom in the new house, and we somehow squeezed your cot into the built-in wardrobe. You were quite literally in the closet. My computer was in another corner. Slowly but surely, I was beginning to write again, as a means of escape. I began the first of many abandoned novels, which were always about the same thing – a woman who is stuck, and in order to become unstuck, leaves. Runs away. Legs it.

The novelty of everything – now that we were no longer up against it – started to wear off more quickly than the euphoria of a pill. Now that we were where we had set out to be, it turned out I didn't actually want to be there after all. I had all the things I thought I'd wanted – a husband, a baby, a dog, a house, and in a household that was not your typical nuclear unit, but a more interesting one, with two mummies, a dad, and five kids. What was not to like?

I remember Bertha asked me if I was happy, and I deflected the question, saying that you were very happy being surrounded by four other lovely children. Yes, but are *you* happy, Bertha persisted. I couldn't answer her. I had no idea what I was, or how I felt, other than fat, trapped and hungover, most of the time.

Of course I loved you, the way all creatures love their young, but I did not love being a mummy. I would sit through toddler groups feeling like a huge, trapped animal, an alien who did not speak the common language, writhing in my own discomfort. I couldn't relate to the baby drivel that came out of the other mummies' mouths, the endless fucking chat about teething and immunisation and breastfeeding and solids, all the normal, ordinary, reassuring communication between mothers of very small children. It all seemed so brain-dead, so bovine. I would sit alone, hiding behind the *Guardian*, avoiding eye contact, ignoring you as you crawled around the floor of the church hall or wherever we were that day. The other mummies cooed at you as I pretended not to be there at all. I would look up every now and then and smile at you, and then go back to reading about the outside world, praying nobody would smile at me and say, 'So how old is your little one?' Wasn't it obvious? You were a baby. What more was there to say?

I was drinking. Drinking, drinking, drinking. Babies, hangovers and a dog that wanted walking every morning at 6 a.m.; what had I done?

I gave Carmen the dog away. Even writing these words, more than a decade later, I still can't believe that I actually did it. Our dry-run baby, our first born, our puppy love who was now a big, bouncy bundle of muscle. Leo was sick of being the chief dog walker, and I couldn't deal with you, and a big energetic dog, and hangovers most mornings. Something had to go. Getting rid of you was not an option – I hadn't kept the receipt. (Just kidding, okay? But this was not my finest hour. I'm grateful you won't remember it.) Giving up drinking never crossed my mind, but if it had, it would have been instantly rejected in horror – it was wine that was keeping me going. Or as that book *Great Lies to Tell Small Kids* says, 'Wine makes mummy clever.' So by a process of elimination, the dog had to go.

I put an ad in the paper and was swamped with offers. When I took her to a family in West Sussex and left her there, something inside me cracked and broke. I couldn't believe I was doing this, giving her away, this beautiful dog with her dark, liquidy eyes who adored us unconditionally. And yet I couldn't look after her the way she needed. Life had gone from being completely without responsibility to being nothing but crushing, burdensome, humdrum obligation. Every day for weeks afterwards I rang the family who took Carmen to make sure they were looking after her properly, until they stopped answering my calls. I missed her so much. I was so afraid they wouldn't love her as much as I did.

'I am not going to the offie for you again,' Leo would say around ten to ten every night. By then I would have finished my second bottle and be desperate for the third before the shop shut. He would often go though. Or I would go, staggering slightly and slurring a bit. Once, when we were still in the homeless place, he came back one evening to find me passed out on the bed, with you screaming next to me. He said you looked as if you had been screaming for a very long time. I have no memory of it whatsoever.

'Are you happy?' Bertha had asked as we sat on plastic chairs in the tiny back garden, smoking. I remember shrugging uncomfortably. She never asked direct questions like that, even though we spent so many hours together talking and smoking, talking and drinking tea, talking and drinking wine. I didn't know how to answer her question. What did she want me to say? I didn't know what I felt about anything any more. I poured another glass for each of us; I'd drained mine before she'd even picked hers up. Was I happy? How did you answer a question like that?

Of course I wasn't happy.

It came to a head one morning, after a dinner for some friends down from London, when I woke up on the sitting room floor in a pool of puke and piss. All my own work – nothing to do with babies or dogs. Luckily it was laminate flooring, which Bertha and I had laid ourselves throughout the whole house, referring to ourselves as the Lesbian Laminators. Anyway, I woke up, and there were Leo and Bertha standing over me. Afterwards, I sat in the tiny garden, shaking and rattling, as Bertha told me she would look after you when I went into a treatment centre for alcoholism. No matter how long I had to stay there. Even if it took six months. But I definitely needed to go into rehab.

What? *WHAT?*

No. Something primal, buried under the layers and layers of numbness, stirred and creaked deep down in the pit of my gut. No. No, I would not be doing that. I would not be abandoning my baby. I had already abandoned my dog. I would not be abandoning you, even if it was to Bertha, the person who loved you most in the world apart from Leo or me. No, no, no. I was horrified and grateful in equal measure for Bertha's offer. I might be a switched off, emotionally unavailable mummy who only ever wanted you to be asleep so that I could sit and drink and read and drink and write and drink, but that did not mean I wanted to leave you. So I had to do something. Something unthinkable. I had to think about stopping drinking. It was like thinking about signing up for an amputation.

Leo had always told me I drank too much, but lately he had been saying things like, 'I'm going to leave if she doesn't stop.' He just never said it to me directly. Bertha told me that he had said it to her. Nobody had ever told me to stop drinking, at least not to my face. 'Bloody right we didn't,' River said years later. 'You'd have bitten our heads off.' Which of course I would have. Getting between a drunk and their bottle is like trying to wrestle a corpse from a crocodile: only a fool would try.

So that was the day I stopped drinking for the first time. I had to – I was backed into a piss-soaked, vomit-stained corner. I could no longer get away with it. Out of shame, and to keep everyone else happy, I stopped. Obviously, if you stop drinking solely to keep other people happy, you will not stay stopped, but I knew nothing back then, other than how to drink.

Luckily, there was a diversion at hand to distract me from the awful, wrenching loss of stopping drinking. I stopped on the day that you, your dad and I got on the plane for a Christmas holiday in Madeira. It was your dad's idea, to go to Madeira. I think he had seen an advert for it in the travel section of the newspaper. It was an odd, staid kind of place, a cross between Jurassic Park and Eastbourne in terms of geology and tourist demographic, all soaring sea cliffs and stuffy hotels that did afternoon tea for ancient chaps in blazers and ladies in sensible sandals. And it was cheap.

It was our first holiday together, the three of us. You sat on our hotel balcony in the setting sun, little red sunglasses and chubby brown arms, always smiling. It was a beautiful place, lush and green and full of banana plantations, and pathways so high that we were walking through cloud. We explored together, taking buses all around the island, going for walks in the funny old Seventies capital, buying a Monopoly board in Portuguese because there was nothing else to do, and all the time I craved a drink with every cell in my body. I craved a drink with an intensity that I thought would crack me right open and spill me all over the floor. I craved a drink from the moment I woke until the moment I shut my eyes.

Your dad was heroic. Every evening as the sun was setting and wine o'clock approached, and I was desperate to sit back with a full glass in my hand, softening into the drink as the evening light changed to golden, he would go to the local supermarket and come back with gallons of alcohol-free beer. I would sit on the balcony chain smoking and drinking can after horrible, gassy can, crushing the empties and cracking a new one straight away, slugging back the useless boozeless booze, in the hope that if I drank enough of it, I might somehow get some relief from the craving. Instead it just made me feel like a human waterbed. But I kept drinking it. So did Leo, in solidarity. When we arrived back in Brighton half an hour before midnight on New Year's Eve, Bertha had filled the fridge with alcohol-free champagne, which tasted like carbonated piss and made my heart ache with gratitude.

They really, really didn't want me to drink anymore.

And I didn't. I didn't drink. At least, not then. Not yet.

Leo began to work part time, which meant he could spend more time with you (and I could spend more time with me). He used to take you to playgroup – you'd wander off together hand in hand, into your private world. I stopped being hungover all the time, which meant Bertha was relieved that she was no longer sharing a house with a drunk, who was very often vile to be around the next day, and who was very often vile to the children, or at best, indifferent. Life looked a bit better, even though I still felt that I had accidentally wandered from my own into someone else's life, through some looking glass, and couldn't quite find my way back. On the outside, I lost a bit of weight, so I went from enormous to just large. I still thought about drinking every single day, but because of Leo and Bertha, I gritted my teeth and resisted. I would not give in, even though I felt like someone holding their breath, waiting to turn blue. White knuckling it.

It wasn't all bad, of course. Your dad and I had some fun together too, although it was essentially platonic in nature. We snuck away to the Hotel Pelirocco on the seafront once or twice, staying in Betty's Boudoir, where we didn't have sex, and the Absolut Love room, where we also didn't have sex. Your dad and I almost never had sex. On one of the very, very few occasions when we did manage it, one of Bertha's children walked in to our bedroom, and stood there, staring, too young to know better and too old not to gawp. Thankfully, his psyche was not permanently scarred thanks to the fortuitous positioning of a duvet, but it kind of killed the moment.

The thing was, Leo wasn't very interested in sex. At least, not with me anyway. I used to ask him jokingly if he had a lover, and he would look at me, with that increasingly tired, increasingly long-suffering face, and ask me just where I thought he might find the time. He would say that he could barely cope with the woman he already had. Sorry, I know this is probably making your toes curl, but it's part of what happened later. Because it's not just love that makes the world go around – it's sex as well. At least, it is for me anyway.

When we lived in the basement in Kemp Town, we almost never had sex because he said I was too aggressive and too frequently hungover. This was true. While I was a fairly average drunk (annoying, repetitive, over-sentimental, occasionally funny), I was evil when badly hungover. I emanated a toxic vapour, like Chernobyl, like Fukushima, and radioactive poison leaked out of my mouth before my brain could cool it. But then I stopped drinking. So he didn't have that excuse any more.

Then, after you were born, he said he didn't want to have sex with me because I was too fat. This was also true. I was fifteen stone, and I wouldn't have wanted to have sex with me either. It was not an attractive proposition, unless you were one of those people who liked to feed their women custard pies and ice-cream because their drastic weight gain turned you on. Your dad was most definitely not one of those guys. So I went to the doctor and got some appetite-suppressant medication, which has since been banned because it was driving people around the bend, and I lost a few stone.

I was no longer very fat. So he didn't have that excuse anymore either. But he still didn't want to have sex with me. I used to wonder what his next reason would be – that I was too old? Too familiar? Too mumsy, now that he had seen you being lifted from my innards? Too saggy? Too mouthy? The wrong star sign?

It wasn't as if we weren't affectionate with each other. We were big into hugs and endearments – it hadn't yet begun to fade to neutrality; we were very loving, but in a basket-of-puppies kind of way. There was no heat, no fire, no spark. We didn't devour each other, which is why I devoured all that cheesecake; we didn't get drunk with lust for each other, which is why I got drunk on all that cheap red wine or cognac or tequila or anything that made me feel all warm and soft inside.

And then, in New York, I had a terrible epiphany.

Leo and I had gone to stay with someone we had met on Half Moon Beach, leaving you behind with Bertha for five whole days. I could not bear to leave you for five days now – I would start to get twitchy after three – but back then, I was still deep-frozen, and left you without a backward glance. Sorry. That sounds horrible, but I really was a long way from thawing out.

So we went to New York, your dad and I, and had fun trawling around weird little shops and eating giant pretzels. Your dad had manicures while I waited in the record shop next door, and we gawped at Ground Zero from the top of a bus, and ate cupcakes from the Magnolia Bakery (and wondered what all the fuss was about), and wandered around Greenwich Village and walked the length of Manhattan while getting neckstrain from staring vertically up. I love New York. Even when snotty, model-actress-singer bartenders sneer at you while demanding a dollar a drink tip; even when you have to meekly submit to a clipboard-wielding dominatrix just to access your pre-booked restaurant table; even when the cabbies are rude and gruff and doing you a big favour just by letting you into their yellow taxi; even when smoking a joint in Central Park could get you the death penalty, I still love New York.

One night, we went to see Timo Maas play at the Bowery Ballroom, and later, wide-eyed from our first pills in ages (I reckoned after such a long break, it would be mentally safe to have one), we were in the queue to get into the afterparty. And then the big black bouncer on the door asked me for ID. I laughed, assuming he was joking, and told him how flattered I was. He remained stony faced. He wasn't joking; without my passport, I wasn't coming in. So I gave up, and took a cab back to Williamsburg, Leo gallantly accompanying me. Back at the apartment, I was still wired, so I rolled a spliff. Our host, who had told me where the stash tin was before we left the club, only smoked strong weed, in those tiny little one-skin joints favoured by Americans, as they are so much more discreet than the traditional British Camberwell Carrot. In keeping with local custom, I smoked a tiny, supercharged one-skinner before lying down next to Leo. As the weed hit me, so too this did this crystal clear thought:

I am not in love with him.

I am not in love with him.

I am not in love with him.

I am not in love with him.

I am not in love with him.

I am not in love with him.

I am not in love with him.

I am not in love with him.

Obviously, I tried to bury the thought immediately, in a deep hole where nobody would find it. I closed my eyes tight, and pretended to sleep. He was still awake from the pill; I froze when he reached over. No. No, no, no. There was no way. This never happened, and here he was, initiating intimacy as I lay there frozen in horror at what I was feeling. The clarity of the moment – the undeniable acknowledgement of my feelings – felt like a bucket of icy water being hurled in my face.

Now that it had finally made its way from my unconscious to my conscious, I couldn't push the knowledge back under again. I couldn't unthink the thought, unrealize the realization. I loved your dad, because he was so lovely and lovable, but I finally had to face up to the idea that I was not in love with him, that I did not feel for him in the way that lovers feel about each other. I knew what that felt like, and it was not this. Had I ever been in love with him? Or was I just going through a phase, my feelings ebbing before they would flow again? In truth, I had no idea. I had no clue about how feelings worked. I'd always drowned them, or drugged them, or denied them. As I was doing now. I could hardly turn around to my husband and the father of my little two-year-old girl and say, 'Actually, I'm not in love with you. Sorry. My mistake. Move along now. Nothing more to see here.' And yet there it was. What should I do with this terrible knowledge? It had been there for ages, but I had always swallowed it down, pushed it down, covered it, ignored it, hoping that it would go away. I had never admitted it to myself out loud in my head before.

There was no way I was going to dismantle our little unit. We were a family, and we were going to stay a family. The idea of traumatizing anyone, or ending anything was just not something I could contemplate; we were, after all, married now, and parents now, not just some pilled up strangers who snogged at a party once, in another lifetime that was really only three years before. We were a trio. We would stay that way. Apart from all of that, I had no desire whatsoever to join the legions of women I knew who were bringing up kids away from their dads, the ones where the dads had weekend access, where the mums and dads were always arguing on the phone about logistics and pick-ups and drop-offs and dates and times and places, and where the mums never seemed to have enough money. I didn't want to be one of those women. Ever. 'Let's have another baby,' I said, soon after we got back from New York.

When your dad pointed out – quite reasonably – that we were already bursting at the seams, that our two year old already slept in the wardrobe and that there was not room for even a pet gerbil, never mind another baby, I pooh-poohed him. It had been two years since I had given birth, and the baby hunger was on me, gnawing at me from the inside. Even ambivalent mummies like me weren't immune from attacks of the screaming broodies. It was a basic biological imperative, without sense, rationality, or logic. (Apart from the fact that without this crazy irrational urge, we would have ceased to exist some time ago.)

It was on me like a demon, clamouring inside my head to do it, do it, do it, demanding that I make another one of you. I became so consumed with the desire to get knocked up that I actually told your dad if he wouldn't do the job, then I would bloody well do it myself. I hadn't quite figured out the details of this threat, but I think he realized then how serious I was; or at least, how stubborn my biology was, because even I couldn't have talked myself out of it – and I can convince myself of most things, that black is white, that day is night, if I put my mind to it. So, as usual, heedless of consequence, I got my own way. I got you, my beloved second child. And with just cosmic seconds to spare – a year later, there would be nowhere left inside me for you to have taken root and grown.

7   'NOT SIGNED TO AVOID DELAY'

'There's a penis growing inside me!'

There you were, floating upside down, your giant head, your curved back, your little, waving limbs, like a deep-sea creature. And there was the irrefutable proof that you were not another daughter. It blew my mind to think that there was a mini-man living south of my belly button, to see him there in front of me in black and white. To see you. I don't know why it amazed me so much; I think it was the precise moment when I realized that men come from exactly the same place as women, and not from some weird, alien planet. Seeing you blew Leo's mind too – he was going to have a son. A little boy, just as he had once been. And just as we were about to become homeless again. Yes, homeless. After all those months of going through all that homelessness hassle. But events, despite my becoming pregnant with you, had continued to hurtle forward at warp speed, without due consideration for my condition, or yours.

That winter, during the hormonal psychosis of early pregnancy, someone told the council that an adult male, an individual neither lesbian nor disabled, was living in the disabled lesbian household. We never found out who, or why, or what for – it was a curiously Eastern Bloc informer sort of thing to do.

To this day, I have no idea who it might have been. But if I had, I would thank them – we needed a kick in the right direction. We were already hideously overcrowded in the shared house. There was no way a new baby, a two year old and an adult couple could sleep in one smallish bedroom, and share a smallish sitting room and smallish kitchen with another adult and four growing children – no matter how much we all liked each other. Which we did. A lot.

So we moved out. Not being quite as penniless as the last time we had been made homeless, we managed to find a big old flat in a posh square on the seafront, which had unnaturally cheap rent because it had been empty for ages. The flat was on two floors and had a little roof terrace up amongst the chimney pots, with the sea sparkling between them. I loved it. Leo loved it. The place seemed enormous, with infinite acres of pale carpet and creamy walls, vast empty rooms with nothing to clutter them. Everything was wide and open plan; you could run around without braining yourself on any sharp corners or falling over baskets of laundry or skateboards or buggies. It was empty. Zen.

And you had your own enormous bedroom, which you would share with the new baby when he was born, but for now it was all yours. It never dawned on me that you'd probably have preferred to continue sleeping in the same room as us. But you seemed happy enough, with your sun and moon wall lights, your little wooden bed, your toys scattered across the miles of soft blue carpet.

Best of all, there was a tiny narrow room that lead out to the roof terrace; it was just big enough for a desk, a chair and a computer, and a potted palm. At last – a room of my own where

I could write and rewrite my unfinished novels, where I could smoke a thousand cigarettes with the doors wide open onto the terrace, and where, apart from the keening and screeching of seagulls, there was huge silence. I had no idea until then how necessary space and silence were to my sanity, which is why I had always lived with lots of people – I had never known myself well enough to realize that this is not what my inner self needed. But there we were, suddenly surrounded by space and silence. It was a multi-occupancy house, but one so enormous and grand with walls so dense and ancient (like many of the neighbours) that you couldn't hear a thing even if they were murdering each other to the strains of Motorhead. Actually, no, not Motorhead. Mahler. And I loved it.

The first night in this heavenly new place, I lay in the bath watching snow spatter and slide down the windowpane. There was nothing outside except freezing, heavy sky. I lay in the hot, scented water, a cloud of bubbles softening everything, steam floating against the whiteness of the room, and it felt like being inside a womb of wet warmth and safety. Inside me, that's exactly where you were. In your underwater garden by the sea.

On Valentine's Day, still thrilled at having a bigger, more comfortable place to live, I thought that your dad and I could maybe create some kind of spark between us, now that there was no likelihood of anyone walking in on us, or hearing us doing anything through paper thin walls. Normally people say 'rekindle', but this implies traces of sexual heat, some softly glowing fire in need of the faintest breath of desire. In our case, we needed napalm.

The unthinkable thought from New York had kept bubbling to the surface of my mind, no matter how hard I tried to hold it down and drown it, to strangle it before it bobbed up again. It – that is, the unthinkable thought – manifested itself on a shopping trip to Ikea, where I bought the biggest widest bed in the whole warehouse. I no longer wanted to share a bed with your dad anymore. Or even a bedroom. But as this was unthinkable, given that we were just about to have our second child together, I dealt with the situation by placing myself on the far side of a mile-wide bed with an acre of cotton-covered no-man's land between us.

I had no clue of the psychology of sexual relationships, because I had only ever been with men who definitely wanted to have sex with me, and with whom I definitely wanted to have sex; it had never been more complicated than that. Then again, I had never had babies with any of them, or grown fat while with any of them. During this pregnancy I gained back all the weight I had lost on the appetite suppressants – and more. The fat had spread around my body, creeping up my back, swelling under my armpits, pudging my legs and inflating my bosoms, widening my hips and inundating my waist. Your dad, while stocky and muscular, was a slim man. Side by side, we looked like the number 10.

Nor had I ever experienced extreme domesticity with any of the men I'd been with before. Beyond my ability to beautify a space using imagination and fairy lights, I am not a domestic goddess. I could barely work the washing machine. Thankfully, your dad was a domestic dream; it was like sharing a home with a very evolved cat – he was neat, contained, and took up very little psychic space, allowing me to crash and leak all over the place. And he always did the washing up and the hoovering. But we did have conversations about putting the rubbish out and buying nappies and all those things that seemed a long way from passion and desire.

If you add weight gain and the daily domestics together you can turn even the most ardent lovers into flatmates – temporarily at least. Everyone knows that without sex you can't have babies, but that equally with babies you can't have sex. But if the sex wasn't there in the first place, apart from on birthdays and blue moons, then you're fucked. Or rather, not fucked. But both Leo and I were big on gesture. So that first Valentine's Day a month after we moved into the new flat, on the day the world is instructed to be romantic, I did what I thought I should do and he did what he thought he should do. I dutifully scattered rose petals on the giant new bed, strung heart shaped fairy lights on the bedroom wall, and gift-wrapped loads of silly heart shaped gifts for him to open: a mini heart shaped frying pan, a heart shaped bath sponge, a heart shaped unidentified thing made of red feathers that had no discernible use, except that it looked nice. I put heart shaped chocolates under his pillow, and wrote him something nice in a heart shaped card. He was similarly thoughtful in his offerings of beautiful flowers and fancy chocolates – all red, my favourite colour. 'I love you', he said.

'I love you', I said.

We exchanged our Valentine gifts; he admired the red glow of the vast empty bedroom with the bed covered in petals; I put the red flowers in a vase, and then we – well, we went to sleep. In the huge bed. We went to sleep with a mile of cotton between us. I don't know if I felt relief, or resignation, or rage. Or just desperate for a good fuck, but not with your dad. No, not with him any more.

We didn't have sex for the whole of that second pregnancy. Not once. I was drowning in my own hormones, huge with need. But what could I do? Beg, demand, nag? This was the one area where these tactics didn't work. So I crawled the walls, and the bed got wider and wider and wider.

It's very important that you know just how much your dad adored you. God, how he adored you. He was the loveliest, kindest, gentlest, most patient dad you could imagine; he would spend hours toodling around with you, playing with you, taking you places, looking after you, loving you. He would dress you, feed you, crawl around the floor with you. He never got bored, like I did. (Then again, he was at work half the time, in an all adult environment, where he was being paid for his time. He wasn't *that* much of a mummy.)

We had hundreds of days out, because I had somehow managed to pass my driving test after six fails, and got a crunchy little Fiat that chugged us around the countryside. We would drive to Middle Farm and Seven Sisters and Drusillas, rattling along at fifty miles an hour, or we would walk along the Undercliff Walk to Ovingdean to the café there, the one with the lovely people and the lovely cake, and on Sundays we would eat sushi at Moshi Moshi, and go on the pier afterwards to let you ride the carousel. Leo adored you and I adored you and inside me there was the other one of you already growing and I am so glad about that, particularly given all that was about to happen. You weren't even born yet, and people would stop and tell us what a lovely little family we were.

But I'm getting ahead of myself again. It got hotter and hotter and I got bigger and bigger. You grew and grew inside me; Leo and I had been to have the twenty week scan together, and we saw that you were a boy, and it felt unreal, because I had never imagined that I would have a boy. I was programmed for girls, even as you astonished me. All over again.

By the time you were born, we had grown into our new home. We had come up in the world – in every sense. The flat was up six flights of stairs, which got steeper and steeper the more pregnant I became. The neighbours were old and snobbish, and seemed to have been writing letters of complaint to the Residents' Committee since the time of the Prince Regent; the rules were many and petty, and there seemed an unspecified terror that the genteel elegance of the square might be tarnished by common renters. Like us.

One ancient neighbour kept himself alive by vigorously interfering in our lives. He particularly objected to your buggy in the hall. 'We don't like buggies in the hall', he would say querulously. He didn't like shopping left in the hall either, or your tiny scooter, or other people's children, or adults, or dogs, or anything that suggested that other people lived in the multiple occupancy building with him. He would monitor our comings and goings, and if I left a buggy, bag, or baby in the hallway while I struggled sweating up the stairs with twenty tons from Sainsburys, he would appear at once, with surprising agility, and say in his trembly old voice, 'We don't like things left in the hall.' Certainly, I could see his point – for about a tenth of a second. It was a very grand hallway, with a heavy old front door and a giant gilt mirror and thick red carpet, but come on – what do are you supposed to do when you're eight months pregnant, coming home with a two year old child and ten bags of groceries?

That summer was the hottest of my life. I thought I would accidentally induce labour, heaving stuff quickly up those stairs to avoid the frosty tap-tap-tap on the door of the flat, and the old boy asking me with such extreme politeness if I realized that I had left some 'items' in the hall. And I would stare at him, this tiny, shrivelled creature in his velvet trousers and cravat and little gold rimmed spectacles, like Rupert Bear's infuriating great-uncle, and even though I was basking in happy hormones and delight at our new home, I would still fantasize about wringing his stringy neck.

Once, soon after you were born, and I was struggling with the usual tons of stuff, but now with an infant strapped to my front and recovering from a caesarean, he snuck up behind me and said it again: 'We don't like buggies in the hall.' This time, insane from sleep deprivation, heat exhaustion and new mummy malaise, I snapped at him to back off. Except I didn't say 'back'. The next day there was a letter from the Residents' Committee informing me that they didn't like buggies in the hall either.

Still, I didn't care. Not that long ago, we had been in emergency homeless accommodation – now we had the keys to a magic garden – acres of beautiful flower-filled communal garden that went all the way down to the sea. The old neighbour was nothing more than a lone fly at our picnic. Ironically, as your birth approached, such was my inability not to pee every twenty minutes that the garden became out of bounds; I would waddle down the six flights of stairs, heave across the road, unlock the garden gate, find a shady spot, and by the time I sat under a tree, I would need to hoist myself upright and huff back up the six flights again, sweating wildly, desperate to pee as you pushed down on my bladder.

I gave up the garden, and would sit instead on the tiny roof terrace, under a broad black straw hat, reading. Reading, reading,

reading. Or I'd lie on the huge bed, the windows open, fanning myself as the tall candles in the glass candelabra next to the bed bent like bananas in the heat. I had heat rash. I was more enormous than I have ever been in my life – I weighed more than sixteen stone, more than a prop forward, more than a catwalk of waifs.

Six weeks before you were born, I heaved and puffed, red faced and gigantic, to London, to see Public Enemy at the Festival Hall as part of Lee Perry's Meltdown, and to meet up with a few old party friends from East London. The looks on their faces, as I lurched down the concrete steps of the South Bank, said it all. I felt myself scorching in shame. I remembered the last time I'd seen Public Enemy, in a Barcelona club in the early nineties, and I felt suddenly like an imposter, a giant mummy zeppelin accidentally blown off course into a place where only cool people were allowed. I shouldn't have been there, but my feet and my head wanted to be here, to be energized by the beats, the power, the fury. I had split off into two beings – my old self, and this giant body snatcher who had stolen my real body and turned it a bloated container.

Still, I bet you enjoyed the bass that night; you would have been vibrating in there. I could feel you kicking around inside me.

All through that summer I became more and more uncomfortable, inside and out, as though I were gestating a microwave inside a space hopper whilst wearing a fat suit. This was not a dream pregnancy like the first one; I might have been healthy as a horse, but I was also the size of one. This bothered me greatly, but at no point did I feel able to do anything about it. Then again, that's what happens if you inhale comfort food to numb your ragingly unmet needs. I was also trying to push down my rising fear, my rising discontent; I was about to have our second baby, and my relationship with your dad was falling apart, dying a slow polite death. I was eating my feelings, because I couldn't drown them in drink. Not while you were onboard, anyway.

And then you were born.

You were a little black hairy beauty with scrunched up eyes and giant, red balls, and when they laid you on me as they sewed my stomach up (again), my response was automatic; this time, I knew what to do. I knew how to hold you. I knew what to expect. Instead of being terrified, like the last time, I was overwhelmed with a sense of everything being exactly right. I knew that I didn't want to breastfeed you, because I had screwed it up so traumatically the last time I had tried it (your sister, said a midwife at the time, was just hours away from losing consciousness from lack of food, when she was only a week old); knowing that made things easier. I bottle fed you, you drank it down, it went into you, I could see it going into you as you sucked it in, the white liquid disappearing into your tiny face. You were fed, bish bosh, job done.

I do wish I had breastfed both of you. It would have been more bonding, better for you both, blah blah blah, but it didn't happen. I didn't have the confidence, the patience, the selflessness. I hated the cowness of it. I wanted my body back, rather than handing it over for further months and months. I never thought of it as maintaining the connection that we had made when you lived inside me; I had never heard of oxytocin. The difference between the second birth and the first was that with the second one, involuntary tears ran down the side of my head when they placed you on me; the first time, I had been too numb with shock to react at all, other than to ask for more champagne and more morphine. You and I bonded that first night though, you asleep on me in the hospital room, me awake all night staring at you in wonder and joy, and it was easy because I was not afraid, and so could just enjoy the feeling of you. This time, I'd had some practice. I knew which end was which.

And then the next morning, you met each other for the first time. It would be fair to say that it was not a joyous experience for the older of you, who looked horrified at what was lying on the bed. 'Look, your new baby brother.' Poor older you. I had managed to wangle a private room, and we had erected a magnificent princess castle, with a princess costume and princess shoes. (You were going through your princess phase at the time, which despite the fact that we dressed you in dungarees as a toddler, you still seemed to discover all by yourself, and so we went with your sudden violent interest in pink.) There is a heartbreakingly funny photo of you sitting on the bed, all dressed up in your princess gear, and staring at the new baby with an almost cartoonish expression of shock and dismay. Poor girl, your world was rocked that day. (Just as Carmen the dog's had been rocked the day we arrived home from the hospital with you – Leo had run out and bought Carmen a whole roast chicken, but she had been so horrified at the new baby that she didn't even glance at it until the next day.)

You got over it though. You two are lucky, because even though today you seem to want to kill each other on an almost hourly basis, your bond is deep. You really look out for each other. That you will have a shared history when you are older is a gift that you cannot yet imagine.

As a footnote to your birth, something small but telling had happened moments before you were surgically removed from me. The anaesthetist, instead of being the nice man from the last time, was terribly haughty and something of a princess herself, albeit the middle aged, heightened-sense-of-entitlement kind. She refused to let me have both Leo and Bertha in the operating theatre, standing at my head, holding a hand each, as they had done at the first birth. Instead, as the guys in green scrubs wheeled me in for the epidural, she made me choose who could come into theatre with me. I hesitated for just a second before choosing Bertha. I hurriedly explained to Leo that it was because Bertha was a midwife who had facilitated hundreds of births, and her presence felt more reassuring. But really, it was because, in the split second pressure to choose, I chose the person I felt closer to. Your dad waited outside, his nose pressed to the glass.

It was rare that Leo ever really said what he thought. If I had been locked out of the birth of my own child, I would have hit the roof, stamped my foot, and insisted on being there. Leo, though, as I've already said, was like a particularly agreeable mirror who would say back to you what he thought you wanted to hear. His politeness was unbreachable. Occasionally his mask slipped, and he said what he really thought, before he had a chance to think about it. One weekend we were flat-sitting for some friends, and in my hurry to shoo him and you out the door to the playground so that I could have some peace and quiet, I accidentally locked us out of the flat. Moments before, I had turned the taps on to run a bath. The flat was on the first floor of the building, so in about ten minutes, the flat below would be flooded. The only way back in was to climb up the scaffolding wrapped around the building next door, and shimmy across onto the windowsill, where the front room window was open. But when I suggested this to Leo, as he stood there with you in his arms, locked out on the landing outside a flat that wasn't ours, he forgot himself. He forgot to be polite, and deferential, and diplomatic: 'How could you possibly do that!' he exploded. 'You're too *fat!*' It was his friends' flat – they had entrusted it to him. He was clearly in the horrors. I recoiled, humiliated, because what he'd said was true – it's just that he had never been quite so blunt about it before. (In the end I called the fire brigade, who came, all yellow hoses and heroism, and one of them leapt up the scaffolding in seconds, and let me back into the flat – only to discover that I hadn't put the plug in the bath in the first place. They were very nice about it. They thought it was funny.)

Leo bought me a gift later that day, a beautiful pair of hand-made flip-flops that I never wore because they were so uncomfortable, and said sorry for hurting my feelings. I apologized too, for generally charging around like a bull in a china shop, but it disconcerted me – not the shock revelation that I was fat (it wasn't really something that I could avoid noticing) but the fury with which he told me.

What else was going on inside his head that he was hiding so well?

I can't remember exactly when your dad started making an awful lot of visits to the doctor, and having an awful lot of tests done at the hospital. He had always been terribly worried about his health. When we first met, he told me that he had annual checkups, which seemed like an extraordinary thing to do when you were young, especially when you were young and caning it on the dancefloor every weekend and extremely fit from doing martial arts.

But then I discovered that your dad had been born very prematurely and had spent months in an incubation unit. This was back in the early sixties when neonatal care was as underdeveloped as he was. Nobody had expected him to survive, yet somehow he had made it, even though he had been born with much of himself not properly formed. Maybe this was partly why suddenly, when you two were small babies, he had a plethora of health problems. High blood pressure. Dodgy kidneys. A fatty liver. His risk of diabetes growing by the day. None of this was lifestyle induced – he barely drank, unable to tolerate alcohol beyond a lone gin and tonic (I'd seen him drunk just once ever, and his normal mildness had curdled to irritating, repetitive belligerence. I know, I know. Pot, kettle, black. I know). He didn't smoke tobacco either (unless something stressful was going on, in which case he would buy an emergency pack of ten Marlboro Lights), and he had a reasonably good diet, burnt toast and fish finger sandwiches aside. He no longer did drugs, and he was not overweight. And yet he began taking pills that you usually don't have to take until you are much older. He began suffering from terrible fatigue, terrible headaches. And sexual dysfunction. It was all to do with the super-high blood pressure, which was genetic, his doctors said. Now he had a water-tight, bona fide reason never to have sex with me again.

One evening, after we had been having one of our going-around-in-a-circle conversations about the seemingly unsolvable issue of his career (his job was causing him problems, as usual – I can't remember if it was the hours, or the pay, or the management, or a combination of all three), he suddenly looked stricken. 'I don't want to become ill,' he said, his voice choking. 'I don't want to be the old man in the corner.' And I briskly dismissed his fears with a swift don't-be-daft comment, rather than comfort him. It seemed that our conversations were entirely dominated by both his bad luck on the job market, and now his bad health as well.

Your dad finally solved his work dilemma by getting a job with an international human rights charity in London. He was very happy with this, and so was I. He'd been moaning about his work life for so long now that whenever he talked about it, I would mentally start making throat slashing gestures. At last he had found something that he liked. Working for the charity, he felt like he was amongst the right people, doing the right thing. He had friends there. He had become part of a group of people he respected, and being part of an organization like the charity gave him a sense of self. It turned out that it was his entire sense of self. I had no idea how much his job and his identity were entirely intertwined until it was too late.

Working for the charity also meant he had to commute, which he hated. To spare himself from commuter meltdown, he stayed with River in Hackney one night a week; it was during those nights when they ate dinner together at her place that she got to know him a bit better. Or as well as anyone could get to know your dad. River loved Leo. Everybody loved Leo.

Back in Brighton, I was left at home with a baby and a toddler. I was freaked out, on account of still not being a natural mummy. When Leo started his shiny new job, which involved his leaving at 6 a.m. and not getting back until seven or eight at night, I became slightly concerned that I might lose my mind in the company of two tiny children. While I adored you both and could sit staring at you, soaking in your absolute gorgeousness, for whole moments at a time, you weren't exactly stimulating company twelve hours a day. My oxytocin levels were clearly far lower than my boredom threshold.

No offence, but babies and toddlers, while gloriously funny for short to medium periods, are not such fun 24/7. Especially if, instead of the splinter of glass in the heart that Graham Greene says all writers must have, I seemed to have an entire heart of glass. This did not, however, mean that I was upstairs writing the next *Finnegans Wake*; no, I was upstairs hiding, wondering why I wasn't like the other mummies who spent all day cooing and gooing.

I remember being at someone's house on a playdate with you. It was the same as all those other playdates: wooden toys, wooden floors, wooden conversations; raisins and rice cakes. I wondered how long before I could leave, as the other mummies talked brightly and lightly about co-sleeping and active birth and breast-feeding, and soon I had to stop myself physically bolting, hurtling through the door to the street outside, gasping for air. As we left, all smiles and thank yous, one of the mummies followed me into the hall and asked me if I was all right. She had green eyes, direct and open. Later, I heard how the mummies were worried that I did not seem very bonded with you. They were right of course. I wasn't. All I ever wanted was for you two to be asleep or else-where, so that I could get on with what I loved doing best – writing in my little room, a lit Marlboro in the ashtray. My main focus was myself and my writing.

Something had to be done. So I found a nanny. When I say 'nanny', I don't mean Mary Poppins. She was an ageing rock chick who charged rock bottom prices, and I soon learned why – she wouldn't always show up, because she would have been out the night before; it was like employing an incarnation of myself, which meant I got a taste of the frustration that a string of former employers must have experienced when I used to phone in sick again, over and over. But when the rock-chick nanny did manage to turn up, you would laugh and smile as she walked through the door, and spit-spot, she would make you two magically disappear to the playground for hours on end. This meant I in turn could disappear upstairs to my little eyrie amongst the chimney pots and write my unfinished novels.

And then I opened a letter, at five in the afternoon, on a Friday, the day before Gay Pride. I'd just had a colposcopy as a result of a dodgy smear test (my first in years – I hated speculums, and had subsequently been avoiding a test for ages), and the hospital needed to speak to me to discuss their findings. Along the bottom it read 'Not Signed to Avoid Delay.' I froze, as the five words vibrated before my eyes. Jesus Christ. Not signed to avoid delay? I jumped in the car and drove to the doctor without even stopping to click on my seatbelt, but the surgery was closed. So I rang the emergency number, but they couldn't tell me anything. They said I just had to wait it out until Tuesday. They told me not to worry. Ha. *Not signed to avoid delay.* How could I not worry?

The next day at Pride I drank so much cava that two strapping homosexuals had to heave me, legless, into a taxi and take me home, because my legs had stopped working. One of you was with me. Luckily our friends were not so drunk, and made sure you didn't get lost in the early evening crowd of mashed up people who had been hard at it all day in the dance tent.

I suppose now is as good a time as any to mention that I had started drinking again. It just happened. Well, no, it didn't. But at the time it seemed like it just happened. There I was, sitting in a café in Brussels, about to have lunch with old friends. Someone asked if I wanted a beer, and I heard myself, after a year of saying no, suddenly saying yes. No reason. I just said yes. Yes, why not. Yes, a beer would be nice. Yes, I think I will. Yes, yes, yes. And so I had one beer. It was delicious, one of those gorgeous, blond Belgian beers that manage to taste of vanilla and coriander at the same time, and I drank it slowly with lunch, savouring it, and that was that. 'Look,' I said to Leo as we paid the bill after finishing coffee. 'One beer. See? I'm cured.'

And so I had begun a period of controlled drinking. I would have one drink. And then I would stop. It involved enormous amounts of self-control, but as I had been completely alcohol-free for what felt like five centuries, I thought that I could now drink like a normal person. You know, the people who put half full bottles of wine back in the fridge with the cork jammed in, or leave half their drink on the table unfinished when they're leaving the pub? I wanted to be able to drink like those people, despite secretly thinking they were total freaks for walking away from half full bottles or glasses; I imagined it was just a question of retraining myself after a period of abstinence. I was wrong, of course, but I didn't know that at the time. Or should I say, I didn't *want* to know. I wasn't ready to know, although deep, deep down, I did. Like Diane Arbus said, nothing is easier than self-deceit. And so I would drink a glass of wine, and then I would stop, the way a train jams on its emergency brakes, and screeches reluctantly to a halt. Or sometimes I would think, fuck it, and have two.

*

'So will I die?'

Bertha burst into tears. Automatically, I handed her a tissue from the box on the desk. We were in the office of a Mr Fish, who wore silver fish cufflinks and whose name was making me inwardly crack up with the giggles, because he was a gynaecologist. Mr Fish the gynaecologist. Like a character from *Viz*. He was in the middle of telling me that I had cancer, and in between trying not to laugh at his name – something of a hysterical reaction, perhaps, because it wasn't *that* funny – I was asking him if I was going to die or not. Actually, I was watching the entire proceedings from the ceiling, which is where I always go when things get hairy. I was watching Bertha quietly weeping into a tissue, watching the man with the fish cufflinks talking to me, and watching myself sitting there – how calm I looked – because actually I had flown right out of my body and was hovering somewhere high above it. I had zoomed out.

The gynaecologist looked alarmed. 'Oh goodness me no', he said. 'You won't die. But you must have a hysterectomy. Right away. This week'. This week? *This week?* I was aghast. That was impossible. This very weekend, Bertha was getting married in the beautiful communal garden where we lived. And two days after that, Leo and I were going to Paris because it was our fifth wedding anniversary.

'If I didn't have the hysterectomy until next week, rather than this week, would I still not die?' I asked Mr Fish. I was being perfectly serious, but I wonder if there wasn't just the tiniest hint of a smile around his lips as he reassured me that no, I still wouldn't die. But that it was still best to get on with it as soon as possible.

Today was Tuesday (you tend to remember the day of the week you find out you have cancer). So diaries were consulted, and I was booked in the Friday after next. Booked in – as though I were going for a bikini wax. Which I kind of was – a prolonged, ultra-violent bikini wax, that would hopefully remove the mutating threat of premature death. In the meantime, there was a wedding to attend, and Paris to visit. And to think I had been complaining that life was boring and samey, with too many nappies and nights in, and not enough excitement.

Bertha got married in the beautiful communal garden that led down to the sea, to the love of her life, whom she had met online. It was the only wedding I have ever cried at, including my own. Not because I had just been told I had cancer, and would have my reproductive organs hacked out within the week, but because it was moving to feel so much love in the air.

The ceremony was at the Unitarian Church, because as the vicar pointed out, 'This church recognizes love' (Bertha was marrying a woman, at long last). Afterwards we moved to the gardens at the square, where Bertha and her love had dotted little white gazebos around the lower part of the lawns, and filled paddling pools with cava on ice, and organized delicious homemade food under the shade of some trees. It was a perfect day, full of friends and love and joy. Sunshine and flowers, hugs and kisses. You two were there in your beautiful wedding outfits, one of you like a little fairy in a gauzy winged dress, the other one of you in a tiny blue cotton pirate shirt; you were both beautiful and joyous that day, my little honeys, one of you four, the other just weeks after your first birthday, both of you with your huge dark eyes and your beautiful smiles.

And throughout that beautiful love-filled day, there was a drum-beat inside my head, a looping rhythm that was going around and around and around, reminding me over and over: '*I have cancer... I have cancer... I have cancer.*'

After the wedding, I took my cancer to Paris, on a trip your dad had organized. It was five years since we had been married amid fairy wings and mariachi bands and drug meltdowns. Paris would be our last ever trip away together as a couple, and, as usual, not even being in the lovers' capital of the world could induce us to have sex. But even if Leo had somehow transformed overnight into Mr Lova Man – which was about as likely as his waking up white – I was way too tightly wound to even contemplate anything so intimate; all I wanted was to focus my mind away from what was going on in my mutating undercarriage. It wasn't even conscious. That's the great thing about denial – you can apply it to anything. So even though I couldn't deny that I had just visited a man called Mr Fish who told me that I had a life threatening illness for which there was no cure, just walking around the city sucking in the external meant I could temporarily deflect the knowledge. I could pretend I didn't know about it, for whole minutes at a time, so long as the external stimuli didn't let up, even for a second. Plus, I was in the middle of my last ever period, and bleeding like a halal goat. What a couple we made – me fat, cancerous and bloody, your dad neutered by medication.

That didn't stop Paris being fabulous. Unusually, it was your dad and not me who had done everything to make this trip happen: found the hotel, sorted the Eurostar tickets, arranged childcare for you two, the lot. I had never been to Paris properly before – years earlier, on the way back from a two day party at a big house in the countryside south of the Peripherique, I remember being lost and disorientated on the Metro on a massive pill comedown, after a night of non-stop ecstatic dancing, but I had never done the Paris tourist thing before now. Leo's invitation – written in his slanting all-capital handwriting – had come several weeks before the 'not signed to avoid delay' letter, yet the timing was so perfect it was almost psychic.

He'd found us a hotel near L'Opera, which had such a tiny room that I felt like I was nineteen and back in my first ever London bedsit, where you could stretch your arms out and touch the walls on either side, but it didn't matter. We were in Paris, it was a hot summer, and everywhere you looked there was something beautiful, like walking through a late period Woody Allen film, years before *Midnight in Paris*.

It was as if ugliness had been outlawed in Paris. We walked miles along the river, which was all decked out for Paris Plage, with sand and deckchairs and vaporisateurs that sprayed cool mist on you as you walked past, and temporary swimming pools packed with shrieking kids stuck in the hot August city, and very good food in cafes all along the winding route, at knockdown prices subsidized by the city council. We sat in cafes and sipped proper coffee and smoked – yes, I know how offensively stupid it is to smoke, especially when you have cancer, but I was still locked in instant gratification mode – and we drank very careful, moderate amounts of wine, and were completely entranced by our surroundings. We squeezed into the Louvre to see the *Mona Lisa* – don't bother, it's tiny and brown and dull – and marveled at the Polynesian tribal art in the cool, uncrowded basement. Or at least I did. Your dad said it was like something you could get at Camden Market, only bigger. Back at the cloistered café by the glass pyramid, we were condescended to by a waiter so snotty he was funny, who tried to make us buy the most expensive wine,

which made us laugh, and we went to the Pompidou, where I ha
multiple art orgasms as your dad sat it out. I lost myself for a
while, darting from wall to wall, from Picasso to Kandinsky, Warhol
to Matisse to Miró, like a pinball.

We did all the touristy things – took a boat along the Seine,
trekked to Pigalle and Montmarte and the Sacre Coeur, and
wandered for hours around the twisty hilly streets where that
Philippe Jeunet film, *Amelie*, had been shot. Your dad hated that
film. You only had to whisper the word 'Amelie' and he would
start snorting in disgust and making vomiting noises and sick
bag gestures. (It's not *that* bad, is it? Sometimes he had very strong
reactions to the most innocuous stuff. He hated walnuts too, and
football.) We even got as far as the Eiffel Tower, although we drew
a line at going up it.

The day we were getting the Eurostar back to London, we walked
through some gorgeous sculptures in a formal garden around
the Palais Royal. There was a café on a long, canopied, stone terrace.
We sat down for a sandwich and a coffee, but when we looked
around, we realized we were the only scruffy people there, and
the only foreigners. Everyone else was an elegantly dressed
Parisian, with expensive shoes and hair, having a three course
lunch. Then the waiter, with icy froideur, handed us the menu.
He waited pityingly for us to scan it, see it was not tourist fare –
or indeed snacky prices – and leg it to the nearest McDonalds.

We looked at the menu. 'Um,' said your dad. 'I don't think they
do cheese toasties here.' The waiter hovered, exuding just the
tiniest breath of impatience. The *prix fixe* for lunch was extor-
tionate, and the wine list was savage. And then I thought: I have
cancer. I might be dead this time next year. 'Fuck it,' I said to the
waiter. 'I'll have the *saumon fumee*. And the terrifyingly-priced

dad looked alarmed, until I told him to relax, that
He was quite afraid of my ability to spend first, and
, or worse, to expect him to cough up for half of my
ances. Don't worry, I reassured him. My Visa bill will deal
his – after all, it could technically outlive me. I was starting
to view cancer as quite liberating.

Everything was exquisite, and perfect, and delicious. The wine
was the best we had drunk in years. The salmon, the bread, the
salad – every morsel was melting heaven. And the very best of
all was when the dessert came. It was a rum baba, served by a
young black waiter of such godlike beauty that I almost collapsed
and died right there at his feet. Like a cheek-boned deity in a
white apron, he landed an old-fashioned corked glass jug filled
with clear liquid next to the angel-soft slice of cake. All it needed
was a label saying 'Drink Me'. He uncorked the jug, and gestured
to the liquid. 'You peurrr it,' he said in a black bass baritone. 'Peurr
it oveurr.' It was rum syrup, sweet and strongly alcoholic. Perhaps
I was already dead, and this was heaven. I kicked your dad under
the table, squirming with the sheer pleasure of it. It was the most
wonderful lunch. It was the lunch to end all lunches. And although
neither of us knew it, it was our last really special lunch together.

'Count backwards from ten,' the anaesthetist said, as I lay pierced
with plastic tubes on a gurney in a small, frightening room full
of silver gas canisters that felt like the control room of a subma-
rine. The stark, metal operating theatre was waiting to devour me
on the other side of the swing doors. I remember thinking how
surreal it was that they actually ask you to count backwards in
real life and not just in hospital soap operas, and wondering if I
should warn them that I had experienced strong dissociative drugs

before, just for fun, and might therefore be immune to theirs. 'Ten, nine, ei...' I needn't have worried. Utter blackness.

The operation took two and a half hours – the surgeon said he knew it was time to retreat when my liver began twitching back to life as the anaesthetic wore off. That poor liver. It is by far my most heroic organ. I feel I ought to write it a long letter of apology, and have it cast in bronze and placed upon a plinth in Trafalgar Square for its unwavering bravery in the face of relentless assault. Unlike my cervix, which fell at the first hurdle.

Your dad was great when I was sick. He took time off work and was entirely supportive. I'd had to go into the hospital the night before they did me, and he stayed with me for hours, as I stuffed Guatamalan worry people under my hospital pillow, and necked whole bottles of Bachs Flower Remedies with names like SOS and Letting Go, and made a little altar to Lakshmi, the goddess of good fortune, on the blood pressure monitor next to my bed. It was as close as I could get to praying; I was petrified. 'You won't die,' he said, when I asked him if he thought I would, as he prepared to leave the hospital the night before the op. I think he was trying to convince himself as much as me.

When I came around, too fucked even to raise my head, and in a foul mood from the anaesthetic, your dad was there to bear the brunt of that foulness. He and Bertha brought in delicious healthy food every day, so that the hospital dinners, unlike the cancer, wouldn't kill me. He helped me shuffle stiffly around the hospital corridors in tiny painful steps with frequent, exhausted stops where I would lean, ashen and nauseous, against shiny hospital walls, as I determined to make it from the bed to the magazine shop and back again with collapsing. (The nurses had tried to get me to use a bedpan, but the idea had so appalled me that I had more or less crawled to the ward bathroom on all fours, as they laughed at my uptightness. I didn't care. No matter how sick I was, I was not doing *that*.) And when, the day after I came home, I insisted on walking into town despite being under medical instruction to do absolutely nothing – I needed some more fairy dust from Neal's Yard and Infinity Foods, and was desperate for some kind of fresh air and normality – your dad got me into a taxi when I started to keel over in the tofu aisle. He was good, your dad. Good and kind. And I was headstrong and bad tempered. Although I do think that he was secretly terrified I would die, because if I did, he'd be left in the shit.

It took *ages* to recover from the cancer operation. It felt as if I had been run over by a steamroller. My only points of reference were your two caesareans; before that, I had never been in hospital since my own birth, back in the days of whalebone corsets and gas lamps. (Apart from that stint in a psychiatric hospital in Ireland, but that's another story.)

What I learned very quickly after a lifetime of perfect physical health is that firstly, a hysterectomy makes a caesarean seem like merely a flesh wound, and secondly, the female stomach never recovers from three lots of slasher surgery. (You are left with a floppy lip of flesh that hangs like a wobbly overbite beneath your belly button, above your bikini line. It's very far from beautiful.) But the rest of me did recover. Fully. I was aware that I might not have – lying in that hospital bed, I heard the woman on the other side of the thin NHS curtain being told that her cancer was unstoppable, and it was just a question of pain management until she croaked. She was being eaten alive by her self-generating Pacman, whereas mine had been sliced out in time, and popped neatly in the bin.

I had to wait ten days for the chopped-out bits to go to pathology in a plastic bucket and sit under a microscope to see if the cancer had gone long-haul, or stayed local. Those ten days went on forever. If it had spread, I would need to have chemo and radiotherapy on top of a huge operation that had already left me feeling half dead. It wasn't so much the idea of losing my hair as losing my mind that worried me, as I imagined the horrors of dealing with nausea and exhaustion on top of already feeling like death on toast, while balancing two small children on my head. Finally, I got the call. 'Have you got any champagne in the fridge?' the surgeon said. 'Because you can crack it open now.' That was the only time I cried. Ever since that moment with Mr Fish and his fish cufflinks, I had been holding my breath. I stood there, the phone hanging in my hand, hot fat tears burning my face.

I didn't have cancer. I didn't have a uterus or a cervix either, but I didn't care – the work of those specialist areas had already been done. You know how people have a magic number of children in their heads? Well, mine was two. That you were already both out of me, alive and kicking, by the time the cancer revealed itself, made me almost faint with relief; what if the second of you hadn't yet been born? I would have gone through life missing you, longing for you, never knowing you. And, more importantly, you wouldn't have had each other. You wouldn't have had a shared history; nobody would have known what it was like for you to be a child, without another child to share it. If you grow up unable to afford therapy, at least you can bitch about us to each other. By making two of you, I'm probably saving you a fortune in therapist bills.

Had that small lump of mutating cells not been removed, they would have devoured me from the inside out, so that I would not be here now, writing this for you, but would be buried some-where, or in an urn, or floating in the cosmos. But I'm not, I'm still here, alive, even though your dad isn't. Cancer is weird, the way it makes you turn on yourself, and devour yourself without any help from an external virus. Then again, with the disconnect between my head and my body, it probably wasn't that surprising that I got cancer; I had been turning on myself for years. It was only a matter of time before the disconnect became a medical formality.

In truth I was reasonably Hindu about death – in that I believed that when your number's up, it's up, and there's no point in prolonging things with machines. Far smoother to surrender to the great recycling process. Nor was I particularly afraid of dying, because I'm sure that when the moment comes, nature will take over, as it does with birth. This was not to be macho about death – I wanted to stay alive as long as possible, like everyone else (well, almost everyone else). But I was not in denial about its inevitability. And that it could happen sooner as well as later.

I believed this ever since a near-death experience I'd had in India, when I experienced such a huge level of disassociation that I felt like I had left my body and was moving towards death. It was the nearest I ever came to astral travel, quite extraordinary and unforgettable, and involved a single large dose of ketamine. There was a raggle taggle group of us around a fire on a remote moonlit beach – this was not the honeymoon trip with your dad and River, but the one before, where I had wandered around India on my own for five months, very far out of my comfort zone, and in exhilarating free fall. On that Karnatakan beach with a small group of hippies, the experienced ones who knew what they were doing measured out the correct dose of clear liquid ketamine into a syringe (all purchased perfectly legally from the village pharmacy a mile inland), and cooked the liquid on a metal spoon over the camp fire. Then they chopped the flakes of crystallized liquid into snortable powder. The more adventurous had injected the liquid ketamine into their thigh muscles, but I was too chicken for that – I just snorted mine. Not everyone did it that night – one or two stayed behind on earth to watch over us as we left our bodies.

It was a beautiful, powerful experience. I was flying through blackness, and there was light far away in the distance, and hurtling through the starlit space felt serene and magical and intense, and it left me feeling differently about death and dying. I was fully disassociated, fully out of body, in another dimension entirely for around twenty minutes. It was space travel, with zero gravity. I have no idea if this was just a bog standard K-hole experience, or if I was lucky enough to experience a genuine near death thing, but either way it didn't matter. It left me with a feeling of calmness and acceptance around death.

That, and seeing dead bodies all over the place in India, where you can see corpses lying unremoved on country roads after accidents involving motorbikes and bullock carts, or bodies burning on funeral pyres on the ghats along the Ganges in Varanasi, where the corpse ash floats up and catches in your hair and you end up inadvertantly inhaling bits of someone's dead relative, like Keith Richards once told a journalist he had done with his dad – albeit chopped out with a line of cocaine. (He hadn't really – it was just a wind-up. Great story though.)

But. But, but, but. Death was all very well if you didn't have two small children whose four small hands needed yours to hold, who needed bedtime stories read and socks found and hugs given.

There was no way I could possibly even contemplate dying when I had the two of you. No way at all. It was unthinkable. Preposterous. I might not have been much of a day-to-day mummy when it came to winding the bobbin up or watching the wheels on the bus going round and round, but my instinct to survive and protect were the same as any other female animal. Innate.

Afterwards, people kept asking me if I felt less like a woman, now that there was a yawning chasm where the baby-making equipment had formerly been stored. Was I mourning my loss of femaleness? Was I fuck. What a hysterectomy meant was (a) no more periods, which I had started when I was ten, and for which I had no fondness whatsoever and (b) no chance of accidentally getting knocked up aged forty-five, just as life was starting to get easy again, because you two had learned to tie your own shoelaces and had become a little more self-catering. So no, I did NOT mourn the loss of my uterus, any more than I would have mourned the loss of my appendix. Goodbye, bringer of monthly discomfort, your work here was done. And thanks for waiting until the kids had both been born. There was one thing I was worried about, though. You mightn't want to read the next bit because it's about my vagina, but now that you've had a warning, you can always skip to the second next paragraph. But it's part of the story. Sorry.

You see, I was terrified that I might be a eunuch after the operation. I knew that logistically – that is, geographically – this could not be the case, but there had been an awful lot of heavy industry going on in the region and I was petrified that there may have been permanent damage. I was beginning to wake up to the idea that sex might be something I would have to go through life without, and I didn't want this. I desperately didn't want this. And yet because of whom I had married, because of illness, because of what felt like a cosmic conspiracy to wall my sexual self in like some nun in a doorless turret – or was that the toxic ash of Catholicism still faintly staining my thinking? – a life without sex seemed to be rushing towards me. It was an unbearable thought.

Turns out I was fine. Six weeks after my op, I was fine. Good to go. All systems fully operational. Thumbs up. As it were. Yet the horrid irony was that while I made a full recovery, sexual and otherwise, your dad had been chemically castrated by all the medication he was taking. While boarding school had repressed him psychologically, his blood pressure pills had now finished him off physiologically. Sexually, he was a dead duck. And somehow, that seemed really final. All along, we had not been having sex because he had not been interested, but now he actually couldn't, even if he'd had a sudden change of heart, even if I became attractive to him again. Or attractive to myself again. But by now our sexual connection, always gossamer fragile, was irreversibly broken. The truth was that even if he had suddenly accessed a font of explosive passion for me – and a wheelbarrow of Viagra to make it happen – I was not interested in him anymore. I was now in an officially sexless marriage. Until death did us part.

Oh dear.

8   CHRISTMAS

Getting cancer though, when you've just turned thirty-seven, well, you'd think that it would be a bit of a shove towards taking better care of yourself, wouldn't you? A giant sign with blindingly flashing lights: get yourself healthier. Change your lifestyle, look after yourself better, revise how you treat yourself, how you regard your body. No more lame-ass jokes about your other body being a temple, or about your current body being an amusement park.

The odd thing is, I actually longed to be someone else. Well, not some*one* else, but some*thing* else. I would see the other mummies at your kindergarten, and they were all fresh and healthy and light, and beside them I felt so toxic and lumbering. They all drank camomile tea and did yoga and used flower remedies, and made homemade bread from spelt and avoided dairy and sugar, and I smoked Marlboro Lights (which I considered the healthier option) and ate plenty of cake, and once again couldn't imagine life without booze. So long as I maintained the whole controlled drinking thing. Which I was. Kind of. Mostly. Sort of.

Sometimes though, I would go for a proper night out, rather than just a polite supper somewhere restrained, and conscious of being on a rare night off from mummyhood, I'd go nuts. As if I had to cram fifty nights out into one. Once, at a techno bash at the Scala in Kings Cross, having not been out for ages, or touched drugs for even longer, I necked a pill, got off my head, smoked a huge spliff as though it were a cigarette, then unceremoniously threw up without even making it to the loo; I just did it fairly discreetly in a corner. It was like puking on opium – I was in such a heavenly state from the E and the weed that it was a mere moment's unpleasantness – but still. I don't think my friends were greatly impressed. You'd think I would have been old enough to know better. I *was* old enough to know better. It was a bit unseemly.

There was a shift in me after that. It didn't manifest itself externally, or consciously – I still smoked roll-ups, though not very many, and people would say things like, 'How can you *smoke* after just having *cancer*?' And I would shrug, and not be quite sure myself. I just couldn't quite seem to stop. Or if I did stop, then I would start again the minute I had one of my controlled drinks. Nor was my drinking quite as controlled as it was supposed to be. But since I'd started again, I had new rules for myself – no more weekday boozing. I didn't automatically uncork a bottle at 6 p.m. every evening, like I used to. I would wait, and only drink at weekends. When your dad was around to look after you both. Sometimes weekends started a day early. But there was a subtle internal change. I honestly didn't even notice it, but it was there all the same. It was a feeling, faint but alive, like the first time you feel a baby moving inside you, a distant tickle that you know won't go away, that will only grow and grow. And the feeling was this: *Life is short. Don't waste it.* Hardly a profound revelation – most people are born with this kind of basic emotional intelligence – but not me. My emotional intelligence came slowly, in dribs and drabs, generally via personal disasters. I didn't realize this feeling consciously, but it was down there in the depths, fully formed, this first sense of mortality, this tiny awareness that I would not live forever, that I was not invincible. That nothing lasts forever. That sometimes you have to act, rather than just react. That if you're not careful, you could wake up one day, middle aged, your face criss-crossed with disappointment and resentment.

'You *bastard*!' he shouted at me, as I pushed him out of the way.

What a strange inverted insult, I thought, even as we yelled at each other. It was as though he were reliving some school bullying incident – which he mostly likely was. And I *was* the perfect bully – domineering, manipulative, like a bulldozer flattening anything foolish enough to remain in my path. My resentment at him was beginning to peak. All I could see were the things he couldn't do – even the petty things, like playing scrabble (he was too dyslexic), or riding a bicycle (he was too scared), or having the guts to stand up to me, rather than present that weary 'yes dear' exterior that hid Christ knows how much resentment. It seemed obvious to me that the only thing we had in common was you – and you were just babies. This wasn't meant to be happening.

'I feel scared when you fight,' you said in your smallest voice, as Leo and I shouted at each other in our loudest. We rarely argued, so when we did, it must have been deeply disconcerting. Especially today, when we were screaming at each other, really roaring and screaming. There was even a bit of pushing and shoving going on, as our mutual frustration exploded. You'd hidden in the bathroom of our lovely flat, watching wide-eyed around the door as we fought in the bedroom. You still talk about it.

Things were falling apart. Take away the crises – the forced house moving, the cancer – and there was nothing left to distract from the reality of collapse. Like a souffle in a gale, our marriage was caving in on itself. All we were left with was your dad complaining about his deteriorating health – moaning about being tired, moaning about needing another blood test, moaning about the consultants. And I shut myself off from it because it wasn't dramatic, because it wasn't cancer or a heart attack or necrotizing fasciitis. And because I was struggling with my own incessant heartbeat of *'Is this it, is this it, is this it?'*

I remembered the words of an old boyfriend who had said, 'Well, you *did* want to get out of London and breed...,' and it was true, that's exactly what I had wanted to do, even though I had spent years denying it, mostly to myself, and here I was, doing it. I had escaped dreary, toxic, old London and was living in a place more beautiful than I could have ever imagined back when I was still being poisoned by all those E numbers – E7, E6, E12, E15. Here I was, here we were, with our little family, living in a beautiful place, except that your dad, my husband, felt like nothing more than a flatmate, someone I had once been close to, but who was now getting on my nerves. Why? For not putting the cap back on the toothpaste? Always being tired? Never being quick enough? Having a persistently can't-do attitude? No. It was more than all of those put together. It was for not being man enough. Actually no, it was for being the wrong man. I was angry with myself for mistaking him for the man I really wanted. I'm sure he wasn't too overjoyed about the mix-up either.

If only he had stood up to me. If only he hadn't turned out to be so weak, so easily bullied. I needed someone stronger than me to keep us on the rails, to make me feel more secure – and your dad was not stronger than me. Nobody was as strong willed and wrong-headed as me, but I didn't know that at the time – I was too busy being right, and being up against the world, charging into things head first, flattening things like a snow plough. I didn't know it at the time, but my thinking was fucked. And underneath the fucked up thinking and the fucked up drinking, there was this little voice, this plaintive but insistent little voice – my submerged intelligence, my true self – calling up faintly from the core of me, from the bottom of the well, even as I tried to drown it out with wine. The voice was telling me that this wasn't working, that I no longer loved him, that perhaps I had never been in love with him, that it was wrong to stay together, that it was okay to not want a life of no sex, that it was okay to want to be crazy in love, to feel passion and connection and for your whole being to light up in the presence of the person with whom you share your life. That *life was short, and you shouldn't waste it.* But instead of listening to that little voice, which was weak and muffled and buried, yet would not go away, I ignored it, and poured wine onto it to make it shut up, and poured my resentments onto your dad.

You remember those fights, and talk about them as though you had witnessed actual domestic violence, even though it wasn't physical at all, it was just raised voices a handful of times – but they were some of the few times when your dad's suppressed anger made its way to the surface, when he lost his usual politeness. Of course, we reassured you that it was okay, that sometimes grown ups fight like kids, but you didn't look convinced.

...I don't know who you are. Who are you? Do I know you? And the husband would be vaguer and vaguer in her mind's eye, a one dimensional character who looked familiar, whose voice she knew, but behind the voice and the face there was a

great blankness, like those movie sets that look real from the
front, but when you look behind them, they are completely
flat and held up by supports...

All the time I was writing like a woman possessed, writing to
escape, writing a story about a fat woman who lived in a flat at
the top of a tall, tall building, who was married to someone she
was realizing day by day, hour by hour, she hardly knew: the more
time she spent with this man, the more of a stranger he was. She
realized that time was running out. She was plotting her escape.
I gave this made-up woman the opportunity to have lots of adventures – she was a total fuck up, but at least she had adventures.
I was writing myself in the third person with a different name
and different details, though you could hardly call it fiction. Yet
I was not conscious of that. As far as I was concerned, I was making
it up as I went along.

I knew almost nothing about Leo, where he came from, where
he was coming from. Nothing. All I knew was that he was kind
and sweet, but by now that was no longer enough. I had been so
self-absorbed for so long that I hadn't even realized that I didn't
know him. We just hurtled along, then plodded, then began
grinding to a halt. There was nobody I could speak to about him
who had known him before I did– his connections had seemed
fleeting, or superficial, or both. He was still in touch with one or
two old friends from his party days, but there no trace of anything
before his time in Little Venice; there had once been a girlfriend
somewhere, whom he said grew frustrated with him. There were
no university friends, no school friends. No siblings, no cousins.
Just him, and the void inside him that I couldn't begin to understand.

Not that he ever talked about how he felt. He didn't talk about anything, other than the surface things, the here and now things like work or domestics; we were as emotionally crippled as each other. My emotional inarticulacy manifested as anger; his as politeness. His politeness made me want to murder him. That time he grabbed me and called me a bastard, I had almost wanted to cheer – look, he's showing some feelings! – except I was so pissed off with him that instead of cheering, I think I shoved him against the nearest wall then stalked off in a rage. But that was a one-off, as extreme as it ever got. The toxicity between us was largely unspoken, and manifested itself in my sniping, and his sighing.

'You're such a lovely family,' people would say, and we would smile, and hug each other, and you two – you were so adorable, so sweetly appealing – and on the inside I wished that your dad and I could just be friends, that we could stop carrying on with what felt to me like the biggest lie of my life.

Christmas that year was very low key.

You were four and you were one-and-a-half, and because you were in this magical age of make-believe, I was getting over the fact that I had never liked Christmas. I still can't bear the endless build-up, the obligatory bonhomie, the horrid overheated shops with their blaring Christmas music and demands to spend; I hate it that everywhere you turn, there are tinsel and mince pies and plastic reindeers and Jona fucking Lewie. All that buying and running around, just so that you can spend a single day stuck in doors overeating food you wouldn't normally consume unless there had been some kind of global apocalypse and it was either plum pudding and sprouts or a radioactive dog carcass. Before you existed, I had always made sure I was very far away at Christmas, in countries that didn't bother with it.

But then Santa Claus began visiting, which made the whole thing come alive – you two meant that we could connect to the magic heart of Christmas. Preparing for Santa Claus with you two was joyous. We would leave out mince pies and cognac (this was before we realized that encouraging Santa to drink-drive was unethical – because he always drained that big fat brandy glass), and in the morning there would be mysterious trails of glitter and sparkles coming from the fireplace, and sooty bootprints, and piles of giftwrapped boxes for you full of goodies, in two separate piles wrapped in different paper. It was also the only day of the year when I would legitimately start drinking at 10 a.m., making the first batch of festive cranberry cocktails straight after breakfast (cava with cranberry juice and a drop of cinnamon cordial – a made-up recipe that was just an excuse to pop a cork long before noon), and the day you were allowed to eat chocolate for breakfast. Such decadence. Chocolate for breakfast on Christmas morning. You still do it, even now.

River would come down, and we would all get up when it was still dark and begin the endless present-opening ritual. Instead of tearing into the pile of interestingly-shaped objects in their shiny wrapping, we always made a great show of handing things out one by one. 'This one's to you from River,' and 'That one's from you to Dad' and so on, until every last present was unwrapped, cooed over, held up, examined, admired and hugs exchanged. It could take hours. It was your favourite part of Christmas. And mine too – I got a huge kick out of watching your faces. It was such a ceremony.

Anyway, that year, despite being gladder than usual to be alive just months after the cancer thing, and glad to be spending our first Christmas in that big open plan flat with the football pitch bedrooms and the writing eyrie upstairs, our present opening ritual did not quite go as well as usual. Not your pressies – they were many and wondrous, as always – but when it came to the adults, there was something wrong. Specifically, when your dad gave me my present, after I had showered him with his. I took the small slim rectangular package, did all the ritual shaking, feeling, sniffing, and privately wondered what delight was on the other side of the shiny wrapping paper. A bracelet? A pen? A necklace?

It was an electric toothbrush.

Somehow, I managed to restrain myself from walking to the window and hurling it out so that it would splinter into a thousand tiny plastic pieces on the pavement six flights down. I can't remember what I had given your dad, but I do know that he had wanted it and was pleased with it – books or films or something. I was aghast. He might as well have given me a pair of Marigolds, or a set of spoons. What was going on? Had he lost his mind? But you were there, and River was there, and it would have been bad form to make my displeasure too obvious – it was, after all, Christmas. Instead, I made a toothy joke through gritted teeth. Ha ha, I said to him. An electric toothbrush. Just what I always wanted. (Now, rereading this, I suddenly remember the joy I'd felt when he had presented me with a tiny tube of Vo5 hot oil for my hair, soon after we first met – how caring it had seemed, how progressive and tuned in; six years later, an electric toothbrush felt like a veiled insult.)

It got worse. You know the way our Christmas stockings are always filled with fun things like posh chocolates and DVDs and little toys and bits and bobs? That year, I had filled your dad's stocking with the usual stuff – chocolate hearts, fancy soap, manly cosmetics, jokey things, useful things, useless things, a stocking full of stuff that I had picked out for him over the past few weeks, squirrelling it away in anticipation of the little present opening ceremony we enjoy once a year.

My stocking from him was full of *blank floppy discs*.

The thing was, your dad was usually a wonderful present buyer. As a long-term metrosexual, he knew his way around the shops. He had a Good Eye. Bertha used to say that he was her favourite man in the world to go shopping with, because he was as at home in the make-up and lingerie department as he was in menswear. His presents were always thoughtful and generous and just right.

Blank floppy discs? *What the fuck?*

'I thought you might need them to back up your writing,' he said lamely, as I stared into my stocking, my jaw dangling a bit. River was starting to look uneasy. You two just stared – even in your extreme youth, you could probably tell that blank floppy discs were not what you gave a mummy in her Christmas stocking. To me, floppy discs on top of a toothbrush just felt insulting – I was his fucking *wife*, not Brian from IT. It was as if he had forgotten me, in between getting gifts for River and you two. Later, Leo told me that he had left my bag of stocking-fillers on the train. Yet rather than just yank me to one side and explain that he had lost them, he pretended that actually floppy discs were his present of choice for me; that this was his decision, that this was what he thought I needed.

Looking back, I remember a hideous moment in Barcelona years earlier, very soon after I had just met him and I was at the height of my paranoia, my serotonergic nerve terminals at their most fucked. We returned to the place where we were staying earlier than planned, and our hosts had taken some of your dad's silver platform trainers out of his open bag and were mincing around the flat in them, in a sneering, mocking kind of way. I froze, mortified. My new boyfriend, being mocked by a bunch of bitchy queens, one of whom was an old friend whom I trusted. And yet I was so desperate for people to like me, and so insanely paranoid, that I just stood there, frozen. So did your dad. Then he acted as though nothing had happened. It was excruciating. I still cringe, still bloom in hot sweat, when I think about it. I wanted to kill those queens for their meanness, just as much as I craved their approval. Neither Leo nor I could protect either ourselves or each other from anyone else. His policy was stiff upper lip to the death. What was most bizarre was that afterwards, having been openly ridiculed by people he had just met, supposed friends of his new girlfriend, neither of us ever mentioned it again. To anyone. *Not even to each other.*

Yet as far as I know, Leo never suffered from the drug-induced paranoia which had taken me over, and which took three solid years to recover from. I know when I was in the thick of it, imagining that the walls were whispering about me, that he did not share the same headspace. In other words, his worldview, his actions and reactions, were not as a result of chemical over-indulgence. It was, I think, something far more deep-seated – perhaps the result of being a small black boy dropped from a great height into the British boarding school system and trying not to sink. But his self-taught swimming was fundamentally defective. He seemed to have built up a defence system that was a faulty version of the never complain/never explain model; along the way, he seemed to have become convinced that pretending something wasn't happening (even when it clearly was, right there in front of his face) was the best way forward from a sticky moment. Either way, he certainly lacked the confidence or the presence to calmly own a situation. And anyway, he was afraid of me. He was afraid of my rages, afraid of my contempt. Afraid of my merciless 'humour'.

After the toothbrush and the floppy discs, we moved on swiftly to Christmas lunch, and to the usual festive mooching after a brisk walk on the beach. Then something even weirder happened. Around five o'clock, your dad reached up into the Christmas tree, which was enormous and groaning and covered in millions of sparkling things, and pulled an envelope from high up in its dense branches. 'This is your real Christmas present,' he said, handing the envelope to me. Why had he waited until now? We'd all finished with the present opening hours before, and I had just about got over my feelings of confused disappointment. Your poor dad. No matter what was inside this envelope, short of a cheque for a million quid or a round-the-world ticket, it would have been the wrong thing. Inside was a voucher for a women-only erotic boutique in North Laine that sold an eye watering variety of sex toys. Given that we no longer had sex, this present was telling me, quite literally, to go fuck myself.

I ended it just after New Year.

It happened much sooner than I could have ever imagined. In fact I had never imagined it, because – and here's the selfish bit – I didn't want to be a single parent. Had it just been Leo and I, we would have probably called it a day long before. And it wasn't just about us – I didn't want you to be all fucked up and traumatized by split-up parents, although you would probably be even more fucked up and traumatized if we didn't split up. But I'd reached tipping point, without even realizing it.

I visited friends in Barcelona for a week after Christmas – the first trip away on my own since before either of you had been born. The night I returned, slipping my key in the lock on our landing, I felt as if I were entering a morgue. I walked into the beige lifeless hush of our flat, where your dad and you two were waiting for me, and the silence – the deathly silence of our married life – wrapped its stranglehold around me, just as the colour and clamour of Spain had hit me in the face like a joyous splash of rosado a week earlier. I was walking into a forever-after that I didn't want.

I couldn't do this anymore. I wasn't ready for a life of quiet desperation.

The decision hadn't been conscious. I had not gone away to think things over. Quite the opposite – I had gone to Barcelona to stop thinking about anything at all except having a laugh and enjoying myself with old friends, none of whom had kids, none of whom spent their days in the playground or the toddler group or the park, none of whom were trapped in a marriage of politeness. And I did enjoy myself. Hugely. I thought about nothing whatsoever except the moment I was in.

Although I had lived in Barcelona in the early nineties, I hadn't been back since before either of you were born. It had been five years since I'd walked under the yellow Llegadas sign in the airport, and whizzed along the dry highway in a black and yellow taxi, past Placa Espanya and the university and Placa Catalunya onto the Rambla. The city came rushing back at me, as if I had never left.

I plugged straight in – the bars and cafes, the endless lunches, the midnight dinners, the sunshine, the art shows, the pockets of culture embedded everywhere in the life there. I visited the two big new galleries had opened since the last time I'd been; and, out of habit, I trekked up to Montjuic to the Foundacio Miro, and to Parc Guell just for the sheer joy of being amongst the Gaudi curves and lizards and seeing the city spread out below – the perfect square blocks of Eixample with the Sagrada Familia sticking out of the symmetry, the beautiful houses on Passeig de Gracia, and the sea glittering at the bottom of the Rambla. I love that city, it's my favourite in the world, the only city where you can live without your soul dying. It's not a giant city like London, whose overwhelming citiness would kill you if you stayed too long; Barcelona is a big fabulous village in between the mountains and the sea.

I walked around, like a dog sniffing out all its old favourite places, the Gothic laneways, the gargoyles, the old men in the bars, the café in Placa del Pi, the ladies in frilly aprons in La Boqueria who sold avocados by the kilo that melted like butter on your tongue. My old neighbourhood, the stinking Barrio Chino, had changed. It had had a facelift, entire blocks flattened, filthy old narrow streets opened up to the wide shiny new Rambla del Raval. I stood outside my old flat, on the corner of Sant Pau and Junta de Comerc, two minutes and a million light years from the sunny touristy Rambla, where the old whores and the drunks used to converge outside my window, screaming and roaring and keeping me awake all night, and the occasional stray tourist who would fall out of

Bar Marsella further down the curving grime of the street, puking bright green absinthe into the gutter as the ropey old drag queen inside mimed to Edith Piaf and seventies' disco. Outside the Marsella, a youngish man with withered legs would roll his wheel-chair into the middle of the narrow street, blocking any vehicle that drove down that way. He would not move until the drivers got out of their cars and gave him a coin; he was fearless, not moving even for taxi drivers. At night you would see him rolled up in some old bit of rug in one of the doorways, his wheelchair folded next to him, with his ghetto blaster padlocked to it, empty bottles all around him. There would be piss running down from his jeans to the gutter. He's probably dead now.

I breathed in the smell of chicken grease from the Pollo Rico, the spit-and-sawdust chicken rotisserie opposite my old front door, where you could get half a roast chicken, a chunk of bread and a glass of cava for 500 pesetas – about two quid. I would buy the chicken and feed it to the mangy ferocious street cats that skulked under the giant stinky bins beneath my balcony, and drink the cava myself, and the men behind the counter, sweating pure chicken grease themselves, would scoff at my foreign madness. Those cats were in an awful state. So were the junkies who shot up in my hallway. I used to step over them; sometimes my plat-forms crunched on their needles. The smell of chicken grease hung in the air and mixed with the stink of rubbish and drains in the heat.

It was a long, long way from where I was now, in polite English mummyland with my polite English husband and my polite English neighbour who didn't like buggies in the hall. I wondered if he'd have liked junkies in the hall.

*

The night I came home, after just a week away in another life, everything crystallized. My heart lifted when I saw the two of you, your upturned faces, your huge eyes. And my heart sank when I saw your dad. I didn't want to hurt him, but I knew I couldn't ignore it any more. This time I not only had to think the unthinkable, but I had to say the unsayable. It was time. Had I not been honest then, our relationship would have degenerated into contempt and resentment; I could not let that happen. I didn't want to do that to me, to you, or to him. The reality was that it was already happening. Bertha would say things to him, like 'How can you let her speak to you like that?' Any longer and it would have curdled, soured into something horrid, into something the opposite of love and affection. Into hate, maybe.

'I need to talk to you,' I said. My voice sounded so deadly serious, he looked uneasy. As if he already knew. We sat down opposite each other at the table after you two were in bed, and I said it all out loud. Quietly, and as kindly as I could manage. That it wasn't working anymore. That we had tried our best. We had done Relate – twice – spending long hours in cramped rooms with earnest therapists, who did their best despite not possessing magic love potions, and whose faces remained neutral as I ranted and raved, and you dad sat, bewildered by it all. We had made babies – twice – but even you two could not save us from our mistake, the big one where we had mistaken each other for the other's ideal life partner. That we loved each other, genuinely loved each other, but not in the way that a husband and wife need to love each other. That the most important thing was to protect you two, to pull together with a common purpose – that is, not to fuck you up – while accepting that as a couple, he and I no longer worked. I had begun to wonder privately if we had ever worked, but that was hardly the point at this stage, so I kept that thought to myself. What I didn't say was that I had started to resent him, that I could no longer pretend that I even much liked his company, that I was beginning to despise him, that I was sick to fucking death of his endless problems, that I was sick of being in charge, of dealing with everything. That I was not his fucking life coach. That even *I* knew that nobody should leave me in charge. But I didn't say any of that. I felt no animosity, just exasperation, resignation, and a strong feeling of enough being enough. I was done.

The conversation was unnervingly calm. There was no anger, no how-dare-yous. He was very quiet. The only thing your dad said which stuck in my mind and bothered me quite a bit was that he would rather stay in a bad relationship than be in no relationship. That was like shining a torch on the unacknowledged chasm between us. I would rather have chewed off my own leg than stay in something that could only degenerate. The model of sticking it out and hating it was the worst option of all.

'You'll have to move out,' I said, because this was probably the next thing you say when you are ending your marriage. He looked up, panicked. I think he thought that we would just stop being a couple, but continue living together. When I pointed out that we had already been doing this for years, he couldn't really disagree. And then, because he looked so stricken, I went into mummy mode, and promised him that everything would be all right, and I'd help him to find somewhere to live in London, that we would work together to make the transition happen gently and smoothly so that there would be minimal fall out for either him or you two.

Which is exactly what happened, externally at least. He got a room in a lovely old house in Islington with a big back garden; it was owned by somebody's dad from your class at school, who had split up from the mum, so it couldn't have been a better household to live in. It was twenty minutes from his work, instead of two hours on a commuter train, and the house was geared up for kids. Given the circumstances, it was pretty damn good. It could have been a bedsit in Tottenham, if it hadn't been for the mummy network.

If that all sounds too neat, too tidy, well, I can only tell you the facts from the outside. How your dad felt inside his head I have no idea. All I know is that he didn't tell anyone we had split up. He still referred to me as his wife. And most importantly for you two, who were now aged one and four, he came down every single weekend. He never disappeared from your lives, not for a moment. Nothing changed. He was in London during the week, and in Brighton at weekends.

Very soon after this, our rented flat was to be sold, and once again we had to move. The punctuation of this move was almost sublime; it was an ironic full stop before the start of the next installment. For once I didn't mind moving, because it was more than a house move – it was a restructuring. A fresh start in a new place. And it was only a few doors away. I'd found a flat through word of mouth in the square, an extraordinary place with a giant, ballroom sized sitting room with twenty-foot high ceilings, and some higgledy-piggledy bedrooms up the steep wooden steps of a mezzanine. We overlooked the square and the garden, through giant floor to ceiling windows, but again because the place was so utterly wonky and Bob the Builderish, the rent was relatively low despite its scope and grandeur. I didn't bother taking the giant wide bed that had been your dad's and mine. That had been the bed of doom, the bed of no-sex, the bed of broken dreams. I dismantled it and left it behind, and went back to sleeping on a mattress on the floor, which is what I have always preferred. I hate beds, and I especially hated that one.

Neither of you questioned why your dad disappeared every Sunday evening. Initially we explained that Dad had to live in London during the week because he was spending too much time on the train and it was giving him a headache; I remember one of you asking tearfully why there couldn't be beds on the train, and that made my heart ache for you. You missed him tucking you in at night, reading you stories. You missed his cuddles. But he always came on Fridays, without fail, and you got used to it, to his not being around the other nights. Looking back on it, your getting used to him not being around five days out of seven was something of a gift, because it made things – I was going to say 'easier', but that's not the right word. Not easier, but when he did vanish for good, at least you had been weaned off him a bit, eased away from his full-time presence to part time, a year and a half before he went for good. It was part of a letting go in stages, except of course nobody knew that at the time.

After a few months of our pretending everything was normal – Leo came down on Fridays, we ate together, we had family outings together, we socialized together with other families in the shared garden – we thought it might be time to explain what was really going on. Eventually, one night as we were cosying you both up in bed, your dad and I told you.

'We are not a couple anymore, but we are still a family, and we will always be a family,' we said, carefully, terrified of your eyes welling up or your face sinking heart-broken under the duvet. But the show of unity between your dad and me was strong; I think we would both rather have stuck pins in our eyes than presented anything but a calm, united front. So we explained that we loved you completely, that we were always your mum and dad, and that your dad and I were still *best friends*. 'Best friends,' you echoed, trustingly.

So careful were we of your feelings that really, other than his not arriving back from London minutes before your bedtime during the week, there was hardly any change between life before and after our separation. The only discernible difference, which you preferred, was that Leo slept in your bedroom when he came down every weekend, and I slept alone in mine. That was it. That was the extent of our break-up. I had lots more childcare and domestic responsibilities, and less time to focus on writing, but Leo's job had always taken precedence over everything anyway.

Because things weren't already overloaded enough, I decided to apply for a master's degree in creative writing. I was terrified of my brain atrophying, or of being mistaken for one of those smug, complacent women I would meet all the time around our smug complacent neighbourhood, whose total immersion in parenting as a semi-competitive sport left me feeling more isolated than ever. Had you been born in East London amongst the kebab shops and the flyovers, it would have been a different kind of disconnect; I was beginning to wonder whether I would ever truly be able to connect with anything, wherever I was, other than a good book. Meanwhile, being a full-time parent meant that my brain cells, already compromised by three-for-a-tenner offers down the offie, were being horribly underused – all they ever had to do was remember where your other sock was, or which friend was coming to tea on Tuesday, and whether they were lactose intolerant or not.

I was desperate for brain food. I didn't want to do a jewellery making course or learn baby massage or study aromatherapy –

I wanted to read books that I couldn't understand, that would make my brain ache in a different way from hangovers. What I would do with this degree I had no idea. It's not as if I thought any of it through. I wrote an essay and got on the course, even though I don't have a degree (years earlier, I had run away to Spain with a man who broke my heart, halfway through a literature degree, but that's another story). God, it was bliss, using my head again. For one whole day a week, I would sit in a prefabricated room on campus and listen to people talking about thinking and ideas and how ideas and thinking work, and nobody talked about playgroups or playgrounds or playdough, and nobody needed anything from me except what I thought about things that were abstract and conceptual and cerebral. It lit me up.

I hardly noticed Leo, even when he was right in front of me.

Maybe I should have noticed. Maybe I should have paid more attention. But we were a couple whose marriage had just ended after several years of limping along. As far as I was concerned, we were doing all right – there were no lawyers involved, no court orders, no fights over custody. There was no home to divide and sell, no new partner causing chaos in the heads or hearts of either of us. We were on speaking terms. We hung out together with you two, doing family things, the way we had always done. He was there every weekend, as he had always been. He still paid half the rent. Any anger or resentment was suppressed, suppressed, suppressed.

Did I notice him changing? Not really. Was I tuned into him? Not much. Did I care any more? Not a lot. All I wanted was for him to arrive on Fridays at 6 p.m., so that I could clock off until Sunday night. By clock off I mean drink, unhindered, without needing to get up for anyone or anything in the morning. It didn't really involve other people. I used to whine a bit that I had been in Brighton for five or six years and hardly knew anyone, but I knew the offies very well, the wine racks and the chiller cabinets and the supermarket aisles floor to ceiling with bottles and bottles of everything I wanted. I would finish my day at university – eight hours of brain bending, after a week of childcare and writing – and I would get quietly, profoundly drunk, because the controlled drinking was becoming less and less so. Goddammit, if I didn't deserve a little drinky by 6 p.m. on a Friday evening, then I never would. Wine makes Mummy happy. Mummy deserves a reward for all the nappy changing, spoon-feeding, playdoughing, cake baking, song singing, buggy pushing, handholding, needs-meeting. Mummy needs a drink.

Leo could barely drink any more. He looked different – duller, less shiny. He never listened to music any more, ever. Just Radio 4. Before we'd met, he had been into psychobilly, and had a large blue quiff – it looked fantastic against the black of his skin (he'd shown me photos). His favourite album was The Cramps *Stay Sick*; his CD collection was tiny, and all over the place, from the Temptations to the Buzzcocks, with loads of awful cheesy house, even though his preferred dance music was at the dentist drill end of things. It was as if he didn't really quite know what he liked.

The first summer we moved down to Brighton, there had been an illicit party on the beach at Ovingdean – you know, where the café is. Back then the café had a flat roof. There is a picture of your dad dancing on it at sunrise, wearing someone's pink glittery top and a pair of platform trainers; that was the Leo I had originally met. By the time we had been married, had both of you, and broken up, he was wearing dark grey anoraks and t-shirts from Primark. He was no longer Mr Man About Town. He had gained weight, even though he didn't eat much; everything was forbidden as the threat of type 2 diabetes loomed ever closer. His doctors told him he had the liver of an alcoholic, which seemed dreadfully unfair, especially as he had paired up with someone with a liver that appeared capable of processing nuclear waste. Maybe our livers had been swapped at birth – how else could I drink myself under the table so regularly without developing cirrhosis, while he only had to glance at a wine glass for his liver to bulge. He had those dark shadows under his eyes that I had thought were connected with parenthood, but were really a sign of malfunctioning internal organs. He would have to fast for twelve hour stints, then go to the hospital and get his blood tested for all the things that were increasingly going wrong with him. And in his last year or so, he began getting worse and worse blood pressure headaches.

Did I hear any of this? No. All I heard was 'Blah blah blah.' After six years of listening to him complaining about his health, his work and his finances, I had gone deaf. All I would do was to suggest things that might help him, over and over. Therapy. Counselling. Acupuncture. Yoga. Tai chi. Someone's Tibetan doctor, who was apparently magic, and worked in conjunction with Western medicine, of which he was on shedloads by now. Sport, swimming, walking, cycling. No, no, no, no. A bicycle would have eased things, made him less reliant on buses, but cycling was for him like driving – out of the question. I don't know why, but I never queried it. I do now, though – why was a man in his early forties scared of cycling and driving? Why was he so helpless, so fearful? What was that about?

'Where are you?' I would demand, at one minute to six on a Friday evening. He'd always be stuck at Haywards Heath, or London Bridge, or somewhere really stupid like Wivelsfield, and I would be in a rage, because I had been mummy for five days straight and would be desperate – *desperate* – to clock off. He'd look exhausted when he came into the new flat, but then he would light up when he saw you two and I would light up when I saw him because it meant it was finally wine o'clock.

Those Friday evenings were actually quite amicable. I would pour him a glass out of politeness, secure in the knowledge that he wouldn't want any more, and then sit down in the wide expanse of crumbling grandeur that I had filled with hippie tat from my travels. The neighbours all had fancy furniture and fabulous art on the walls, and million dollar surgical kitchens, while I had an Ikea sofa from which I would get good and drunk. In a way, I think Leo was quite secure with that. I was there, on the knackered sofa with its sequined Ganesh blanket covering, pouring myself endless glasses of three-for-a-tenner, reading until my eyes blurred, then toddling off to bed in the next room. He knew exactly where I was, and what I was up to. It wasn't as if I was out there on the pull.

And so it went on. For a whole year, this is what it was like.

Once he had had settled into his new Monday to Friday life in Islington, Leo invited me to come for dinner there one Friday evening. Everyone was around the table together – the man who owned the house, his sons, and other lodgers. They all seemed to like Leo a lot – because Leo, with his charm and courtesy and kindness, was very easy to like. It was a lovely house, chaotic and ramshackle, stuffed with pianos and plants and books and cheerful mess. You remember the big back garden – in the centre of London! – with that giant trampoline which the man used as a destresser when he came home from work. His work was benign and involved pianos – your dad had not been sent to live with an arms dealer, a banker or a butcher. It was not that kind of household. The kitchen, which overlooked the lush, unmanicured garden, was large and cluttered and full of whole foods; Leo and the man and the sons and the other lodgers all ate together in the evenings. It was the kind of place I would like to have lived, had I ever accidentally ended up back in London. And what's more, it was cheap.

Leo's room was next to the kitchen. It wasn't very light, and there was nothing in it apart from his bed, and some pull-out beds for when you two came to visit. Your bright, simple paintings were scattered around, and there was a mosaic heart on the wall, which I had made out of dozens of pieces of broken red tile and broken mirror, in an art class I'd done, and of which I was very proud; one night, in a fit of drunken generosity, I had given it to him as a moving in present. Or a moving out present. Slivers of broken glass, arranged to form a heart.

You two liked going to visit him there. You still talk about the pancakes your dad would make you for breakfast on weekend mornings, and how he got you a family pass for London Zoo, which was quite near. You must have gone there a dozen times. I went once, that time I visited with you, but I hated it. Those bears, rocking their heads from side to side, insane from confinement. The elephants, huge and stuck, the giraffes with nowhere to go. It was awful.

'Nothing I do is ever good enough,' your dad would say to me on the rare occasion he felt sufficiently needled to complain. He was right of course. Nothing he could do was ever going to be good enough. Not now. He was doing his best, but was not remotely resourceful or flexible. Despite living five nights a week near the centre of London, a city he had always professed preferring to Brighton – he'd said he had moved to Brighton only because it had been my idea, which sounded more like an abdication than a re-location – he didn't seem to have much of a life now that he was back in the city and had the freedom to do as he liked. The old rave friends had slipped away, had babies, moved on. Some were still at it, still putting on parties, still caning it, but Leo's party days were over. He didn't seem to have replaced them with anything else other than work and you two. And me. The man he lived with said that Leo always still referred to me as his wife, as though the only reason he was in London Monday to Friday was for work purposes, rather than because we had split up. He never called me his ex. Ever.

I didn't know any of this – I was too busy being self-absorbed, being a parent to you two, and counting the days until Friday. And writing. I didn't have much of a life either, at least not compared with now. I interspersed the monotony with grand gath-erings – every summer, we would have a party in the garden to celebrate my birthday, then yours, which was the day after mine. Cake and cava, the sugar rush of the summer, with gazebos to keep the sun off, borrowed from the garden committee. One year everyone got so drunk that the gazebos got trashed, and a committee member was knocking on the door at 8 a.m. the next morning to ask with icy politeness what we were going to do about it. I was unconscious, so River had to deal with it.

That last Christmas – the one after the electric toothbrush Christmas – was actually quite good fun, providing you didn't look under the carpet where all the feelings had been swept. There is a photo of us – a great big gang of us – gathered under a giant tree in the sitting room. There were fourteen for Christmas lunch, several of whom were unexpected – it didn't matter. Christmas Day was a great day for drinking. Unexpected guests just meant more people to drink with, even if they didn't drink. Most of them didn't. I'd left all the hardcore boozers behind in London and Barcelona. 'More?' I would always ask solicitously. 'Freshen your drink, sir? Ma'am?'

I remember, one birthday or Halloween, surging with fury when someone from the neighbourhood whom I had never much liked remarked jokingly that no matter what the occasion, I would always be sloshed. I remember wanting to smash their face in, as they sat there in my sitting room, drinking my champagne, listening to my music, their children playing with your toys. Fuck you, I thought furiously. I was a convivial host. (Although I now fully acknowledge that convivial is just drunk in four syllables.) But it was a given that any of my gatherings would involve loads of drink; I just never got completely smashed until everyone had left and I could fall over in peace. What was the point of socialising, if not to drink? The people, unless they were proper drinkers too, were little more than props. I always did food, because I was not one of those people whose idea of a party was twenty cases of lager and a few packets of cheese and onion. No way. I did proper food, so that nobody would ever go hungry, and if there was lager present, it was Japanese and in glass bottles. I had standards. Sort of.

That last Christmas, there are photos of you two in the blurry December dawn, one of you riding a sparkly bicycle across the endless white wool rug in that huge front room, the other of you still in nappies, lying on the floor playing with a big wooden pirate ship. The tree looms gigantic, like those trees outside shopping centres. Everything is twinkly.

Later, with that big crowd of us around the lunch table, there were gallons of bubbly. I don't remember the rest.

PART TWO

'It's the ultimate hissy fit'

JOHN WATERS ON SUICIDE, *Observer*, 15 MAY 2011

7 September 2011 – Five years later

It's five years today. What would I say to him now? Five years to digest what he did. For a long time, the only thing I could think was that if he were't already dead, I would have killed him myself, strangled him with my bare hands, more merciless than any rope.

It's five years since that full moon, since the lunar eclipse, when I stood by the window at midnight in parallelograms of powerful moonlight, knowing for certain that big change was coming. I remember mumbling a prayer to the moon. Mother goddess, look after us. I had no idea how to pray. I am not mystical or psychic. But I knew, standing there, that something was happening.

It's five years since that day.

I had said to him – I had actually said the words out loud, in the preceding months, words that should never have even formed in my brain, never mind left my mouth – that we would survive without him, that we would be absolutely fine without him, but he would never survive without us. Imagine being told that you are expendable. Imagine how that would have felt.

I bloody meant it too, at the time.

9 SOBER

After that faux-jolly last Christmas I became increasingly isolated and miserable, caused by nothing more sensational than alcohol. I know I keep banging on about drink, but we are reaching the end of it soon. This is almost where I stop. Drinking I mean, not banging on about it. Stopping drinking – for good this time – was to have a bigger impact than I could have imagined.

Unless you are one, it's hard to fathom addiction. For instance, I cannot imagine what it feels like to gamble addictively. The idea of pouring my scant cash into fruit machines or poker games or onto roulette wheels is baffling; why on earth would anyone do that? The only time I have ever gambled was in a Kitzbuhl casino years earlier with Joseph and River, and it was Joseph who had paid for the chips I placed on the table. Certainly it was a buzz when River and I both won a few hundred quid that night, but not such a buzz that I was ready to gamble my winnings away; instead we both scooped our chips from the table and went straight to the cashier. The idea of splashing money, without getting something guaranteed back (like drunk or high), seemed insane to me. When I hear how people gamble their homes away, I am left as puzzled as everyone else by their actions. I just don't get it.

But here is the difference between someone whose need for instant gratification supercedes all else, and someone who isn't like this: whereas River kept her winnings to pay for her ski lessons, rather than expecting our dad to foot the bill, I took my unexpected fistful of cash straight to the casino bar, and bought overpriced champagne for the three of us. Instant reward, instant gratification, instantly more, more, more.

For most of my adult life, the idea of not drinking was as nonsensical to me as gambling. I loved it. I loved the anticipation, the warmth, the comfort, the ease, the disinhibition, the exhilaration, the way it made me feel differently about myself and the world around me. Even if that world had shrunk to the size of a postage stamp by the end of my twenty-four years of getting drunk. But when it has become a source of misery and isolation, why would you continue? Why, once you have sobered up, would you deliberately restart the whole cycle again, knowing that you don't actually want to? This is what normal drinkers find difficult to understand – why anyone would continue drinking when it is so clearly causing them (and everyone around them), at best distress, at worst, total fucking chaos.

Here's an illustration, which I found in a recovery book, of the incomprehensibility of addiction. Imagine someone obsessed with playing chicken in the traffic. For years, they get away with it, nipping in and out between speeding vehicles, enjoying taking chances, finding jay walking fun and exhilarating, even as friends roll their eyes and offer friendly words of caution – which the traffic-dodger cheerfully ignores. Then they get hit a few times, nothing too serious, just a few scares and bruises, but enough to make any normal person reconsider their actions. Except they don't. They carry on, and get hit by a bus, and are badly bashed up. Having left hospital, they soon re-engage with their obsession, and get hit by two more buses. Back in hospital, everyone remonstrates with them – their friends, their loved ones, the medics – but to no avail. As soon as they can, they are at it again, limping towards the traffic, more insanely than ever. No matter how much they want to turn back, no matter how many promises they make to themselves and others, they cannot stop stepping under the wheels of trucks, and getting more and more mashed up every time, long after everyone around them has backed away in horror, bewilderment and anger. That sounds nuts, right? Nobody would do that, would they?

We are going to zoom in now, and you will see a close-up of your mother swimming – drowning – in a poisoned sea of alcohol. You will see how removed she had become from everything, as we look at the minutiae of her shrunken life. You will see how she saw nothing, how she missed the disintegration of your father as he fell apart almost in front of her, because she was too busy falling apart herself. Here's why:

An Unremarkable Weekend At Home

Thursday:	6 cans of beer @ 2.5 units each	15 units
Friday:	3 bottles of wine @ 9 units each	27 units
Saturday:	5 cans of beer @ 2.5 units each	12.5 units
	1 glass wine @ 2 units each	2 units
Sunday:	2 bottles of wine @ 9 units each	18 units

My weekend consumption	74.5 units
Recommended weekly alcohol units for women	14 units

On **Thursday** evening I'm not drinking, so I drink six cans of lager after you have gone to bed, even though I don't like canned lager.

It reminds me of East London, and searching for coins down the back of the sofa. That was a long time ago, but its metallic ting transports me back to woozy evenings of giro cider, crushed beer cans on ashy carpets, cheap spliff and blokey banter. From my elegant sitting room overlooking the sea, I have no need to be transported back there. Anyway tonight I have no intention of drinking; it is a school night. I don't drink midweek, because this is when I am home alone with you two and I cannot be drunk in charge. When I first became a mummy, during that initial head-spinning year, I was drunk in charge every night; luckily Leo and Bertha were around too, had I ever accidentally set the house on fire or dropped you out the window. Although I never did, because I was still able to function. Kind of. These days I am far more responsible, especially now that there are two of you and your dad sleeps in London midweek. But after the dinner-bath-bed rush hour, as I reach in the fridge for the milk to make tea, I see them, the cans of Stella lying there on their side, two gold circles facing me from behind the yogurts and the salad, lassoed together by opaque plastic loops. I'd forgotten they were there, because I had not put them there myself – maybe they're left over from the weekend. I feel suddenly elated. Fuck it, I think, I deserve a nice cold beer. Just the one. Just the two.

So I sit in the big high-ceilinged room with its tall old windows overlooking acres of communal garden, and the sea if you crane your neck, and I read the newspaper and listen to The Dandy Warhols, and pop the two cans of Stella one after the other. The beer is gassy and tinny, but I chug it down, barely tasting it. My mood quickly lifts. I feel lighter, mildly excitable. I want more. But the whole point of drinking on a school night was that I would only have two beers, two weak pissy little beers, and that would be enough. Enough, I tell myself sternly even as I put on my jacket and reach for my keys. I draw a note for you two – because you're too young to read – of a cartoon woman taking out the cartoon rubbish, which I colour in with fluorescent pens and leave propped up on the kitchen table.

I check you're both asleep by sneaking upstairs and popping my head around your bedroom doors, seeing your two small faces flushed in the glow of their nightlights, pink for her, yellow for him – and then I leave the flat, run down the stairs, out the front door, down the street, across the road, to the garage. I am sweating at the thought of you waking up, of not finding me there, of not seeing the note, of screaming the place down, of someone hearing you. I buy four more cans of Stella – I decide against wine, in case I accidentally get drunk – and race back across the road, up the street, through the front door, back up the stairs, into the flat, and am back popping cans on the sofa as though I have never left. When the last can is crushed and thrown in the recycling box – I shove them down under the newspapers, their thin tin crunching as I try to compress them – I go to bed. I am not drunk as much as sloshed, my stomach lurching gassily like a carbonated paddling pool.

On **Friday**, I'm a bit tired and thirsty, but not debilitatingly so. I spend the day at university, hoping throughout that I smell of intelligence rather than Stella. It's super intense, and I am exhausted when I come home so I drink three bottles of white wine. I drink the first one in half an hour, while watching *The Simpsons* with you two. It's amazing how quickly I go from tense and tired to relaxed and giggly. When your dad arrives to spend the weekend with you, I am feeling most convivial. I mentally clock off – ching! – and immediately uncork the second bottle.

I'm glad Leo doesn't drink, because this is my wine. It's mine. I'm glad when the three of you go upstairs and I am left alone. I drink the second bottle a little more slowly – by now, I'm starting to feel quite squiffy – and listen to The Dandy Warhols again, loudly, and as usual am filled with a terrible yearning, an ache deep inside that I can never soothe. I drink the third bottle as slowly as I can, eking it out, sipping the last of it like a normal drinker. But of course it doesn't last. When it is finished I feel bereft. I consider asking your dad to go out and get me another, but it's too late. The garage has shut. Why do I never, ever have enough booze in the house? I need to start buying it by the case – but you only buy cases when you're having a party, don't you? Or can you buy cases just for yourself? But you'd just drink them all at once, wouldn't you? How do people keep cases of wine in their homes? How do they manage to have a drinks cabinet? I never have any drink in the house. Ever. It never lasts more than an evening.

On **Saturday**, I wake up with a proper hangover. Throbbing head, dry throat, tight skin, raging thirst, and a feeling of absolute detachment, like a hot air balloon breaking from its moorings, floating away. Inside my head is what Martin Amis calls the poisoned yolk of my hangover, sliding slowly back and forth across the tightened drum of my skull. You two are watching loud bright Saturday morning cartoons; Leo is making your breakfast. I want you all to leave. Right now. Go on, piss off the lot of you.

Eventually you do, and I make my own breakfast. I am ravenous, my blood sugar has plummeted. I have already drunk two bottles of cold, burpy Diet Coke – I always buy Diet Coke when I buy wine – but my thirst is at cellular level, unquenchable. After breakfast I still have huge sugar cravings, so I drive the two minute walk to the garage, and buy the Saturday *Guardian* and a family sized bar of Galaxy. Then I sit on the sofa, mechanically eating the chocolate, and reading the paper. I doze, fuzzy brained and pacified from all the food, a Diet Coke within reach.

As the day progresses, my mood deteriorates. I am snappy and short tempered and distant with you two and Leo, but you are all used to it, and keep out of my way. By the afternoon when some friends pop around, I desperately need a drink. Someone produces a bottle of red wine – one bottle between six of us, which seems both preposterous and vaguely insulting, as if they don't realize that I could easily inhale the bottle all by myself while they are still fumbling for the corkscrew. I drain my glass in seconds, my back turned. My shitty mood is mildly alleviated, but of course it's not enough; my switch has been flicked and I want more, immediately. Again I curse myself for not having a house stocked to the ceiling with drink of all kinds. Why do I keep thinking that I won't want any more when I always, always do?

We go out to see some fireworks, in a big group of adults and children, and I drink five more cans of beer in the following hours. I am drinking cans of Stella again in an effort to not get drunk; I realize that when I am in company I can't get as drunk as I'd like to, because people might find it disconcerting and think less of me, and so I stick to beer. It's comforting, holding a beer, knowing there are plenty more in the rucksack. I relax and get into going 'ooooh' at the fireworks.

On **Sunday**, I am sweating and lethargic, and so I spend the afternoon drinking white wine. Blossom Hill. I couldn't find any Pinot Grigio, and I couldn't be bothered to go to the supermarket. I laze around the big sunlit room, friends popping in and out, you and other kids playing with your toys on the floor, food on the table. None of it matters so long as my glass is full. Leo leaves on Sunday evenings, and I am on mummy duty again until the following Friday – it's a bit like being a coal miner, or a junior doctor: five days on, two days off, five days on, two days off. Five days sober, two days drunk, five days sober. Of course when I say 'sober', I mean 'sober*ish*'. I mean dry*ish*. I read you stories for ages, animatedly doing all the actions. You stare at me, enjoying this excited, enlivened mummy, wondering how long she'll last.

On **Monday**, I feel like shit. Total shit. I always feel like shit on Mondays. Not for the same reasons lots of people feel like shit on Mondays – I am not going off to a horrid job that I hate, and staying there for an indecent chunk of my day – God, no. I feel like total shit today because over the weekend I have consumed seventy-four-and-a-half units of alcohol, which is sixty units more than those government teetotalitarians would strictly recommend. Maybe I'm overdoing it a bit.

My skin is flaky, my face is puffy, my nose is runny, and my lungs feels as though I've inhaled a bucket of quick-drying concrete, which of course I haven't – that's just silly – but instead I've smoked two pouches of Golden Virginia and a pack of Marlboro Lights. Which is a lot more than just silly.

It's not as if I don't realize I have a drink problem. Of course I fucking know, I'm not daft. But knowing it isn't enough to make you stop. Junkies are more than aware that they are junkies when their arms are falling off from gangrene, yet they still stick a dirty needle in. Drunks will drink even when they are desperate not to. Self knowledge affords us nothing.

Finally, it comes to an end. Nothing dramatic. No arrests, no police cells or social services, no public nudity or driving pissed down the wrong side of the motorway, no smashed windows, no screaming, no bleeding, no punching, none of that. Just the end. The end of a twenty-four year relationship, the only one in which I had ever been truly devoted and faithful.

It's a full moon – because things seem to happen on full moons – cold and clear, the wind gusting and rattling against the window panes and the ancient sash frames. The moonlight glares on the dark gardens outside, and bounces off the white fronts of the houses around the square. Faraway at the end of the gardens, the sea is lurching. You're in London with Leo for the weekend. It's lovely when you leave, your little overnight bags filled with pyjamas and toothbrushes and teddies and storybooks. Goodbye, I call happily, as your small hands carefully clutch the bannisters down to the front door. Off you go, little honeys. Goodbye! Goodbye! Then I close the door behind you and exhale into the sudden blissful stillness.

River and Syd are coming from London for a girly chill-out; that's what we do these days, we chill out. The stay-up-forever nights and lost next-days are long gone. We're all grown-ups now. We're going to relax around a roaring log fire, chatting and lounging. Nobody knows, because I haven't told anyone, but I have given up drinking. I haven't had a drink for two weeks now. Not since New Year's Day, when I was so hungover I had pins and needles in the tips of my fingers all day. Peripheral neuritis. Winos get that a lot. So when my guests arrive with several bottles of cava and white wine, I am discombobulated. I've made an unnaturally healthy meal – tofu, quinoa, seeds, spinach salad, fruit salad – and have poured myself a glass of fizzy water. I wasn't expecting them to bring wine. It unnerves me. Here is my alcoholic voice, the one that shouts the loudest once I'm in its grip: *What are they playing at, don't they realize that I made a secret decision not to drink tonight?* Syd doesn't usually drink, and River is super-moderate unless she's on a big night out, which is not tonight. Even as I pour myself more fizzy water, a small, needle sharp thought pings through my head: *If I drink tonight it won't be my fault. They bought the booze, not me.*

All through dinner there's a private argument going on inside my brain. I wear myself down in the end. This is what it sounds like: *Go on, why shouldn't you? You've been on fizzy water for a fortnight, go on, you deserve it. Why should they drink and not you? That's hardly fair, is it? Go on, what harm can it do? You're not drinking on an empty stomach – what can go possibly wrong? Go on, go on, go on.*

It's all starting to go a bit Father Ted. Worn down, I pour myself a drink.

Soon we're having a really nice time, talking and laughing and enjoying each other's company and the intimacy of its just being the three of us, without men or kids. Or maybe the other two were having a perfectly nice time all along, and I'm playing catch-up. We open more cava. It flows. We're animated, happy. I love cava. I love the way the bubbles go straight to your brain. I am not thinking about how I have given up drinking. I am only thinking about the next drink.

Later we watch a film. I open another bottle, although by now the other two seem to have had enough – their 'off' buttons are kicking in. I don't have one of those. We put on a second film – *Desperately Seeking Susan* – and I automatically reach to open the next bottle, but the cava is gone and the white wine is gone – I hadn't bought any, because I'm not drinking. Fuck! Fuck, fuck, fuck. So I go into the kitchen, leaving the other two contentedly sprawled in front of the film, and begin my desperate seeking. I search with a quiet, intense urgency. Nothing in the fridge. Not even lager, which is undrinkable once you've been on the bubbly, but I would have drunk it anyway. Just bowls and bowls of fucking tofu and salad. My eyes sweep the work surfaces. Could there be a forgotten bottle of anything lurking anywhere? Behind the cook books? In the vegetable box? The cupboards? I scan the pesto, the pine nuts, the penne, knowing even in my drunkenness that there is nothing there, yet compelled to complete this ritualized search anyway, so that I can resign myself to its fruitlessness. 'Oh well, at least you tried,' I can tell myself later, as the cravings still ride me in waves. It's like when you're stoned and you lose your last pea-sized piece of hash on a swirly carpet and you end up disman-tling the sofa looking for it – except with drink, it's far, far more urgent. I hate this feeling, it overwhelms me, I cannot relax until it has been sated, and only passing out makes it stop – but in order to pass out, I need more drink.

And then I find it. In another cupboard, amongst the brown rice and the kids' sugar-free biscuits, behind the school lunch apple juice and the organic muesli bars, I find it, lying on its side: a bottle of mulled wine left over from Christmas. I check the proof on the label – it's 12%, the same as proper wine – so I open it and pour a mugful. I start to drink it in big, cold, disgusting gulps, standing in the kitchen with the lights off. I can hear the other two murmuring in the sitting room – I hope neither of them comes out. I don't want them to see me doing this, even though it looks like I'm drinking tea. I gulp faster. There are sticky purple stains on my chin. I wipe them off and hope they won't notice my purple teeth. I empty the bottle in under five minutes. It's not that I would have minded sharing – well, no, actually, that's a lie, I would have minded a lot – but I know quite well that River and Syd wouldn't have wanted any. They would have said no, politely, and kept their faces neutral. After all, who on earth would want to drink cold, sugary, mulled red wine on top of white wine and cava? Who would want to do that?

I am really drunk now. The film blurs. Madonna becomes a cartoon, and I forget how to follow the plot. The other two recede away from me, as though I am on shipwrecked on wine island where everything is foggy and faraway. I'm shutting down. I stagger off to bed, slurring excuses, before the film ends. I don't remember passing out.

Next morning my weekend hangover is bad. The usual components are there – dying of thirst, sweating filth, cranky as hell, imbalanced and uncentred, but this morning the poisoned yolk has taken on a sweetish purple sheen as it slides across my brain, and I almost retch as I suddenly remember the mugs of mulled wine. *Christ. What the FUCK was I thinking*? For a moment, I am engulfed in – what? Shock? Disgust? Self-loathing? Fear? Well, yes. Obviously. They're all normal hangover feelings. But this morning the fear is all-consuming.

It breaks over me in toxic waves, rippling through me so that my breathing is ragged, my sweat icy, and I feel like Chicken Licken having a panic attack. I can't even make eye contact with myself, never mind anyone else. Do I have the Fear because I drank myself insensible when I had been entirely determined not to drink at all? That after two weeks of mineral water and salad, I couldn't stop myself getting shitfaced?

Obviously, all this Fear needs suppressing as quickly and efficiently as possible. After swigging my way through three or four Lime Diet Cokes and half a packet of Neurofen – I'm out of dihydracodeine, which is the only thing that really works – I persuade River and Syd to let me take them to lunch. This is not altruism – it just means that I can choose the venue. The only thing that can fix me now is cold beer and sushi. That will be my cure, my leveller. After a good feast of sushi and delicious dry, cold, light, fizzy Asahi – bottles and bottles of the stuff – I will become human again. All will be well. I just need a drink.

'Are you all right?' They watch as I chug down more Neurofen. Their expressions might be mild unease. Or wariness. Or resignation. Or maybe all three. I can never tell. I do my best to hide my hangover, just as I always do my best to hide my drunkenness, but of course it manifests itself as clearly as if it were a giant green boil on my face.

I almost pick a fight with the front-of-house person who doesn't have a table for us at the sushi place. After a brisk walk along the seafront, my anticipation – and thirst – intensifying with each step, I was horrified to find my favourite place closed; raging, and taking their seasonal refurbishment entirely personally, I redirect our march towards another sushi place that I don't like as much. By now I am actually shaking with a need for food and drink. Or maybe just drink. Whatever. I just want a fucking table, and even though there's an empty one, the manager won't give it to me, because she says it's permanently reserved for disabled people. 'We'll move if any come in,' I say again, through gritted teeth. 'Any disabled people. We'll move.

'I'm sorry,' she smiles coldly again, although she isn't sorry at all.

'It's fine,' River says directly to the manager, bypassing me. 'Really.'

'No it's bloody not,' I say out loud.

The thing is, I know I'm being an arsehole, but I really want to sit somewhere comfortable, where the convivial around-the-table atmosphere will help my companions relax into maybe getting a bit drunk with me. Except they won't, because they're not interested in getting drunk. It's not their thing. I remember that Irvine Welsh comparison between drinking and taking heroin in *Trainspotting*: 'Whereas the pissheid in the pub wants every cunt tae git as ootay it as he is, the real junky disnae gie a fuck aboot anyone else.' I feel desperately self-conscious; my hangover is so jaggedly visible, my nerve-endings so stretched and raw. For a fleeting moment, I wonder if it wouldn't be easier to be a smack-head. At least then you wouldn't care about what people thought. And you wouldn't be bothered with stupid fucking restaurants either.

We sit, three in a row at the conveyor belt, the little plates trundling enticingly past us. Bright coloured plates and jewel-like fish under clear plastic domes, everything exquisitely miniature and delicious. The air hums with bright, lively Sunday afternoon chatter. I glance up and am filled murderous rage. The disabled table has just been filled up by a group of people without a wheel-chair, a walking stick or a prosthetic limb between them. 'Look,' I hiss, raising my arm to call the front-of-house gorgon back over. 'They've taken our table and there's nothing wrong with them.' Before I can attract her attention, River grabs my arm and reminds me through clenched teeth that not all people with disabilities are in wheelchairs. Syd nods, and says that we're fine here. I open my mouth to argue, but I know it's useless, so instead I just glower, and leave it. It reminds me of a joke I haven't heard yet: What's the difference between a Rottweiler and an alcoholic? A Rottweiler will eventually let go.

Once River and Syd have started eating, I call the manager over on the pretext of ordering more miso soup, and whisper that I'd like three glasses of champagne. It's my way of saying sorry to the other two; just saying the word 'sorry' with any degree of sincerity simply wouldn't dawn on me. I'd just feel embarrassed, and besides, what would be in it for me? Anyway, who can resist champagne? The gorgon comes back and says that they don't have any cold champagne, that if I want it cold I'll have to wait an hour while it goes in the fridge. *You stupid cow*, I want to scream at her, *What kind of fucking place serves warm fucking bubbly? I bet it'd be cold if it were for those fucking people at the disabled table!* Jesus. Waves of rage are breaking over me, as real as the waves of poisoned sweat prickling my back and armpits, and I feel like pure murder: I'd murder the manager, for being such a cold, fish-eyed bitch; I'd murder my sister, for being so eternally fucking sober; I'd murder my friend, for being so oblivious to my pain; and I'd murder those bastards sitting at the disabled table without a care in the world, waving their able-bodied arms around and visibly enjoying themselves. Probably about to order a bucket of ice cold Krug. I hate them all. I hate everything. I hate feeling like this. I just fucking hate it. Hate hate hate it. I am poisoned.

So I order a hot sake – a 500 ml flask, meant for sharing. It comes, warm alcoholic vapour rising like a genie from the neck of the white porcelain flask, three little white egg cups on the black tray next to it, two of which will remain untouched. River and Syd are drinking water. I drink the sake and order another. It's hot and potent and I don't even know if I really like it or not. I just drink it. The other two continue to drink water. I don't eat much – I'm on a January detox, after all – and so I soon feel quite drunk again. The sake feels strong and floods warmly into my blood. I begin to unfurl. With each egg cup of it, I feel the distance growing between myself and the other two, because I've set inevitable sail towards Alcohol Island again and they're resolutely on the shore. But now that there's a litre of strong hot booze coursing through my veins, I feel more able again; able to converse, able to communicate, able to relax, able to enjoy myself. So what if I'm slurring a bit, or that my face is hot and pink. By the time we leave, my murderous hatred of the front-of-house woman has dissipated quite a bit, although not so much that I bother to leave a tip.

It is dark outside. We wander through the twinkling lights of the Lanes, and stop by Monsoon. It's the January sale. There's a scrum of women in there, even on a dark late Sunday afternoon. River and Syd stand around as I make drunken purchases for you two – a pink swansdown cape, an overpriced boy's t-shirt that was not on sale. On the way home, I stop at the video shop for another film, and at the offie where I buy two bottles of Pinot Grigio. I never drink Chardonnay if I can help it – the Bridget Jones-on-a–hen-night connotations are too strong. Although, obviously, I'd drink it if there was nothing else in the fridge.

In fact I'd drink anything if there was nothing else in the fridge.

Leo delivers you back from London when we arrive home. Our communication is brief and semi-formal. As usual, I have little idea what is going on behind his immaculate manners. Little interest either. Obviously I will come to regret this lack of interest more than I could ever possibly have imagined, but for the moment I am only interested in getting at my wine before the sake warmth wears off and dips me back into hangover hell. I need a top-up. He leaves again, for the lonely train ride back to his rented room in London, like a ghost passing through the wall. I barely notice him going. River goes upstairs with you to read your bedtime stories, and Syd leaves to go back to Lotus, Vishnu and Ted in London. I open the wine, pour two glasses – I'm being polite, obviously – and chug the rest of the bottle before you've even reached the last page of *Goldilocks and the Three Bears* upstairs. I am drunk again.

When River comes back down, I'm already slurring, and rolling cigarette after cigarette after cigarette. It's not a happy drunkenness either; there's no conviviality. I'm not sparkling or effusive or enthusiastic, all those things I imagine I become when I drink. I'm not witty or amusing or sharp-brained, yet I can't seem to stop talking total shite; it's just pouring out of my mouth – flabby, unconnected, rambling strings of words. I'm slurring and skinning up, slurring and skinning up, except these days I'm not really skinning up any more, just rolling thousands of rollies out of habit, without adding anything psychoactive to make me think. Thinking and drinking don't go, unless you want to think all the wrong thoughts. Anyway I'm scared of smoking dope now. Scared of where it might lead me – unlike booze, it has a habit of showing me the truth, in big flashing letters. I don't like the truth too much. I'd rather avoid it if possible.

As we sit together in the big dark sitting room, another stormy night gusting outside, I feel that River is recoiling, disengaged, frosty. I try to ignore it – am I imagining things? – but I feel more isolated than ever. I have arrived on Alcohol Island again, and scuttled my boat for the journey back. I'm stuck here, alone.

We put the film on – that amazing surfer documentary *Dogtown and Z-Boys* – and I ramble through a lot of it, my synapses not so much buzzing and snapping as flapping wetly like fish dying on a dock. River says little, drinks nothing. When it ends, she yawns and stretches, but I am not ready to let her sleep just yet. Instead I become maudlin and weepy, and tell her how lonely I am, how much I want to be in a relationship, how shit my life is. 'I don't think I'll ever meet anyone,' I wail, wine weeping from my eye sockets as she glances at her watch. 'It's not fair, life is passing me by. I hate my fucking life.' River listens in stony silence. In a few hours she has to travel miles to a university where she will give a lecture to a hall full of undergraduates; she desperately needs to get to sleep, but as she is sleeping on the sofabed on which we're now sitting, she has little choice but to listen to me. She offers some constructive advice – I have no idea what, I am too drunk to take anything in – and the tears continue to flow in great rivers down my cheeks. Like Jesus backwards, I've turned wine into salt water; and now I'm drowning in it. There is no more wine in the house, so I can't even top up my glass and maintain the misery.

It's the last hungover Monday morning of my life, and it feels as though the sky has fallen in and landed on my chest. I wake with that awful jolt, the one where you're suddenly hurled, without warning, back into consciousness from the thick black of booze-sleep; there's always that nanosecond of amnesia, of blissful innocence, before the jagged memory fragments come flying back, like meteorite slivers, slicing into your brain, making you wince. It's the same every time, this feeling of being flung against a brick wall. Every time you leap awake on impact, you have a tiny second – oh no, not again – before you collapse back on the pillows and hastily start plastering over the cracks. You'll have trained your mind to side-step the truth, instead sending messages of false brightness to yourself. *Oh well*, you'll think. *Ho hum. Here we go. Never mind. Quick, have a Diet Coke and a dihydracodeine*. Or, *Hey, at least I haven't woken up next to a total stranger, like I used to in the past. Ha ha, at least I don't have to chew my arm off this morning. And hey, at least I haven't pissed the bed. Phew! Not like I used to. Like I still do sometimes. But not as often as I used to, so that's okay. At least I don't have to scramble around hiding wet sheets and flipping mattresses over. Goodness me, no. See? Everything's fine.*

Imagine a phrenology model of an alcoholic's brain on waking. The denial part will have taken over the whole lot. Except this morning, none of the usual denial-chirrup is working. No amount of la-la-la can alleviate the feelings of physical and emotional desolation. No, this morning, I feel like shit and I want to die. Why do I do this to myself? I am exhausted from this. I am so, so sick of it. I lie in the sweat-damp sheets and groan. I want the day to go away, to leave me in peace. I cannot imagine the awfulness of getting up. Everything hurts: my chest, from the five million rollies; my kidneys, from the vats and vats of drink; my head, from total dehydration; and my heart, from the endless bloody pointlessness of it all. The misery closes in over my head, and I feel myself starting to submerge. I remember that scene in *The Hours*, when Julianne Moore is drowning on the hotel bed, the water closing over her until she is covered. Except Julianne Moore is not lying in sweaty ropes of sheets, her skin patchy, her lips cracked, her liver desperate for respite.

On the other side of my bedroom door I hear you screeching around, fighting as only a five year old and two year old can. I hear River making your breakfast. She should not be doing this. She should be on a train to her new job at a university two counties away. As I stand upright from the twisted pit of bedding, and almost topple from the headrush and the nausea, it dawns on me that very soon I will have to be at the school gates, making small talk with the yoga mummies, the macrobiotic mummies, the reiki mummies, the shiny, healthy, herb-tea mummies. There are no pisshead mummies at your little school. I am sick with terror.

River glances up as I come in. Again, she seems distant, frosty, as though she's pissed off but resigned to the fact that I will always be like this. You two are full of bright morning energy; I lumber around you, a toxic wreck, dreading the day, terrified of taking you to school, terrified of not taking you to school. I cannot possibly interact with Teacher, that kindly, serene mother-figure to whom you rush every morning, to whose flowing skirts you cling; I cannot face it. I cannot face the drive to nursery, the cheery playworkers, the bright colours and happy children. But the idea of spending all of this poisoned, exhausted day with a fresh, energetic five year old and two year old terrifies me even more. I don't know what to do. I can't deal with this anymore. When River says something non-committal like, 'Tea?', I burst into tears. I sit by the kitchen table, and lose it, sobbing, covering my face. You are right there in front of me. Through the gaps in my hands I can see the worry on your small faces, and that makes it worse. I am completely distraught. I say the same things over and over again – *I can't cope, I can't do this any more, I don't know what to do.* I am horrified at what is happening to me, losing control like this in front of my super-controlled sister, my worried little children. I shake. I feel nauseous. I am terrified. 'I have to go now,' River says, not unkindly.

Why don't you stay and look after us? Can't you see I'm sick? How can you leave me like this? What am I supposed to do? Is

your new job really so important that you can't fuck it all up just
to stay and walk me through this hangover? Doesn't anyone under-
stand the pain I'm in?

'I'll phone you,' she says. The sound of the door closing makes
me wince. You look up at me expectantly, then you're off,
screaming and fighting and running around and being normal.
I steel myself to leave the house, covering my puffy eyes with
dark glasses, putting on my lipstick with a shaky hand, realizing
that I probably smell of old tobacco and stale booze. I wear black,
as usual, as though it will disguise me.

Then, late and shaking, I drive you to school and nursery, my
hands gripping the wheel of my tiny old Fiat, my jaw clenched
so tight it makes my headache worse.

The relief of having jettisoned you both, for a few hours at
least, is overwhelming. Now I can get on with being terrified
without anyone swarming around me. The Fear is on me so badly,
swamping me in sick anxiety. I remember the beer in the fridge.
Although I desperately don't want it, I even more desperately
need it, and drink a can in about ten seconds flat. I choke and gag
as I pour it down my open throat. It very slightly takes the edge
off. There is more in there, behind the skimmed milk and the fat
green olives, but I don't dare – I have to drive later. I have not
been driving very long, and am too scared to drink drive.

I force myself to look in the mirror. I see a thirty-eight-year-
old woman sitting at her kitchen table at eleven o'clock on a
Monday morning, crushing a can of Stella between her shaking
hands. Her breath is short and jagged, and a light film of poison
sheens her skin. Maybe I am in the wrong setting. My surroundings should surely be dingier: old chip wrappers on the floor,
dirty lino, ugly mismatched chairs, chipped paint, scarred walls.

Empty bottles of White Lightning, maybe some empty tins of Fray Bentos pies or whatever alcoholics eat when they're not throwing up on their own shoes and passing out on park benches. A few crumpled copies of the *Sun*, cigarette burns on the nasty MFI furniture. Perhaps some vomit stains somewhere, some dried blood and piss. Some awful smells. Instead there are crumpled copies of the *Guardian*, carefully placed in the recycling box alongside a dozen empty wine bottles. There is a giant bowl of fruit on the table, and books on the shelves. The floors are wood instead of curling lino, and the twenty-foot ceilings in the sitting room overlook private gardens you need a key to enter. How can there be an alcoholic living somewhere like this? Alcoholics live in bins, don't they?

I get up groggily and go into my room, the raw terror and physical anxiety slightly eased by the Stella, and go online. I scan through lists of psychotherapists and phone one at random, like pinning the tail on the donkey. Although I don't expect to be seen that day, I am given an emergency appointment later in the afternoon. That's what the therapist calls it – an emergency appointment. Fuck. Maybe it's worse than I thought.

And that was the end of it.

'Get yourself to a meeting right away,' said the therapist. She didn't need to say any more. I knew what kind of meeting she was talking about. She had taken one look at me, shaking and shallow breathing raggedly in her soft soothing armchair, and told me that this was where I needed to go. Now. In a way it was almost a relief to be told what to do. What could I do? She was a therapist. Therapists knew more about me than I did. And although I knew I had reached the end of it, that I had finally hit the wall, I was still appalled. Going to a meeting of recovering alcoholics was the end. Once you were in there, your drinking was over.

Now, anyone who is not an alcoholic would read over those last few pages and think, Jesus Christ, and about time too. How much longer was that woman going to carrying on destroying her health, her sanity, her relationships with others, the wellbeing of her children? But if you're an alcoholic reading this, then you'll understand exactly the terrible wrenching terror of saying goodbye to your longest and most consistent relationship. Never mind that it had been an abusive lover for many years now, kicking the crap out of you and leaving you for dead time and again, only for you to rush back into its embrace within hours of your bruises healing. It has always been there for you. From your anguished youth to your early days abroad , it was there during the coruscating loneliness, the isolation, the feeling of being eternally shipwrecked far beyond the horizon. It never let you down. It never walked out, ran away, hung up, drove off, left you. It never scorned you, dismissed you, attacked you, ridiculed you, abandoned you, rejected you. Well it did, constantly, every time you got drunk, but it never seemed like that at the time. It was your lover, your best friend, your companion, your confidante. Your abuser.

It was fucking weird, going to my first meeting. It was in a church basement opposite the room where you did ballet. There was your ballet teacher, through the glass door panels, and all the little girls leaping and flouncing, as I lumbered to an empty seat in a packed airless room, too terrified even to make eye contact. If I had been naked I could not have felt more self conscious. What I didn't realize was that the alcoholics in the room were all far too self absorbed to notice, but when I sat down, the woman next to me smiled and said hello, which was quite an un-English thing to do.

But then the strangest thing happened. Kept happening, all through the hour and a half I sat there, rigid and sweating and shallow breathing. Every time somebody spoke, they seemed to be saying what I thought. It was as if we all shared the same brain, me and this roomful of total strangers. People spoke about drinking the way I thought about drinking. I sat there, numb and stunned, as I heard a whole room full of people I had never seen before in my life talking about how I secretly felt inside. It was uncanny.

Everything changed after that. I properly stopped drinking, not because I was trying to get anyone else off my back, but because I desperately wanted to. Three small words – 'I don't drink' – changed everything. But initially I didn't really notice the change – all I could focus on was the joy of no more hangovers, on what it felt like to wake up every morning, and not want to either die or at the very least duvet-dive, depending on how much I'd had the night before. To wake up feeling normal every single morning was an astonishing thing. I had never done it consistently before, not for years and years. To finally realize that I had a treatable malady – alcoholism – was such a huge relief. Now that I knew what had been wrong with me my whole life, I could deal with it. So *that's* why I had spent years falling off all those barstools and fucking up relationships. What a relief to know what it was that had been wrong for so long. I did not have a hard time and therefore drank – I had a hard time *because* I drank. Glaringly obvious, of course – but not when you're in the thick of it. Not when you're drowning in a river of denial.

I had thought that going to meetings would be like Weight Watchers for booze, and initially it was, but soon the obvious poser arose: if you take the brandy out of the fruitcake, you're still left with the fruitcake. What do you do then, Miss Fruitcake, with your lifetime of twisted thinking, of normalizing the abnormal? Although I was no longer some human hamster trapped on the hedonic treadmill, it became apparent that it wasn't just about always wanting to drink – it was about how I felt. I'd never had any idea how I felt about anything (beyond anger and frustration, obsession and craving), but when I heard words like 'restless, irritable and discontent', I had a lightbulb moment – *yes, that's me*. I had always been restless irritable and discontent. Always. And lonely. Lonely like you would not believe. Lonely to my core, for as long as I can remember. A great gaping hole of loneliness, no matter where I was, no matter who I was with. Even with you two, my most beloved, I was still so fucking lonely. Not to mention self-obsessed, but that's addicts for you.

Once the drinking stopped, though, I began to thaw out. By being honest about how I felt, and listening to other alcoholics, I began to realize that I was far from unique. I started to experience what feelings felt like, without automatically chucking liquid anaesthetic down my neck to numb them. I began to wake up a bit, defrost a bit, come alive like some frozen stunted thing that had been trapped in ice. Inside the melting ice was something, raw and new. Fucking hell, I thought, I may actually be human after all. This had never happened before. I had never been this desperate to change direction.

All through that winter and spring of 2006, I embraced my not-drinking with the same dedication and obsessive fervour with which I had embraced my drinking. Instead of trying to do it on my own, which always felt like holding my breath, and invariably ended with a massive drunken exhalation, I was doing it with a group of other people who had the same screwy relationship to drinking as I did. It was like learning how to breathe for the first time, learning how to feel, how to be. People say that your emotional development is put on hold around the time you started drinking, which made me a fourteen year old trapped in a thirty-eight-year-old body. I always knew I had been unable to empathize and was emotionally immature, but at least now I knew why. I suffered from a compulsive disorder, a mental illness, an addiction, whatever you want to call it. All that mattered was that I could get treatment for it now, in the rooms of recovery, rather than trying to do it on my own. What a relief.

That summer, in June, I went on holiday. Some friends rented a villa on the Greek island of Skopelos, and invited me along. I had never been on holiday sober before. You two stayed at home with your dad, and I swanned off with five other women to a beautiful island full of pine forests and secret beaches. It was a proper holiday, with sun lotion and fat novels – I remember the uninterrupted bliss of Alan Hollinghurst's *The Line of Beauty* – and it was hot. Hot, hot, hot. The heat woke up my dormant desire. That and not drinking made my sexual self slowly come back to life. When I got home, I knew it was time to do something about it. I'd had enough of living like a nun. I was thirty-eight and a size eighteen, but I was a sober size eighteen, and I no longer smoked. I had given up the day I stopped drinking, because I hated it, and had wanted to quit for years, but every time I got drunk I would chain smoke. Now I no longer smelled of ashtrays and beer cans and wine bottles. I was fat, but I was healthy, and tanned, and bored of being celibate.

It had been a year and a half since your dad and I separated, yet nothing had really changed. He was still there every weekend, and I was still there every weekend, and he still wasn't referring to me as his ex, and I was starting to think that it was time for things to move on. Any residual guilt I'd had at dismantling our marriage had long passed. Now I just wanted to get on with things, to make up for all the time I'd lost floating upside down inside a wine bottle. It seemed like a reasonable length of time had elapsed – if formal, how-soon-after-your-marriage-do-you-fuck-someone-else etiquette existed, I would be well within its borders of decorum.

When I was a long-term castaway on Wine Island, I would just sit there, half-cut and lonely, and fantasize about a man who would find a fat, chain-smoking drunk devastatingly attractive, a man who relished the stink of cigarette butts and booze breath, who didn't mind a bird who would only ever remember the night before up to certain point; this unlikely knight would ride in on his horse – a strong horse, mind, with a reinforced back – and whisk me away. Then everything would be all right. (See? This is why you should never read fairytales to small girls. Once the idea of male rescue is introduced at a formative age, it can remain lodged in an unconscious part of the female brain for decades. Anything seemed better than self-rescue, which might involve reading books with words like 'inner goddess' and 'feel the fear' in their titles.)

But as my internal fog cleared, burned off by the Greek sun, I began to realize that no man was going to turn up on my doorstep and declare undying love or even unrequited passion. I reckoned, quite logically, that if this were to happen, it would have happened by now. It was time to stop playing Rapunzel, and blast my own way out of the tower.

Finally, an opportunity to make some changes presented itself. You two and Leo went away for a few days and left me home alone. This provided some physical and mental space, where I could think about what to do. I had no idea of how to go about anything, because I had been out of the loop for so long, and in my absence, the loop had remodelled itself entirely. All I knew was that I had an itch I could no longer postpone scratching, but the idea of forming an intimate relationship with another human being was terrifying. Apart from your dad, I had not been with anyone since 1998. I had not been with anyone at all in a couple of years. I was clueless about what to do, or how to do it.

I went online. Not to the *Guardian* Soulmates or any of those proper grown up dating sites where everyone is solvent, bubbly, tall, slim, vivacious, fun, adventurous, outgoing and attractive, where everyone spends their spare time walking in the woods or enjoying a cheeky Rioja in front of a cosy log fire, after a day of snowboarding or hot air ballooning. No, I wasn't ready for any of that – the idea appalled me. So I went on an adult site instead. Don't worry, you're not going to hear any more about that. My mission is to be honest with you, but there's a line between honesty and over-share that I have no need to cross. (Not here anyway. Maybe one day I'll write a novel about it all, and go into eye-watering detail, but I'll warn you in advance.) Suffice to say that sobriety had given me newfound confidence, where the opinions of others didn't weigh so heavily, yet I was still not sensitised enough to be able to feel vulnerable and soft in relationships, the way I do now. Plus, I had watched enough episodes of *Sex and The City* to know that right now I was channelling a plus sized Samantha; forget the roses, just give me the – well, you get the idea.

*

God, I had fun. Adventures. It was extraordinarily exciting, after lying fallow for so long. I felt alive. I had a secret life. I went on secret missions that nobody knew about. For years, I thought that I would never again connect with that side of myself, that I would die a reconstituted virgin, a desiccated celibate, cranky and imbalanced from all that inverted, untapped sexual energy, and thirty stone from eating my feelings (food was all I had left now, in the absence of drugs, booze and tobacco). But now I had sex as well. Oh boy, did I ever. It was a period of intense liberation and exploration, just a few short months after I had sat and cried into my wine because I thought I would never be able to honour that part of myself again.

Unexpectedly, without meaning to, I met someone. A tall, muscular man with intense eyes, with whom I had nothing whatsoever in common. What was meant to be a single liaison turned into a flurry of weekends, neither of us quite believing what was happening. We came from very different worlds, lived in very different places, had different lives, different values, different outlooks; but once we were alone, an erotic alchemy took over, rendering all external realities irrelevant. We were sex tourists visiting each other's planets, and creating our own private world as we did so. During those hot summer weekends of August, I disappeared as soon as your dad arrived off the train, rushing off to another train to visit this unexpected man. 'See you Sunday,' I would tell your dad, wishing him a good weekend the way you would a neighbour or an acquaintance in a shop.

'You too,' he would reply, even more politely, adding a generous, 'Have fun.' I can't imagine what he thought I was up to. He never asked and I never told.

*

It was a bit weird.

Ever since I had stopped drinking, things had been a bit weird between your dad and me. The thing was, I might have been hideously bad tempered during those years when I was always hungover, but overall I was passive. I wasn't going anywhere. My world was tiny, and I was trapped inside it, like Alice after she drinks from the bottle that traps her inside the house, with her arms and legs sticking out the windows. Now that I had unlocked the door to the outer world, it was starting to become obvious – to me, at least – that Leo and I needed to move on a bit. He was still acting as if nothing had changed, as if we were still together.

When I began disappearing for weekends to the man with the intense eyes, instead of sitting indoors isolated in my drinking and writing, drinking and reading, it seemed wrong to tell Leo where I was going. But equally it seemed wrong not to. It wasn't as if I was doing anything deceitful or underhand. It wasn't as if we had broken up the week before. I wasn't bringing a new man home for tea and cucumber sandwiches, or carrying on with his best friend, or foisting anyone new on you two. That private part of my life was exactly that – private, distant, compartmentalized. Yet the situation remained one of entirely uncharted territory – what exactly *do* you say to your husband when you are running away from domesticity for a weekend of pure, uncomplicated pleasure? When your husband looks blankly at you, and seems to be pretending that nothing is happening?

Here are some of the things I said:

'I'm going now, there's some risotto in the fridge.'

'I hope you're having fun in London.'

'I'm back out there again – I recommend it.'

'I think we should get a divorce.'

At no point did I tell Leo anything about my private life, other than that I now had one. Details, even vague ones, would have been unnecessary, as well as insensitive. I would have loved it if he had turned up one weekend with some lovely girl with a bright smile and kind eyes, someone who was really into him. It would have levelled things out between us, neutralized things, and taken his focus off me. We didn't have the kind of cosy relationship where we exchanged confidences; we operated under a kind of weary politeness. But although we had no direct conversation about anything – other than, I think, Leo politely murmuring that he was happy for me – things were starting to feel a bit strained.

Not about my having a private life, although I doubt it helped. No, it was bigger than that. Years of my resentment, previously suppressed with a thousand wine corks, were now bubbling involuntarily to the surface and demanding oxygen. In my newer, freer state of mind, rebellion was kicking in. I was sick of the imbalance between us. When it came to our division of childcare, it was very, very lopsided. I did almost all of it.

Other separated parents, I reasoned, shared their kids a week on, a week off; while this wasn't practical, because we didn't live in the same town, I became obsessed with the idea that instead of being two days with your dad and five days with me, that he should have you for a third day. That way, the ratio would still not be 50:50, but it would be a bit more balanced than it was now. Unlike other mothers, I was not jealously ring-fencing my time with you, guarding our days together and confining your dad to every other weekend. Quite the opposite. I might have stopped drinking, but I was a long way from being emotionally present, from being a devoted mummy. An awful long way.

The colour drained from his face when I first suggested the three days/four days split. Then he began shaking his head. 'Impossible,' he said. 'No way. No way. What about my work?'

'What about *my* work?' I asked him. My writing was starting to take off a bit, after years of bashing away at my keyboard in the small hours when everyone else was asleep. Not to mention my MA work which was balanced on top of everything else. I reminded him that he worked for a human rights organization, one which prided itself on its family-friendliness and flexibility. He looked horrorstruck, as though I had asked him to have a vasectomy without anaesthetic. And I felt a surge of exasperation. Everything – *everything* – was down to me. School, nursery, packed lunches, playdates, childminders, babysitters, doctor's appointments, clothes, shoes, bedrooms, toys, dinners, breakfasts, driving, bill paying, cleaning, shopping – all my responsibility. I wanted more time to write. Or just more time. He wouldn't even consider it.

Not drinking was making me angry at him, properly angry. It felt like I was looking after another kid. We ended up in mediation. It was chilly and strange. The mediator didn't know what to make of us. 'Usually when couples come in here, it's because they're in dispute over access,' she said. 'I have never come across this situation before.'

By 'this situation', she meant two parents who were fighting over *not* having their children. Sorry, kids. Please don't take it personally. We were two immature people trying to play at being grown up and making a right mess of it. He was frozen in terror at the idea of change, and I was seething with previously unexpressed resentment. What a pair. But it was never to do with not loving you – it was to do with a refusal to take on responsibility.

It took me years to get my head around the idea that I was responsible, for myself and for you two. Bloody years. 'Only you can resolve this,' said the mediator, adding – a bit tartly, I thought – that she was not King Solomon.

We were barely speaking after that.

Walking down from the station to catch a bus home at Churchill Square, invigorated after a weekend of secret pleasures, and smiling inwardly, I was stopped short by a sudden thought. Today was your dad's birthday. Fuck! I had completely forgotten. Normally, birthdays and Christmases were a chance to spend hours choosing the funniest card, the loveliest wrapping paper, the best present (addicts are terrible like that – we will do *anything* to light up those little gratification bits in our brain, and if it isn't with drugs or booze, then shopping will do instead, even if it's not for ourselves). Or maybe it's a female thing – women tend to be good at special occasions.

But despite my hardwiring, I had forgotten. You were both too young even to know your own birthdays – it was up to me to make sure that your dad got birthday presents from you, just as, a fortnight earlier, he had made sure I received little cards and gifts from both of you. Today, your dad was taking a train back to London, alone. He obviously had no birthday plans, or he would have said he needed to leave early. It seemed incredibly sad.

And yet I felt impatient that I still felt responsible for him somehow, that it was up to me to make sure he had a nice birthday. I wished again that he had a girlfriend to fuss over him, as I ran into the nearest shop – Mambo, which was having a sale – and bought him a t-shirt with a sheep on the front that read 'I Heart Sheep'. Perhaps there was some unconscious reference to his ancient stuffed animal Daffyd. Or perhaps I was in a hurry and keen to get home to see you two. I grabbed some other small, impersonal items and scribbled a card, and that was it. 'Happy birthday,' I said a bit stiffly, embarrassed that he might realize I had completely forgotten it, that my offerings were rushed and insincere. He made a show of opening his gifts with enthusiasm, and put the I Heart Sheep t-shirt on immediately, and the three of us sang *Happy Birthday* to him, but there was no cake and no candles and given that he was dead three weeks later, I can't imagine he was happy at all.

Something strange happened around this time – very close to the birthday I'd forgotten about – which, although I noticed it at the time, didn't seem that significant until later, by which time it was both significant and too late. Things between Leo and me had not been getting any better; my impatience and frustration were peaking, as were his unresponsiveness, his heel-digging. We had been having increasingly fraught discussions about his being responsible for you two for an extra day. He was absolutely unmoving, and I was becoming increasingly sharp. He would argue passionately that his entire life would implode if he had to have you a third day; I would argue equally passionately that if I could do it, then so could he: that you two were *our* children, a responsibility to be shared. That there was childcare in London too, for working parents – neither of you were yet in school full time, which made things more flexible; that if I had a mummy network in Brighton, then perhaps he needed to get a daddy network in London.

Was I being unreasonable? I don't think so. Selfish, yes, absolutely, because I was only thinking of my own needs and not his or yours or anyone else's. But not unreasonable – I kept thinking about all the parents I knew who co-parented more equally, who did a week on/a week off – and if we couldn't do that, then we could bloody well do this.

(Now, today, five years later, the idea of not seeing you for a week is *horrifying* – the longing would take over and I would have to drop what I was doing and come and find you. But this was when I was just six months sober, after twenty-four years of boozing – I still had an awful long way to go. My heart was softening very slowly, only around the edges, its centre still icy cold.)

Anyway, the strange thing that happened was this. The last time I ever saw him, I was haranguing him – by now, having exhausted all other possibilities of shared childcare, I was pressuring him to move back to Brighton to step up more as a co-parent. In retrospect this was unfair, given how important his job was to him, but at the time I was totally exasperated and no longer gave a fuck about his job. But that's retrospect for you – everything is so much clearer from a distance. So the last time I ever saw your dad, he was standing in the doorway of my bedroom, and I was swivelling around from my desk by the window, where I was sitting writing. I remember my voice being harsh and shrill, all softness towards him gone. 'I don't want to keep having this conversation over and over,' I said sharply. 'It's getting boring.' This in itself was not the strange thing, because this was how I had been communicating with him for a while now, frustrated beyond any pretense of politeness. No, what was strange was his response. Instead of looking angry and defensive, as he usually did every time the subject reared up (and to be fair, I was obsessive, consumed by it – I had not yet learned the skill of letting things happen naturally, of not bashing away at something, of not trying to impose my will with a lump hammer), instead of looking pissed off and pained, his response to my last ever words spoken directly to him was – a blank. 'Mmm hmmm,' he said, blankly, neither nodding nor shaking his head. He was blank. Blank, blank, blank. Disengaged. Elsewhere. Then he nodded imperceptibly, and made some vague noises, but I could see by his face that he was just mouthing a form of 'yes, dear', instead of getting all antsy and prickly as he usually did. How odd, I remember thinking at the time. Maybe he's re-evaluating his priorities. He seems almost detached. Removed.

10 FULL MOON LUNAR ECLIPSE

Joseph and Mary were coming from Ireland. You never call them Grandad or Granny, because the idea of being called such grandparenty names makes them feel old; they kept their own names instead, thus avoiding being filed under 'ancient'. Mary is a dedicated *Hello* reader rather than a bootee-knitter, and Joseph's main concern is that you have not been baptised Catholic, and are therefore destined for hell; but eternal damnation aside, you and your Irish grandparents adore each other. You've always looked forward to their visits with excitement, given that they usually involve lounging around in hotel bedrooms watching cartoons, being drip-fed chocolate, and being taken out for lovely dinners where you stay up late eating giant ice-cream sundaes and generally being spoilt to within an inch of your lives.

Like everyone in the entire extended family, Mary and Joseph both adored Leo from the first moment they met him, and had been horrified, and totally mystified, when we separated. I didn't go into detail about why we had split, but instead tried to reassure everyone that there would be no nastiness, court cases, custody battles, or anyone taking anyone else to the cleaners. There would be no voodoo dolls or curses, not side-taking, no viciousness or vileness. It was not like that. You have to remember that divorce had only been legal in Ireland since 1997, the year before your dad and I met; before that, couples stuck it out ad infinitum, no matter what. So when Irish couples did split, after years of tearing each other apart, it was generally because the relationship had broken down so badly that each party would have happily pushed the other off a cliff. It was not like that between Leo and me, but Joseph and Mary were still rather shocked that we would not be doing the till-death-do-us-part thing after all.

Anyway, they were coming to visit, and in keeping with long-standing tradition, would be coming over to ours for dinner. They were both keen to see your dad, and I was very happy for him to come down and spend the evening with us – I had always empha-sized that although he and I were no longer a couple, that did not mean we were no longer a family. No matter what our individual situations were, we were both still your parents. And Leo had always seemed keen on that idea too – he was not one of those drift-away dads, one of those fade-out fathers whose presence became more and more intermittent until, like the Cheshire cat, there was nothing left at all but the memory of his smile, as he set up a new life some-where else and forgot he had ever been a dad to anyone ever.

I found this much later on my hard drive. He had written it the day before he died:

FROM: Suzanne Harrington
TO: Leo@gmail.com
SENT: 05 September 2006 06.26
SUBJECT: Weekend

Hi Leo

Mary and Joseph are coming today until Friday so if you do have the Friday off you are MORE than welcome to join us down here Thursday night, I know they'd love to see you. But no pressure, obviously, it's 100% your call.

Suzanne xxx

FROM: Leo@gmail.com
TO: Suzanne Harrington
SENT: 06 September 2006 07:51
SUBJECT: Weekend

Hi Suzanne

That sounds like a great idea, I would love to see Mary and Joseph on Friday. Looks like there is lots going on in Brighton for the kids so best for them to stay.

I'll see you Thursday evening.

Leo

Hardly reads like a suicide note, does it?

Later, the coroner estimated the time of death was around 8 p.m. on that Thursday evening, high on that windswept hillside overlooking the sea. He died at around eight o'clock. Dinner time.

But where were we that evening? What were we thinking, as we stared at the empty chair where your dad should have been sitting? It was very odd. Unlike me, your dad was reliable. In the past, I had been known to invite people for dinner at my house, and then forget to show up myself, because I was still down the pub, but Leo was the opposite of that. If he said he would show up, then he showed up – he had always liked Joseph and Mary, and enjoyed our family dinners because they could be pretty lively compared with his own experiences as an only child. Nor was he under any obligation to come – there was no expectation, just a genuine desire for his company. That was all we wanted from him. I'm so glad that email is in existence, because it seems to provide some kind of strange proof that things appeared relatively normal – I want to wave it at you, and say, 'Look, look, a normal exchange of pleasantries about dinner – with no indication of suicidal intention whatsoever!'

I had ordered food in from Moshi Moshi – lots of lovely bright, fresh sushi plus warm salmon teriyaki with sticky rice and pickled plum. It was a treat, to have such nice food delivered, and spread all over the giant wooden dining table in the sitting room. I had texted Leo earlier, asking him when he would be coming. This is what he texted back: 'Around 8 p.m. See you later.'

Yet when 8 p.m. arrived, Leo didn't. And so we sat down, and waited, and slowly began nibbling at the California rolls, the prawn nigiri, the tuna sashimi, the clean flavours zinging with wasabi and soy and those delicate pale pink slices of fiery ginger. He'd be here any minute. The train was probably stuck at Hayward's Heath. Leaves on the line. Signal failure. Perhaps someone had thrown themselves under a train at London Bridge – that was always happening, and could jam up the whole network for hours. Selfish buggers. We kept nibbling, as the salmon teryaki sat drying out in the oven.

After a while I texted him again. He didn't answer. I rang him. His phone was turned off. This really was quite strange. This was very unLeo.

We ate the salmon teryaki some time after nine, Joseph, Mary and I – you two had gone to bed – and although we chatted away about this and that, inside my head I felt something was up. Something was not right. When they left to walk back to their hotel, I was overwhelmed by a feeling of unease. And that was when I stood by the window in the diagonal slanting moonlight, as that powerful full moon glared down, a full moon *and* a lunar eclipse, and I whispered an unconscious prayer to the universe, because although I had no idea of the details, I had a strong sense that nothing would ever be the same again. Two days later, reading my tarot, I would pick up Death and the Hanged Man.

Let's contextualise for a moment. I am not a flappy, hysterical type who catastrophizes every time someone is half an hour late. I do not imagine mayhem and disaster at every corner, nor death and destruction before teatime. But with Leo it was different. It had happened before. He had disappeared before.

Since he moved to London, his health had been getting worse. His blood pressure was so high that he would sometimes have to go to hospital and have it lowered, which meant lying in A&E all day with a drip in his arm. I have no idea why his blood pressure was so high, or why it was getting worse, or what could be done. All I know is that he necked loads of pills every day and that sometimes he would be blinded by headaches that seemed to split him in half. His father, from whom Leo inherited that same handsome, South Indian darkness, had died of a massive coronary while still in his mid twenties. His *twenties*.

I remember phoning him one day at work, and the receptionist saying that he hadn't come in that morning. So I called his mobile. And his landline. Nothing. No answer. Eventually, I called the man whose house he lived in, but Leo was not at home. He wasn't the kind of man who would be down the pub at noon on a Thursday, or sloping off work for a secret tryst in a King's Cross hotel. He didn't have to. He was a free agent, no longer constrained by

244 • SUZANNE HARRINGTON

marriage vows, but more significantly, he was not the kind of person who would take time off work lightly – his work was his central source of identity. He would not jeopardize this identity by messing around or not turning up. When it came to his job, he was conscientious to a fault. So that first time he went missing, I rang the hospitals. It's not really much of a laugh, ringing around hospitals, although after a while I got used to it. I rang Charing Cross, Guys and St Thomas's, the Middlesex. What do you say? 'Hello, A&E, have you seen my ex-husband?' I eventually found him at University College Hospital. Oh yes, said whoever was in charge of the ward. We have Leo here. We're keeping him in for a few more hours until his blood pressure is back down at a safer level.

Another time, he went missing on the day of the July 7 terror attack in London. No reply from his work, no reply from his mobile, no reply from his home phone. Hours and hours of no contact, as the radio broadcast the horrors of the day. Eventually, he surfaced intact – he had been at a memorial service for the founder of the charity, at St Martin-in-the-Fields. If it hadn't been for his previous disappearances to various A&E departments, his not answering his phone for a few hours would not have been of any significance; but given the state of his blood pressure, it was. Which is why that night, after Joseph and Mary left, I went to bed with a feeling of terrible trepidation. Something was definitely wrong.

When I rang the hospitals the next morning – Charing Cross, Guys and St Thomas's, the Middlesex, UCH, the same order as before – it turned out he had been at one of them. He'd come in in agony with a blood pressure headache, and had been discharged a few hours later with some paracetamol or something similarly inadequate. But he was not back at his house in London, when I phoned there. Nor was he at work. I rang the hospital in Brighton, but he wasn't there either. His mobile was still turned off. It had still been only twelve hours since he hadn't shown up for dinner when I called the police, sitting at my desk in the bright morning sunshine, to formally report him missing. You have to be missing for twenty-four hours in order to be a missing person, but I didn't care. I needed to tell them he hadn't turned up.

The police rang straight back. They needed to come over to get some details to file a missing person's report. For God's sake, I thought. Couldn't they do that over the phone? I had already described Leo in great detail – what more did they need to know? His star sign? His favourite colour? I had stuff to do – I had to drop you two to Mabel's, because she was looking after you that morning, I can't remember why, except that school wasn't open yet and I needed to get on with my day. (I can't remember specifics – my memory is sharp and clear, but only of images and sensations and words, rather than logistics and chronology.) When I told the police woman on the phone that I was going to be in and out all morning, I was a bit taken aback when she said very clearly and insistently, 'We need to you stay where you are. There are officers on their way over.' She paused briefly, before repeating, 'To take some more details.'

This was all getting a bit weird. I didn't want you overhearing any unnerving conversations about missing fathers. I told you that some police had to pop in to about some boring neighbourhood business, and you were quite excited at the idea of real life policemen coming to visit. It was such a beautiful morning, the light strong and September golden, the sunshine warm, the garden still full of colour. There were two of them. Two police with young boy faces, two ink blots against the whiteness of the huge sunny room. The room was swamped with sunlight, the stargazer lilies on the table thick with scent, fleshy and still.

They were very smiley and jokey with you two, mucking about, letting you try on their police hats. I distractedly made them tea, and asked them to wait until Mary arrived before we started doing any missing person stuff; she would take you two out, so that you wouldn't hear me giving them details of your dad, even though I already had. Then Mary came, eyeing the police but too nonplussed to say anything – she knew that Leo had not turned up for dinner, but that was all – and then you were gone, down the wide stone staircase and into the bright sunlit garden across the road.

In the sudden silence, the expressions of the two young police men instantly readjusted from larking-about-with-kids to deadly serious. The change was so instant it was almost comic, as if they were actors. There were their hats on the table, like props, next to their mugs of Earl Grey. Their faces were so solemn. Something was wrong. Something was definitely wrong. 'Is he dead?' It was all I could think of saying. It seemed like the obvious place to start. The logical place.

They nodded.

So there you are. The blood pressure had got him after all. I had pre-empted them, done their job for them – so why did they seem to be almost squirming? I felt winded. He was dead. Dead, dead, dead. Dead. It had actually happened. The voice in my head was instantaneous: *of course he's dead, that's what you were expecting, wasn't it? How could he be anything else except dead? You've been expecting this. You always knew he'd die early. He*

wasn't built to last. You knew that. They don't send coppers over
to fill in forms.

What happened? I asked them, waiting to hear about a heart attack
on a packed train or a massive stroke on a crowded tube or an
aneurysm as he rushed for the bus. They were really squirming
now. The moment hung, and hung, swinging between us.

And then one of them said mechanically, without making eye
contact, 'He took his own life.'

Jesus *Christ*.

I was not expecting THAT.

Everything slowed down and stopped still. I wasn't actually
sitting there any more, but was high above the table now, watching
the scene from the ceiling. It was like watching *The Bill*, or
EastEnders, or some other soap opera involving solemn police
officers straight from central casting, delivering bad news. Yes,
maybe an episode of *The Bill* – low budget, high drama. I kept
rising up out of myself, swooping upwards, and seeing the three
of us sitting at the long wooden table down below, the fat bird
and the two boy coppers, her eyes wide in disbelief, their eyes
fixed on their hands. This could not be real. Of all the things he
could have done, he could not have done this. *Took his own life?*
What the *fucking fuck* were they talking about?

'He can't have,' I said eventually, and then I kept repeating it,
over and over. 'He can't have. He can't have. He has children. You
just saw them. They're his children. He can't have.' The two baby-
faced police looked like they wished more than anything for the
power to disappear, to vanish and be anywhere rather than here.
Raiding a crack house, chasing a joyrider, interrogating a
paedophile – anything, rather than listening to a woman say over

and over again that her husband could not possibly have killed himself because he has two small children.

'What am I going to tell them?' I asked the policemen. I genuinely thought that they would tell me what to do now, because for once, I had no fucking idea. This was so far outside my remit, so completely uncharted. They lowered their gaze to their shoes, as I asked them again, 'WHAT AM I GOING TO TELL THEM?'

Job done, they were leaving. Backing away towards the door, leaving me with this gigantic piece of information – what was I supposed to do with it? My brain jammed, like a frozen computer screen. All I could think of was the immediate impact of the information. It's funny, how your brain can't handle huge chunks all at once. It seizes up, ceases processing. All I could think of was not, *oh my God, my children's father has killed himself and this will affect them for the rest of their lives*, but, *oh my God, I will have to cancel my weekend plans because he's not going to be here*.

The first oh-my-God was too awful to contemplate, so my brain shutdown, and instead all I was left with was that hollow, frustrated feeling that you get when you are just about to walk out the door, all dressed up, and the babysitter suddenly cancels. It seemed like the end of the world to me, that I could not go away for the weekend. I felt that he had somehow done this – this *thing* – to spite me, to stop my fledgling private life in its tracks, to regain control while sticking his fingers up at me and my demands for him to take more responsibility.

That was all I could think.

And yes, I know how that sounds. It sounds monstrous. But at that exact moment, I could not think bigger or longer term than that. I could not digest the information. I could only apply it to the very superficial and immediate. And all I could think was, how fucking dare you, how fucking DARE you—

The police were saying something. Did I have anyone who could come over? Anyone I could phone? And again I was on the ceiling, watching the story unfolding and desperately wanting to fold it tightly back up and nail it away in a box.

I drove you to Mabel's. I have no idea how. I walked downstairs and called to you and Mary, the three of you in the garden, in a voice that sounded normal – my jaw was clenched, but other than that, you would not have thought I had just been punched in the face with a huge hit of horrendous information. Mary looked sick, as if she knew something was up, but had enough sense not to ask. Not until you were safely delivered to Mabel, where you would spend your last ever day of ordinary two-parent childhood.

I forgot your packed lunches, but I remembered my sunglasses, the biggest, blackest ones that covered half my face. I was glad of them, glad of something to hide behind. I wanted the gap between you leaving the car and me having to open my mouth – those few seconds watching you run across the garden, all small brown limbs and floppy sunhats, past the guinea pig hutches and the paddling pool and the sprawling dogs, and into Mabel's house, where you were safe and oblivious, enjoying the last morning of your pre-dead-dad lives – to last forever. I just wanted to hit the pause button. I wanted to hit it and hit it and hit it.

Mary and I sat in my car, in the car park by Mabel's garden. There was debris all over the car floor – a black banana skin, a crushed apple juice carton, an old sticky strawberry Cornetto wrapper next to a dented bottle of Evian, a litre of engine oil, some old Sonic Youth cassettes, lots of grit and some scrunched up parking permits. Mary seemed afraid to move her feet in case she touched anything.

Outside there was a shimmer to everything. It seemed unnatural, as though it might be coming from inside me, rather than from the sun. Like when you don't sleep for days and everything takes on a strange edge, as though you're inside a kaleidoscope but with the colours bleached out. I felt very detached. Numb. Unreal. We were sitting in a hot car with its whiff of banana and Castrol oil. It was an unseasonably hot September day. Leo had been found a few hours ago hanging from a tree on the Downs. The gap – there you were, going into Mabel's house now, through the glass door and out of sight – only lasted a few seconds, but it was one of those car crash moments – everything slowed down and stopped, until nothing was moving except my heart. I felt paralysed, sitting there behind my giant black glasses, in the awful brightness of the morning.

When I did say the words out loud, I couldn't soften it, although I did give a kind of pre-warning. 'I need you to hold it together when I tell you this,' I said. And then, before either of us had time to think, I ploughed on. 'He's dead.' She sucked in her breath, but I kept going. 'He killed himself. They found him this morning.'

'Was it because he had to have dinner with us, do you think?'

We were sitting around the wooden table when Mary said this. It sounds almost comical, but when something inexplicable happens, you grasp at straws. Joseph sighed. He looked old, as if he was ageing by the hour. River was mechanically making tea. She had been making tea ever since she had arrived on the train from London. We had been drinking tea all day, sitting around this table, the calming scent of camomile and lavender and neroli wafting around the room, the fading September light making everything shimmer. Everything had been shimmering all day.

'No,' I said. 'I don't think it was because of dinner. I think it was bigger than that.'

'If only I'd known, if only I'd called around to him more, if only I'd realized,' River said, almost to herself. As if her calling around to his house in London more frequently could have somehow prevented him from doing what he did. A surge of rage broke over me. They shouldn't have been there. Mary and Joseph should have been on their flight back to Ireland after a nice family visit in Brighton, and River should have been on a train going to work, not here, not here sitting ashen and shaken and sick with the fallout of what had just happened. Leo should have been there, not them. This was his weekend. How fucking dare he shirk his responsibilities like this? How fucking DARE he?

See? That was where my brain was stuck, snagged like a stuck zip, unable to move either backwards or forwards. It was his weekend to have you two. And now he was not coming. That was all I could process. That he would not be coming down to look after you that weekend. That you would not be seeing him this weekend. That he had messed up my weekend. Every weekend. I know how awful that sounds, reading it now, five years later; but the truth is I was not thinking of him, and as yet I was not thinking of you, or the three of us – you two and me – as a unit. I was only thinking of me, and how just as my life was starting to get interesting and lively after years of being inert from alcohol and a dead marriage, he goes and does this. He fucks you up, and he fucks me up. *The selfish fuck.* That's all I could think.

Sorry I can't write something more noble, but I'd be lying if I did.

'What are you going to tell the kids?' River asked. It was almost time to collect you from Mabel's. I was sick with dread. You were five and three – what on earth was I supposed to tell you? I had been telling people all day. 'Leo's just killed himself... Leo's just killed himself... Leo's just killed himself.' Phoning people, mechanically repeating the information, absorbing their shock. Like pouring poison from a bottle into the clean air. And now I had to tell you two. I had no idea where to even start.

'I don't know,' I said.

'You'll have to tell them something,' Mary said.

'Yes I *know*,' I said. All I remember is dread and anger. 'I'll tell them he went to heaven at short notice. I'll tell them he's become an angel.'

Bertha and her wife were there, at the table. 'Take them into the garden, and say that you have something very important to tell them,' Bertha said. 'Tell them very quietly.'

We rehearsed what I would say to you over and over as we sat around that great big wooden table. I was terrified and numb and furious all at the same time, and as it neared the time to collect you, the fear was making my guts lurch. I was about to ruin not just your day, but possibly your entire childhoods. This would stay with you for the rest of your lives. This would change the course of your lives forever.

'Are you *sure* it wasn't because he didn't want to have dinner with us?' Mary asked again.

'Oh Jesus Chri—' I said, but River interrupted.

'She has a point,' she says. 'He could have found the idea of having dinner here with everyone humiliating, now that you're not together anymore.'

'Oh for God's sake!' I almost shrieked. 'Don't you think that might be a bit of an overreaction?'

'Of course, love, of course,' said Joseph. 'He wasn't in his right mind. Obviously.'

'Do you think he'd been planning it?' Mary asked, staring outside into the communal garden where he and you spent so much time together every weekend, where you were part of the community, the loving dad with the lovely kids.

'I don't know,' I said. 'I have no idea what was going on in his head. I never did. That's why I broke up with him. I didn't know him.'

It was around then that I noticed one of the paperbacks lying on the side table. It was a Jacqueline Wilson book called *Vicky Angel*, about a girl whose best friend dies and becomes an angel. There were loads of books all over the sitting room – on bookshelves, on the table, on the floor, rows and piles and heaps of them – but this one jumped out at me. I didn't ever remember seeing it before. A horrible sick feeling washed over me, more nauseous than fearful. He had bought that book to read to you at bedtime. Was he forewarning you? I grabbed the book, holding it up: 'Look! He bought her this! He bought her this!'

Instantly Joseph and Mary came over to me, their four arms around me, obviously relieved that I was showing some form of emotion that was appropriate to bereavement, that wasn't pure ice-cold rage. But I pushed them off. What I was feeling wasn't huggable, or touchable, or fixable. The idea of weeping was repulsive. I just wanted to kill him.

*

You probably remember this, seeing as it was the moment your lives changed forever, but given how young you were, maybe it's hazy, a gauzy film shimmering over your memories with some sharp pointy images sticking through. I walked in faltering dread the half a mile to Mabel's, speechlessly grateful to Bertha for coming with me. We crunched over the gravel car park towards her garden gate, and there you both were, on the trampoline, bouncing and shrieking. It was such a warm, beautiful day.

Faking normality made my mouth dry and my head pound as we walked home up the hill, listening to your bright chatter without hearing a word of it, and unlocked the tall spiked iron gate into the garden. There was nobody in there, apart from a lone neighbour – the horrid one who hated children, who ignored us as we passed her, her pinched face scowling like a fairytale witch. As we made our way to a quiet bench under a dapple of trees, you were babbling, chattering, the usual million questions, what's for dinner, when is *Scooby Doo* on, your blissful oblivion making me feel sick.

'I have something very important to tell you both,' I said in my quietest, least dramatic voice. Almost a whisper. As if I was about to tell you a story. To get the next sentence out, I needed giant, super-power courage. I didn't have it, so I went for a distraction instead, dipping in my bag to hand you both a mini Kit Kat. Your eyes lit up. There's a distinct possibility that you will forever associate cataclysmic bad news with red-wrapped chocolate bars, although to be fair, it doesn't seem to have put you off.

So I told you. That Dad had died that morning. That he had been in a park, and had become very unwell in the park, and had died in the park. That he was now an angel. A stupid, dead fucking angel with stupid dead fucking angel wings. I didn't say that. I didn't even hint it. And your faces crumpled, even as you kept shoving the chocolate in. It was so still, so quiet, so warm and fragrant in the garden. I choked down the burning lump in my own throat, because you would have thought I was crying for Leo, and I wasn't, I was crying for you. But I shoved it down, because it felt very important to keep it together at that moment. Getting weepy would have made things even weirder and scarier for you.

You asked some questions – which park, was there an ambulance, where was Dad now, would we see him again – and I answered as simply as I could. There was no point in telling you he'd had a heart attack or a car crash or any of the usual lies people tell to protect children from the truth, because if I lied now, I would have to unlie at a later date, and then how could you ever trust me again? So I was vague. *He-became-unwell* was the chosen term of explanation, repeated over and over in the coming months. And you were too shocked – and too young – to start demanding proper answers.

'My daddy is dead,' one of you said, as we walked into the stillness of the sitting room, where a quiet, numbed group of adults sat around the dining table, empty tea cups in front of them, everyone rooted to the spot like the giant potted plants in the corner.

'Yes,' someone replied. 'He is.'

And the air, heavy with essential oils, was very calm, and nobody freaked out.

We made a Dad table. I had no idea what I was doing, but it seemed the most natural thing to do, to make an altar to him, like you see in Indian houses. It was a table covered with some beautiful orange-gold sari material, with a big picture of Leo and lots of smaller ones, and a lit candle, and incense and flowers, and a drawing from Bertha's kids of a brown man with silver wings and the words 'Leo Angel'. It was something to focus on, a way of honouring him. We went through all the photos and you made a Dad book, picking out your favourite pictures and carefully sticking them on the pages, so that you had a story book of your dad – pages and pages of pictures of him with you, on beaches and in restaurants and on holiday, looking happy, looking normal, looking alive. That book is one of your most precious possessions. He is the least suicidal looking man you could imagine, beaming out of all those family photos.

You know that bit in *Total Recall* – the original, not the remake – when Arnie, disguised as a female tourist on Mars, keeps repeating 'Two weeks... two weeks... two weeks', because her circuits have blown? In the immediate period after Leo died, that's what happened to me too. Only looking back can I see how frozen it was, how shutdown. I could not comprehend the size of what had happened. I could not see the tragedy, the awfulness – only the raging inconvenience, and a sense of crushing responsibility, as if a cement truck had dumped into my chest and my lungs were filling up with quick-dry cement.

I was burning with rage at the sheer injustice of it. I had no idea that I was in shock – all I could think was, I never signed up for this! Who the *fuck* wants to be a single parent? Not me! Not me *ever*! The bigger picture, the feelings of others, I could not feel – I had no empathy. I could only feel my own anger. Cauterized inside my own hot fury and disbelief. *What a cop-out. What a lame-ass, chicken-shit cop-out.* If he hadn't already been dead, I would have murdered him with my bare hands. I managed to hide this from you, but not from the other adults around me, who were all stricken and grieving.

You see, I had made an assumption. My assumption was this. That once you have kids, you stay on the planet. That no matter how hot-air balloon your head goes, those children are your sandbags. They are your anchor to the world, for the simple reason that they exist, and they exist because of you. They were not left on your doorstep. They did not come free in a box of cornflakes. You made them, they are yours. So once you have kids, you stick around; it's the unwritten rule. No bunking off. If you've signed up, you're signed up. No refunds. No get-out clause. That's the rule. At least, I thought that was the rule.

Meanwhile, there was the jaw-grinding, light-headed, nauseous aftermath. For three weeks, we hung, sick with suspended animation, waiting for the suicide bureaucracy to give us back the body. I was consumed by my need to get away, to escape to my secret private life, not for any erotic purpose (believe me, the word 'suicide' has an instantly castrating affect) but so that I could be somebody else, sitting in a different world, watching films in a different home, in a secret private hideaway where I could pretend to be anyone but myself. Instead, I had to make phone calls and say things like, 'My little boy won't be into nursery today because his dad just killed himself', and watch as people curled in on themselves, recoiling from the information.

Three days after the police came, it was the Brighton Burn Up, the annual Ace Café gathering where tens of thousands of bikers rode from London to Brighton for the day to hang around the seafront, showing off to each other along Madeira Drive. I remember pushing my bicycle through the leathery throng, feeling wrecked and numb in the sickening September sunlight, you strapped into the toddler seat behind me, fractious and disorientated. All around us the bikers were having a great day out, with their huge shiny bikes and their naff bandanas and outsize tattoos, their hard-faced women, their beer bellies. Normally I love bikes. I walked between them all for miles, cut off from everything, envious of the simplicity of it all, of the bikers' connection and camaraderie. Lost and fear-sick and shock-sick and adrift. I had never been so terrified of being your mother.

In the middle of it all, there was a funeral. I had never been to a funeral before – only to baby namings and the very occasional wedding. Never in my whole life had I been to a funeral, and now I had to organize one. Where did you start? There had to be an autopsy. Your dad was in the coroner's freezer for three endless weeks before being released to be buried. I became a regular down at the coroner's office, a building I had passed a million times but had never seen before. Until now. They were kind, the coroners. And straight up. They didn't say 'passed away', they said 'dead'. There's a whole language around suicide. You don't 'commit suicide', you take your own life – committing suicide sounds too much like committing homicide, and killing yourself is too harsh. Personally I couldn't stomach the idea that Leo took his own life. Took it where? It was way too vague. No, he killed himself. That is what he did. Nor do people 'pass away' or 'fall asleep'. For fuck's sake. They die.

I remember sitting numbly in a small impersonal office in the coroner's building, being told awful things about blue nylon rope and rigor mortis and toxicology, and how there had been no alcohol or illegal drugs in his blood. No, he had killed himself in cold blood. Somehow that made it even worse. How there had been a packet of anti-depressants in his bag, untouched and unopened. How the only substances in him had been shedloads of various medications for his various physical ailments. Nothing for his head.

I had to register the death. It was at the town hall, where I had registered both your births, and where your dad and I had got our marriage certificate six years earlier. The same rooms, the same forms, the same people. Birth, marriage, death. Telescoped. 'I need to register a death,' I said. The faces were blank. What did I want – for Town Hall officials to leap over their counters, hug me, make me a cup of tea?

People – even official people – go weird around death. They go even weirder around suicide. I remember closed faces, cold voices, briskness, averted eyes, as I filled in forms and ticked boxes. A few acquaintances who had heard the news – because Brighton is small, and bad news travels fast – studiously avoided me. Some still do to this day. I remember telling one woman in the street what had happened, and her backing away and saying, 'Oh dear. Well, thanks for telling me.' You feel polluted, like a ship with a toxic cargo desperately needing to berth somewhere safe but there's nowhere.

And the funeral. I had only ever planned parties. Where did you start? It wasn't as if Leo and I had ever sat down and discussed what kind of funerals we would like. All I knew was that he was a vehement atheist and he was eco-conscious. The idea of a Catholic funeral – the religion he and I had been born into – with all its drear and blackness, would have horrified him. I found a green funeral place run by women, and organized a woodland burial in a biodegradable coffin. Those women, they were so soothing. It was such a relief to be with people who knew about death, but who weren't hiding inside vestments and calling me 'my child'. Those women were strong and kind and capable, and I didn't have to look after their feelings so being in their company, no matter how briefly, was a huge relief, a huge solace.

The celebrant came around. I remember how she liked her tea – two teabags, an Earl Grey and a British Rail, in the same cup. For some reason that reassured me. None of your dandelion and rose petal rubbish. She was like a doula, except for death instead of birth. Together we wrote the words she would say. She took care of all of that. The other woman – calm, open-faced, kind – was the dead-body person. The embalmer. She came with a tiny cloth bag with your dad's silver rings inside – his wedding ring, and another with the words *'toujours'* engraved on it, which made me want to laugh, cry and scream all at the same time. Instead I just took the little bag from her and put it away for you. I gave her your dad's favourite shirt – the purple glittery one he had worn on our wedding day – and his sharp black suit. She promised that she would make him beautiful. She was so kind. But I didn't care what he looked like, because he was dead, and I was a widow.

A fucking widow. Like a poisonous black spider.

This was the bit where people around me expected me to dive back into a gigantic pool of booze, but I didn't. Getting absolutely shitfaced after being widowed by suicide would not be unreasonable, of course, especially when you're only eight months sober after an adulthood of drinking alcoholically, and are now on your own with two kids aged three and five, but the idea of falling back down into that poisoned hole and drowning in it held no appeal. Eight months without a hangover and listening to the shared wisdom of other recovering alcoholics worked in tandem to keep me sober. Physically, that is. Emotionally, I was still toxic. A long, long way from emotional sobriety. Which is a polite way of saying still horribly fucked up. Not engaged with humanity at all.

And it showed. Someone sent a letter after the funeral telling me they could no longer be my friend because I was so selfish, self-centred and self-obsessed. That I had not cared about Leo, and no wonder he died. One or two other friends distanced themselves, avoiding all but the most basic contact in the months after he died. An acquaintence pretended she had become invisible, and hid in doorways when she saw me coming. I kept going to the meetings of recovering alcoholics, who were the only people who seemed to think it was normal to feel the way I felt.

I have no idea what you remember about this time, other than the giant blurry shock of it all. You might remember feelings and sensations – perhaps feelings like loss, insecurity, confusion – and you might remember feeling your mum would have rather been anywhere else on earth than sitting still with you two. It's making me squirm to write this, but those first few months after your dad died, *I was not there for you*. I could only give you the mothering you so desperately needed by regularly getting away from you – which I did, leaving you with friends at weekends so that I could escape to my private life. It's something I regret, leaving you like that, even if it was with people you knew and loved, but at the time it seemed like the only way to stay sane. I wasn't dead, like he was, and I wasn't drunk, like I used to be, but I wasn't really present either. I was still deep inside my own cauterised glass bubble of me-me-me; I could see out, but I couldn't really hear or feel. Yet at the time, I had no idea just how deaf and unfeeling I really was.

Thankfully that was five long, long years ago. More than half your lifetime ago. As you recovered from the shock of losing your beloved, loving dad, I recovered from the mental and spiritual toxicity of alcoholism as well as the shock of bereavement (the physical recovery from alcoholism is the easiest bit – it's sorting your heart and soul out that takes the time). Since then there have been five years of daily recovery, of therapy, of sorting my head out to become what I was meant to be. Free from addiction. Free from fear. Free from rage. Free, free, free.

I have become your mother. Which is just as well, because otherwise you really would be orphans.

We spent a week decorating the coffin. It arrived – plain white cardboard with thick white rope handles on the sides – and we put it in the centre of the big airy sitting room. I remember telling someone on the phone that we had the coffin at home, and were making it beautiful for Leo, and the friend asking, kind of horrified, if we had Leo's corpse in our sitting room, and we had both laughed loudly – hysterically – at the thought. No, I remember saying. No body. Just an empty box. Rapidly, the abnormal was becoming normal.

Leo's favourite colour was purple, so that's what we painted the coffin. There were a few of us – all women – working together quietly, almost ritualistically, transforming this white box into a thing of disco-beauty worthy of Leo; when it was finished, it was pale purple on the outside, with a glittering twist of pink down the middle, and lined with deep purple satin. We put a pair of white swansdown angel wings on the lid, and covered the hard edges with bright fake flowers whose colours glowed; underneath the angel wings there was the word 'love' made from glass. You each painted two small canvases – pinky purple brushstrokes of love – which we stuck on each side by the rope handles. And on top, above the angel wings, there was a glass dragonfly.

As I sit here writing this in our house on the hill overlooking the sea, paid for by his death while downstairs you are lounging around with the dogs on a lazy Saturday morning, a large white feather has just floated from the sky past my window. At exactly the moment I was writing about angel wings. Okay, so it's probably a seagull feather, but very, very occasionally, I get an almost imperceptible sense of Leo. Or maybe it's my imagination.

The dragonfly is where it gets a bit Mystic Meg. A few days after those boy policemen came by, and as we were all reeling around shell-shocked, distractedly making tea and phone calls, there was a dragonfly. It was huge, bluey-green with enormous Tinkerbell wings, and it was flying around the high ceiling of the sitting room. It would settle on the cornicing high above the room, or on the glass at the top of the windows, sitting still for ages before flying silently high above us again. There had never been a drag-onfly in here before, but this one came out of nowhere, and stayed for days. There was no river nearby, no pond, no marshy meadow – just the stony beach and salty sea at the bottom of the garden. This dragonfly was unlike any creature that had ever flown in before.

'Do you want me to kill it?' Mary offered, rolling up a news-paper.

But we didn't. We were sharing the same thought – that it was some kind of Leo spirit. Well, you do think odd things when your brain has been bashed flat by a mallet of shock, and the presence of this enormous dragonfly – out of nowhere, a one-off – was too strange to be normal, if you know what I mean.

I found out later that as a child Leo had been fascinated by dragonflies; years earlier he had bought his auntie a beautiful dragonfly brooch. Dragonflies, it turned out, were something he loved. But after three or four days the dragonfly in the sitting room, flitting weightlessly above us, was starting to do my head in, so I finally got a step-ladder and caught it in the cup of my hands – I could feel its ghostly fluttering – and released it out the open window. I felt relieved when it was gone. We put a glass one on the coffin instead. It was probably just an ordinary, unmystical dragonfly, looking back on it, but it was kind of spooky, especially if you were already weirded out. Which we were. Very.

So many people came to the funeral. There was a whole delegation from the charity, including its deputy director, who made a speech. I did too – I told some anecdote about Leo's metrosexuality, said how he had been a civilizing influence, and gave heartfelt thanks to everyone for their support. I remember saying, 'Because we'd be stuffed without you.' River's words were far more heart-wrenching. She ended it almost in tears with 'I love you Leo.' Right then, I did not share that sentiment.

Thankfully the celebrant was on hand to make the funeral beautiful. She spoke directly to you two, and to all the children in the little stone chapel in the cemetery: 'We've come here today to say goodbye to Leo, to your daddy, he died because he became very ill and we are all terribly sad because we miss him so much,' she said. 'The sadness really hurts inside, it feels like our hearts are broken. When people are very sad they cry lots, even grown ups, and it's fine to cry. It shows how much we loved Leo. If someone next to you is crying give them a hug or hold their hand, look after them.'

And she spoke to the adults too: 'You are repeatedly asking questions in your mind about why this happened, why on earth did this lovely warm-hearted man come to the end of his life in such a sudden and tragic manner. You may feel anger about what has happened. These feelings are entirely natural.' Nobody looked angry though, as they sat weeping in the chapel. So much weeping. We three sat at the front, listening to all the weeping going on behind us, our wide eyes bone dry.

I had longed to cry – not at the funeral, which felt like some kind of awful party that I was somehow co-hosting alongside the funeral directors; but at home, alone in the sitting room, I had really tried to access something resembling grief. I stared at photos of Leo and me, happy and smiley, in Spain, in India, in Ireland. Nothing. I dug out cards he had sent me, old notes and poems and romantic scraps of paper I had kept. Still nothing. Eventually I gave up and played a Sinead O'Connor album that has the ability to unblock me, but nothing. Zilch. Not a single salty drop. And you know what? I have only ever cried once. For you, yes, many times, but for him, only once. It was at the Duke of York's cinema the following spring, where I watched Anton Corbijn's film *Control*, about Ian Curtis from Joy Division, and when he hung himself at the end (which obviously I knew he would), suddenly I was awash with tears. It was as if someone had pulled a release valve inside me. The man I was with gave me a tissue, but I was inconsolable, streaming with tears, gulping, trying to swallow my sobs because I was in the middle of a cinema. It was the only time I cried.

*

It's not even because of anger any more– these days I can think of your dad with compassion and love, and gratitude for his being alive in the first place, for his kindness and loving heart, and because without him I would not have the two of you; but I could never seem to cry for him, except once, via Ian Curtis.

Choosing the music for the funeral had been a bit of a minefield. The obvious choice would have been a thumping slab of nose-bleed techno, to which the celebrant made a gentle reference when reading out the story of your dad's life (as told to her by me briefly enough for it to fit on a single page with large font), but nose-bleed techno would have cleared the church – perhaps resurrected half the graveyard – so we played 'Lola' by the Kinks instead. The song that one of you was named after. Earlier that week, I had thought to include that Velvet Underground song about how I would stick to you like glue, as a kind of reassurance. Then I listened to the second verse and heard the line about someone hanging from a tree, and decided against it.

Instead, I picked the Beatles' 'Tomorrow Never Knows', and a song called 'Chalo' from Ted and Billy's band, which is Hindi for 'let's go', and is a word you'll hear a lot when we get to India.

After the last piece of music finished, we walked to the wood-land burial ground, which was really just a scrubby bit of the cemetery near the Muslim headstones angled east to face Mecca. I can't remember everyone who carried the coffin. The day is lurid in my head, yet I can't remember the details, the faces.

What I do remember is the impossibility of trying to lower an oddly heavy and highly decorated coffin into a rectangular hole in the ground while wearing platforms. I remember wondering if, teetering on the edge of the grave, I might not fall in, like some ginormous Alice in a black, white and red print dress, falling headlong down into the hole and onto the purple coffin, being covered in earth, being buried alive. The ground quite literally swallowing me up. I would have liked that, to tumble deeply into dark quiet earth, rather than remain upright at this beautiful, hideous funeral. It would have been more peaceful underground. In that instance I envied him a bit.

The lowering of the coffin had to be stopped while I bent down and unstrapped my daft red platform shoes and stepped off of them, so that I could take the rope and lower him into the ground without falling over on the uneven earth, easing him down, into the dark mouth of the earth where he could be left alone, in peace, without ever again needing to worry about all those things that were always worrying him: gas bills, cancelled trains, cholesterol tests, overdrafts, job interviews, fatty liver, failing kidneys, type 2 diabetes, high blood pressure, dyslexia, work, upgrading his skills, paying the rent, and rejection from someone he had loved who was bored to death with hearing all about all of this, and just wanted him to get on with it like a normal adult. At last, he could relax. He didn't have to deal with any of that shit anymore. He was free.

11   THE MEMORY BOX

We weren't free though. We were anything but. We were fucked.
I remember one night at bedtime when you were crying for him
again, and I said that it would get better, get easier, less painful,
and you sat up in your little wooden bed with tears running down
your face and wailed, 'When, Mum, *when*?' as though I could give
you a time and a date.

Your sixth birthday came hurtling towards us like a truck, very
quickly after the funeral. Right away. I was sick for you, having
your first dadless birthday party. Everyone came. More than forty
kids. It was a very special birthday, in a big wooden-floored hired
hall, with a really funny guy who did tricks and had you all transfixed for an hour – he cost hundreds, but was worth every penny.
I remember rows and rows of you, sitting stuffing yourselves with
birthday cake, the chatter and screech as normal and happy as
any other birthday party. The photographs show you beaming,
beautiful, energised, loved, happy in the moment. Thank Christ.
Thank Christ for our friends, our community. And for the resilience
of children. Of you. Of both of you.

Something extraordinary happened a few weeks after the funeral.
The phone rang. It was someone from the charity. Leo's old boss.
He was talking about something called a death in service payment.

I had no idea what he meant. Since Leo had died, my dad Joseph had been keeping us alive financially because I was unable to work; all my juices had dried up. Creative, sexual, the lot. I could barely write a sentence. The landlord and landlady, a kind old Polish couple, had lowered the rent quite a bit, which was the kind of practical compassion bereaved people need. I had not given money any thought. All I could manage was to look after you two as best I could, and not drink.

The charity sent me a cheque for more than one hundred thousand pounds. It was like winning the lottery, except without any of the joy or excitement. Just fear and shock. I stared at this vast fortune, boggle-eyed, before hiding it away in my sock drawer, too terrified to think about what it meant, what it was for, what it would do. I had never in my adult life had any money beyond what I needed to live. The cheque stayed in the sock drawer for weeks and weeks. River began making jokes about the Bank of Sockland, and finally Joseph told me to put it in the bank because my sock drawer did not pay interest. I had no idea about interest. No interest in interest. I have never been a money person.

So this is the bit in the story where your dead dad bought us a house. He was the man who turned into a house. What a gift to us, when we were at our most insecure. And I had to do terrifying, grown up things, newly sober, newly bereaved. Stuff from which I had always run a million miles. Mortgages. Estate agents. Interest rates. What the fucking fuck was that all about. I was *clueless*.

After twenty-three years of moving around from rented place to rented place, from city to city, from country to country, from continent to continent, after twenty-three years and dozens of addresses, I bought our house on the hill overlooking the sea, just before my fortieth birthday.

Our own house. We left the Regency Square with the communal garden and the secret tunnel down to the beach and the flat with the giant sitting room and the vast wooden dining table that could accommodate a banquet, and moved up the hill to a sixties house overlooking the South Downs. There was an overgrown garden and a huge hedge, and when you looked out the front window all you could see was the Downs. No other buildings. No demented neighbours demanding silence at three in the afternoon. Just a horizon where the sky met the earth. From the window in my room, where I put my desk and computer, was the sea. All my life I had wanted to look out on the sea as I wrote.

(As I write. This is where I am sitting now, writing this, with the sea view paid for by the death of your dad. Well, when I say 'paid for', I mean 'contributed' – he paid the deposit, and like everyone else I am mortgaged to the tits. I don't care. This is our house.)

Having our very own garden meant we could get animals. We started small, with Betty the hamster who came with us from our old flat and lived on top of the fridge. One morning soon after we moved in, I found her dead in her cage and I cried and cried because her stiff little body struck me as the saddest thing, the most tragic thing – see, I can cry for a hamster, but not for a husband – and I remember being so scared to tell you that she had died, in case you crumbled at yet more bereavement, but you barely glanced up from *Tracy Beaker* or *Horrible Histories* or whatever it was. You told me not to be so daft. She was buried by the hedge with considerable ceremony.

We got four guinea pigs in a chicken hutch in the wild, unkempt garden – James Bond, David Bowie, Iggy Pop and the Ginger Ninja. They were rubbish pets. Every day when we went to feed them, they thought it was the apocalypse and ran shrieking to the other end of the hutch. They were not the cuddly fluffies we had fantasized about, so we gave them away to another family. Cats were the obvious choice, except when we did get them, three out of four got squashed on the busy hill outside the front gate. Only one survived – Firework, the zen master of cats, negotiator of busy traffic, killer of baby rabbits. He's lying on my bed watching me as I write, eyes narrowed. I remember when his cat sister Suki got hit by a car. We rushed her to the emergency vet, who put her in a kitty oxygen chamber and rang me at six the following morning to ask whether to operate or not. It would cost £800 to put her back together – she had a fractured pelvis and various flattened organs. She was your cat. 'First my dad, now my cat,' you said, your eyes full of tears. In despair, I managed to get someone to take her to the PDSA (our money was all gone, swallowed by the new house). A few weeks later, once she was able to hobble around, she escaped again and this time she didn't survive. So we got two more kitties – fluffy little black and white sisters called Fifi and FooFoo. They went splat as well.

In time, we got what we really wanted – big, furry, barky dogs. Ruby the German Shepherd and Betty the Rottweiler. Our beloved dogs. And Firework, of whom they are both terrified. If I could, I would have a sheep, some goats, a few chickens, maybe a horse and a cow. But then I'm an alcoholic. We always want more.

So there we were, settling into our house on the hill with its space and huge sky and fluctuating menagerie. We were doing okay. Things were getting better. Slowly getting better. Slowly getting normal. Whatever normal is. Except there was still one huge thing that needed to happen. A massive thing. Something they don't teach you at parenting class – not that I ever went to one in my entire life. How to tell kids the truth after their dad has hung himself from a tree on the South Downs. How DO you tell kids about suicide? They don't have a chapter on *that* in any of the parenting manuals – not that I have ever read one, but I imagine it's not in there with potty training and nit combing and toddler tantrums.

Here are the questions that were banging around in my head: when you have already been bereaved, wouldn't it make things worse by telling you what had really happened? That Leo hadn't just died, but had died on purpose? But if I didn't tell you, if I wanted to protect you from further pain, how would that work out later, when you did find out the truth? When was the right time to tell anyone anything like this? How to even approach it? If I told you too soon, would it blow your minds? And if I left it too late, would it blow your trust?

Meanwhile, the information sat inside me like a malignant lump, like a poisoned stone blocking the clear path to being honest with you. As those months after Leo's death passed, the secrecy became more alarming, more potentially devastating, like an unexploded bomb. Everyone knew that your dad had killed himself. Your teachers knew, the parents at school, our own close friends, the older kids – everyone except you. I had no idea what to do. Not telling you felt very wrong. Kids aren't daft. You can sense things that are left unsaid, you can feel things that are not quite right; your intuition is in place even before your ability to speak. Already the oldest you was asking about what exactly had happened. My stock response of 'he became very ill' was starting to sound vague and unconvincing.

Yet if I told you what had really happened, how would you take it? Wrapped entirely in self as all small children are, would you conclude that you had somehow caused your dad's death by not being lovable enough to ensure that he stuck around? I was at a loss. If I didn't tell you properly what had happened, you would do what kids always do when any important information is with-held – you would fill in the gaps yourselves, with God knows what (like when adults sidestep telling kids about sex properly, and kids subsequently imagine babies conceived though belly-buttons or nostrils). But what I was most afraid of was that you would hear it the wrong way, accidentally blurted out. Now *that* would have been a car crash.

Still I hesitated, because I was terrified that my instinctive desire to be truthful was wrong and would damage you even more, or that my subconscious motivation was to selfishly unburden myself of the secrecy. Nobody seemed to know what to do – when it came to the possibility of disclosure, friends and family veered between 'later', 'much later' and 'never'.

Then someone told me about a kids' bereavement charity called Winston's Wish, which was specifically for helping the children of suicides. A charity that deals with the children of suicides is not something you'd normally come across – it's not a hedgehog hospital or a donkey sanctuary – so to find that such an organi-zation existed was one of those moments when the sense of relief almost knocked me off my feet.

Tell them, they said immediately. Tell them the truth. Don't let your kids fill in the gaps with their own make-believe. But shouldn't I wait, I wondered nervously, until they are older? Maybe around twelve, or twenty-one, or forty-five? No, they said. Tell them now, because if you tell them later, it will affect their trust in you. They will not be able to reconcile themselves to the fact that you kept such a huge thing from them for all those years and years. They need the information now, when they are still forming, so that they can assimilate it into their being, and grow with it, rather than have it suddenly dropped on them like an anvil when they are older and more formed. Let them grow with it, until it becomes a simple fact within them, a part of themselves.

Christ, was I relieved. At last I had legitimate permission to be honest. I hated the idea of keeping such a gigantic thing from you; you deserved the truth, providing it was revealed to you in a way that you could digest and process. It had been almost a year since those boy police had come. You were healing up a bit. You had just had your fourth and seventh birthdays. We had a new house and kittens and Betty the hamster. Your confidence was coming back, you were calming down a bit. It was time to let you have the information. But how? For fuck's sake, *how*?

The thing is, in children's culture, the good guys never die. Only wicked witches and evil stepmothers, or ogres, monsters and beasts. Thank God, then, for *The Lion King*. We watched it over and over, the younger you especially clinging to it as some kind of validation that you were not the only young son whose dad had died. But how was I to transcend the concept of ordinary death – that distant thing that until recently happened only to guinea pigs and great-grandmothers – and get across ideas of depression and suicide?

Van Gogh saved the day. Remember *Camille and the Sunflowers*? We read that book over and over, the one that tells van Gogh's story from the perspective of the young boy he befriended in the south of France. You enjoyed the detail – the poverty, the wandering, the absinthe drinking, the ear cutting. Kids love a bit of gore – your eyes widened in fascination at the bloody bits. You accepted the ending – the pistol, the early death – the way you accepted the endings of all stories. I told you that van Gogh died because he had been ill, not in his body, but in his mind. How he'd had a serious dose of depression. You nodded, taking it all in.

One Sunday we drove out to Charleston near Lewes, and went for a walk along the river where Virginia Woolf drowned; do you remember my telling you her story of how she loaded her pockets with stones and waded in? I said it was because she had been so unwell within her mind. How she'd had this thing called depression. How it was not to do with her outside life, which was perfectly nice, but with the inside of her head being unwell. We had a big chat about what it must be like to be depressed, and how it makes people's thinking go funny, so that they are not thinking straight, and can't make proper decisions. I kept comparing the mind to other parts of the body – the heart, the lungs, the liver – and telling you both that it too can become unwell, that it too sometimes needs care and medicine.

It all came out one evening after bedtime stories. We were having another conversation about depression, about how ordinary it is to be depressed sometimes, but how occasionally people become very, very unwell with it, and can no longer think straight. Sometimes, if they have very serious depression for a long time and have never gone to the doctor about it, they may even kill themselves. The words hung in the air, quite reasonable and approachable. Then you said it: 'Is that what happened to Dad?'

The relief was indescribable. It surged inside me in a warm soothing rush. The door to the truth was finally opened. What followed was the most serious conversation we had ever had, even though that conversation in the garden with the Kit Kats on the September day of the boy police took some beating. But there, in the warm glow of your cosy bedroom, the three of us piled on the softness of one of your beds, surrounded by stuffed bears and purring kittens, there were no lies, no whitewash, no fakery. No ambiguity. Just facts.

You took the information and asked a million questions. I told you everything I knew – the when, the where, the how. All the details, dates and places. The blue nylon rope, the tree, the person who found the body at 6 a.m., the police telling me, me having to pretend everything was normal as I drove you to Mabel's, not wanting to lie to you, not wanting to tell you the truth, and the reason. That your dad had had terrible, terrible untreated depression. That I had not realized just how bad. That for months before he died, he had become more and more isolated, staying off work, hiding in his room, not asking for help, other than from the doctors at A&E when the blood pressure headaches became too much. That a few friends had suspected that all was not well, but nobody had any idea just how serious it was, because Leo was not good at telling people how he was feeling, unless it involved physical problems. That when he came down at the weekends to see you both, I had not been paying enough attention to notice his mental health was declining, because he was good at masking it. That he was at his happiest when he was with the two of you. I told you the lot.

I emphasized the depression over and over, and told you that he had loved you more than anyone else in the world, which he did. You said – small children though you were – that you were glad that I had told you, that you had never felt quite sure about

what exactly had happened. The feelings of trust, unity and acceptance were huge between us. At last, I was becoming your mother.
About fucking time too. You'd waited quite long enough, and with
such unconditional patience.

But obviously, with the younger you still being only four, this
new knowledge had some grimly funny repercussions. You began
bringing hanging into your playtime at school, so that soon you
and your fellow kindergarteners were using brightly coloured wool
to hang handmade dollies from doorknobs. Your lovely, kind
teacher was horrified, as well she might have been, while your
classmates took it in their stride. But it passed. Everything levelled
out, as the people at Winston's Wish had said it would.

'My daddy killed himself,' you would tell people. Everyone.
People in shops, on buses. Children would say things like, 'Did
he? Why?' while adults had no idea at all what to say and just
looked aghast. After a while, the need to tell everyone you met
subsided, as the idea sank and settled into your minds.

Now that the older you was seven, you were ready to go on a
weekend retreat with Winston's Wish. First someone from the
charity came to our house, and spent the afternoon talking to the
three of us. The weekend – for which there was no charge – was
designed to help you and a bunch of other kids in the same
situation to workshop your way through a programme of play
therapy. It was designed to give you some emotional tools to deal
with the earthquake that had happened in your life. Remember
when you came home with that box full of precious things
connected with your dad – drawings and writing and memories
– and you were a mass of excited chatter about what you had done
and how you were feeling and how much you had enjoyed it?

I've done it too – the adult version. When the older you first went, the year after Leo died, Winston's Wish invited me along as well to participate in a weekend residential for the partners and ex-partners of suicides. I turned it down flat. The idea of sitting around with a group of adults bereaved by suicide was the last thing I wanted to do – I was still too angry, too outwardly detached and inwardly freaked out. I would have felt like a fraud, I told the counsellors, because I had not been in love with your dad when he died, unlike the other bereaved spouses, who were dealing with their own heartbreak as well as that of their children. So I stayed away, waiting for the anger to subside.

It did eventually.

And so two years later, when the younger you had turned seven and was ready for your turn at the residential weekend , the two of us drove over to a West Sussex village on a beautiful golden day, where you were greeted by volunteer carers all of whom had suffered traumatic bereavement themselves, and taken lovingly into a place of toys, chocolates, games, and healing work on your battered little heart. Now that you both knew what had really happened to your dad, you were able to be immersed in truth and healing, and to hang out with other kids whose dads had done the same. A few mums, but mostly dads. You tore off, bouncing with excitement. When they asked you what you most wanted to achieve from the weekend – they meant things like self esteem, understanding, confidence, shared experience – you said, 'Football skills.'

After dropping you at that lovely place, I drove a mile down the road for the adult version of what you were doing. Yet familiar as I was with sitting in a circle emoting (by now I had been sober almost five years, thanks to three-times-a-week meetings with other recovering drunks) being in a room full of people whose partners had topped themselves was something of a new experience. It wasn't as bad as it sounds. There were just over a dozen of us – all women, apart from a lone man whose wife had jumped off a tower block. Almost all of the men had hung themselves. They had been all kinds of men. A naval officer. A musician. A lawyer. A hippie. An office worker. A civil servant. An IT engineer. An army man. A drug addict. It was like tinker, tailor, soldier, spy, except they they all ended up on hanging from a piece of rope.

For the first time since Leo had died, I was in a place where I could hear the real feelings of others who had been through the same thing. Their anger. What a comfort to hear their anger. Their rage and frustration, their how-the-fuck-could-you-do-this-to-our-kids. And we were all allowed to voice it, to shout it out without anyone judging us or backing away. Again, I experienced a feeling of great relief. I was not an evil heartless bitch after all. My cold fury, stinkingly offensive amidst the grief-stricken, was normal.

Although I no longer wanted to strangle Leo myself, I felt vindicated by the real feelings of those who had been left holding the babies, the bills, the bullshit. And their stories made me realize that actually, ours could have been even worse – several people spoke of being ostracized, of being openly blamed, or of being avoided and shut out and shunned. All I had got was one harsh letter, and a few people avoiding me for a while when I was at my angriest and most emotionally toxic. That weekend in the middle of nowhere in the Sussex countryside gave me an insight into what it was really like for other parents eyeball to eyeball with suicide. It was entirely authentic. I was grateful for it.

*

Your dad has been buried under a sapling in that scrubby bit of cemetery for just over five years now. We never visit his grave. Every now and then I ask you if you want to, but you never do. It's as if we don't have to get in the car and drive across town for him to be in our consciousness. We talk about him though. There are framed photos of him in your bedrooms, and he comes up in conversation quite regularly. This is where this book came from – your asking about our lives together, his and mine, before you were born. Like I said all those pages ago, I can only tell you about the time I knew him. Of his life before June 21 1998, I can tell you nothing because I was not there and so it's not my story. All I know is that he turned up alone, unexpectedly, and left alone, even more unexpectedly.

During the funeral ceremony, the celebrant asked everyone to write a memory of Leo on a small white card, which she collected and gave to me in an embroidered white cloth bag. I put this bag, along with the sheets of handmade rose-embedded paper which contained the celebrant's words, into a pink cardboard box, along with the dozens of sympathy cards we received. This week, five years later, and for the first time since the funeral, I opened the box. It had been at the bottom of one of the wooden trunks in my room, buried beneath school photos and birthday cards and your paintings and all the other childhood treasure that I am keeping safe for you, for when you are older.

This pink box, I realize now, contains priceless treasure. Time has softened everything. I dug it out because I wanted to remember details of the funeral which had not lodged in my brain – as I said, the day was an intense, headachey blur of vivid sensations – but I had forgotten completely about those memory cards. There were around eighty of them, written by friends, family, colleagues, neighbours, and small children with wonky writing who drew birds and hearts and flowers all over them. There is one from you, with just two words in your giant spidery five year old handwriting. It says, 'Love Lola', and is surrounded by unsteady kisses.

Some of the cards are directly addressed to you both, telling you what a wonderful father Leo had been and how much he loved you. Others address Leo directly, using the same words over and over in dozens of different styles of handwriting – cheerful, kind, gentle, loving, generous. Even reading those cards now, today, as well and happy as I have ever been in my life, I look back at that time and feel like a poisonous dark smear. My card to him read, 'Leo, for once I'm completely stuck for words. I wish you love and peace forever.' I actually remember staring at that blank white card in the chapel, as everyone else was scribbling away at theirs, and not being able to think of anything to say. Even in death, I could not write something loving about him as a person, only about my own reaction to his actions. Had I written what I was truly feeling at that moment, it would not even have been wishes of love and peace – it would have been something like 'You fucking muppet, what did you do that for?' But these cards were not for Leo – they were for you. One day, you would read them, so even in my funeral haze, I recognized that your mother's last ever words to your father should not be 'fucking muppet'. Even though at the time it felt like he was.

Reading those cards all these years later, I still get a flash of paranoia, as though between the lines there are dozens of recriminations, unspoken accusations. What bothers me is not the idea that I somehow caused his death, which obviously I did not (I was an ex-wife – I was not physical illness on top of clinical depression), but the idea that people may have thought I did. Did they? Or were they merely repulsed by my fury and coldness around his death, because I would not weep along with the rest of them? Suicide is like dropping a poisoned rock into a pond. All those ripples. No suicide note, no formal diagnosis of deteriorating mental health, no previous attempts, no veiled threats – just a body, all alone on a hillside. The ultimate rebuke. I wish I had been a bit nicer to him.

What matters now though – all that matters now – is that I am your mother, alive and properly present and good enough. If anything good could ever come out of something as totally shit as your dad killing himself, it is this: it made me step up as your mum. It made the three of us bond. Yes we scream at each other and slam doors. Yes sometimes I forget how to be a parent (I still haven't read the manual). Yes sometimes you shriek at me that you hate me. But this is normal. This is normal family life, where feelings are not suppressed or hidden or not allowed out. The trickle down effect of my five years of daily recovery work probably makes you the two most emotionally literate children this side of a Californian therapy room. For this I am stupendously proud. You could just as easily be out setting fire to cars or torturing small animals. Although this may still happen.

Obviously, you are still prepubescent. Maybe the fallout of your father's sudden departure will kick in alongside your hormones. Who knows. All we can do is be honest with each other all the way. Truth, honesty and freedom. It will continue to get us out of a lot of earthquakes alive.

One of the steps of recovery involves making amends to those we have harmed when we were still in the thick of our addiction. It's about acknowledging our past, so that we are not haunted by it, and taking responsibility for our present. My amends to your dad are indirect. Were he still alive, he would know someone different than the person he married; it took a while, but once the drinking had stopped and the recovery work began, she began to emerge. Kinder, softer, more conscious, less mental. Your dad never met that woman, so my amends to him are ongoing – I am bringing up his children to be happy, joyous and free. I am bringing you up as a sober mummy.

EPILOGUE

We're away any day now. At last, the long promised trip to India.
Twelve years after your dad and I set off on that wonderful three-
month honeymoon – the one where Syd, River and Gimli came
too – to those beaches in South India, the three of us are finally
on our first trip there. You've had your jabs, you've been taking
your acidophilus and echinacea, and will soon be bunking off
school for a chunk of winter term.

We have been looking at the map, planning our itinerary. South
Goa. Then maybe a trip further south to Karnataka, to Om Beach.
I've heard it's very different now, with a road connecting the sleepy
pilgrim village to the distant beaches, and an ayurvedic spa hotel
built on the cliffs. Half Moon beach now has its own website –
when we were there it didn't have water or electricity.

You are a bit ambivalent about this trip, because you have heard
so many different things about India: palm trees, sacred cows,
tropical beaches, hot sunshine, mangos and coconuts, snakes,
spiders, Delhi belly, beautiful women in saris, hippies, parties,
gods and goddesses, scary toilets, motorbikes, mayhem, beauty,
peace, chaos, terrible buses. How are you expected to form a
picture of such a place? It has been my dream to take you there,
to show you this other world, to open you up to another way of

being. And if you hate it, well, at least you'll have given it a go. You know, like Marmite.

We will be away for Christmas, as I used always be, before you were born and Santa Claus insisted that we stay home. This is the first Christmas since you were born that we will not spend with River. We three will be together, in the places where your dad and I went. If you had told me five years ago that I would be taking you both to India without another adult, without a fleet of handlers and helpers, I would have tapped the side of my head. But we are going. It will be an adventure. We will lie in the sun and soak it all up.

ACKNOWLEDGMENTS

Thanks to my friend Susan Ferguson, who got the ball rolling.

Thanks to my agent Becky Thomas at WME for her enthusiasm and encouragement, my editor Sara Holloway whose energy and patience was immense, and my publisher, Margaret Stead, for taking it on.

Thanks to my friends Annabel Giles and Fran Creffield for being the book's early midwives.

Thanks to my Dad for always believing in me even when I didn't, and to all my family for their unconditional support and enthusiasm – which I hope will continue after they've read the book.

Thanks to my kids for putting up with a mother who spends a lot of the time hidden away upstairs saying 'Shh, not now, I'm working.'

Thanks to Winston's Wish (info@winstonswish.org.uk helpline 08452 030405) and Amnesty International for helping us when we needed it.

And thanks to my beloved friends, every one of you. You know who you are. A special thanks to Pat Hurley, for a life-changing introduction.

A NOTE ON THE AUTHOR

Suzanne Harrington has at various times been a journalist, a TEFL teacher, a dole claimer, a backpacker, a youth worker, a painter, a wardrobe assistant, a washer-upper, a pen pusher, a house cleaner, a comic bagger, a market stall holder and a cake maker. She is columnist for the *Irish Examiner* and also writes for the *Irish Independent*, the *Irish Times* and the *Guardian*. She lives in Brighton.